NOC STORIES

Changing Lives at the
Nantahala Outdoor Center
Since 1972

Wesser Falls on the Nantahala River (photographed by Serge Skiba/Shutterstock)

NOC STORIES

Changing Lives at the Nantahala Outdoor Center Since 1972

Compiled by **PAYSON KENNEDY**
Edited by **GREG HLAVATY**

 **MENASHA RIDGE PRESS**

NOC Stories: Changing Lives at the Nantahala Outdoor Center Since 1972
Copyright © 2018 by Payson Kennedy

Printed in the United States of America
Published by Menasha Ridge Press
Distributed by Publishers Group West
First edition, first printing

Library of Congress Cataloging-in-Publication Data
Names: Kennedy, Payson, 1933- editor. | Hlavaty, Greg, editor.
Title: NOC stories : changing lives at the Nantahala Outdoor Center since 1972 / compiled by Payson
    Kennedy ; edited by Greg Hlavaty.
Description: First edition. | Birmingham, AL : Menasha Ridge Press, 2018.
Identifiers: LCCN 2017050894 | ISBN 9781634041416 (pbk.)
Subjects: LCSH: Nantahala Outdoor Center—History. | Outdoor recreation—North Carolina—
    Nantahala National Forest—History. | Rafting (Sports)—North Carolina—Nantahala River—
    History. | White-water canoeing—North Carolina—Nantahala River—History.
Classification: LCC GV191.42.N72 N65 2018 | DDC 796.509756—dc23
LC record available at https://lccn.loc.gov/2017050894

ISBN 978-1-63404-141-6; eISBN 978-1-63404-142-3

Cover design by Travis Bryant and Scott McGrew
Text design by Annie Long
Front cover photo of Adam Clawson (1972–2017) by Villa Brewer
Photo credits (others noted on page): pages 99 and 179: Villa Brewer

MENASHA RIDGE PRESS
An imprint of AdventureKEEN
2204 First Ave. S, Ste. 102
Birmingham, AL 35233
menasharidge.com

Table of Contents

Foreword

By Clay Courts, Chairman of the Board

In 2012 my business partner, Jerry Harrison, and I were honored to join the Nantahala Outdoor Center (NOC) community as owners. What sets the NOC, an outdoor guide service and retailer, apart from most other companies is that it is a community of people driven by passion. In 1972 Horace Holden, Aurelia Kennedy, and Payson Kennedy founded the company, creating a culture driven by a search for community and the flow state. As Payson states later in this book, "The paradox is that when work feels like play, the person is able to work effortlessly but with full concentration that produces high-quality results and great internal satisfaction." The stories in this book give us a view of how their shared passions shaped the people who led the Nantahala Outdoor Center to its status as the "world's best outfitter."

For more than 45 years, the staff members' love of community and their excitement to share outdoor adventure with others have defined the incredible guest experience for which the NOC is known. Investing in the center has provided me the opportunity to combine my interests in business and outdoor adventure. We are in the business of making memories for our guests, and we could not ask for a greater adventure than this.

Introduction to the NOC Legacy:

Changing Lives Since 1972 By John Burton

W hy write this story of a little company in Western North Carolina that gets people to play in the outdoors? Who cares? Is it important?

Here's why: The Nantahala Outdoor Center (NOC) has changed millions of lives for the better, in ways most of them did not expect when they engaged with us for the first time. It was founded with two main goals: to create a community of like-minded people who enjoyed working with each other, and to engage in work and activities that were so compelling and fun as to not seem like work. In fact, one of our favorite staff T-shirts is "Choose a job you love and you'll never have to work a day in your life."

John Burton guiding on the Chattooga River

To the outside world, it has been a successful yet unconventional business venture, a social experiment, a powerful intentional community, a commune of granola-eating hippies, an industry leader, and a source of personal growth and triumph for many aspiring adventurers—a dream place.

Internally, it has attracted, nurtured, trained, and been molded by some of the finest, truest, most positive and courageous, most value-driven staff members to have blessed any organization. Perhaps 1,000 people either met their spouses working there or have parents who worked there.

What is this company, in simple, declarative terms? In 1972 it started serendipitously as an outdoor adventure company on the perfect piece of land situated where the Appalachian Trail crosses the Nantahala River, at the end of what would become the most popular whitewater river run in the country. The founders and their families, and the Explorer Scouts and students they recruited in that first summer, guided a few hundred folks in rafts down the Nantahala and the Chattooga Rivers. They taught a few kayak and canoe classes, mostly to students at the North Carolina Outward Bound School; fed hikers and paddlers in the riverside restaurant; sold leftover souvenirs and gas they pumped at the store; and put a few folks up for the night in what was the old Tote 'N' Tarry Motel. The staff did everything: They ate their meals together; slept in shared housing; washed dishes; repaired pipes, boats, and roofs; cleaned motel rooms; guided rafts. That was it. Less than $50,000 in total revenue was collected all summer.

Forty-five years later: The NOC has $21.5 million in annual sales; about 700 people on staff at the summer peak; 108,000 rafters splashing down eight southeastern rivers; and $8 million in retail sales in four stores—two at headquarters, one in Gatlinburg, and one in Asheville. We delight thousands of travelers in River's End Restaurant to a total of almost $2 million in sales. We teach hundreds of aspiring paddlers. We teach the highest-level wilderness emergency medical professionals. We send thousands of kids and young-at-heart adults down zip lines and through adventure ropes courses, leading them to places of courage and accomplishment they didn't know they could access. We continue to lead from one of our founding principles of taking care of the environment.

The NOC has earned a respected place in the world of outdoor adventure providers. Dozens of former staff members populate the local school system as teachers and administrators. Many former staff members have left to start their own adventure companies in the region, in the West, and around the world. The NOC brand is associated with quality, value, safety, leadership, and reliability, be it on an adventure, in products sold in the stores or restaurants, or in other services. Various national industry associations have recognized the NOC for its leadership, including America Outdoors Association, which represents the rafting business, and the Outdoor Industry Association, which is the trade association for companies in the active outdoor recreation business.

The NOC's image is also unique among outdoor companies, and perhaps among business enterprises anywhere. Many friends who might be labeled *conventional* or *conservative* consider the NOC a little weird, something like a socialist experiment, and—horrors—a bad profit-maximizer. It has been guided by a one-page written Statement of Purposes (see page 241), developed by the staff in the early years, that has stood the test of time, so that it is relevant and basically unchanged today, more than 35 years after it was drafted.

But the keys to the longevity of the NOC, to its stature, to its adherence to its founding values, are the founders: Horace Holden, Payson Kennedy, and Aurelia Kennedy, all now on the far side of 80 years of age. They remain the inspiration for the thousands who have passed through. They are still vibrant, active, and consistent in who they are, the example they set, what they believe, how they treat other people, how they spend their time, and how they welcome the thousands of former staff members and guests who come back to cross paths with them. They laid the groundwork for the NOC lifestyle, and they continue to embody the memories of many grand adventures. Though many people viewed early NOC staffers as something like vagabonds, many of us have found that we *can* go home again, because Horace, Payson, and Aurelia created a timeless enterprise.

What follows is a compilation of memories, perspectives, impressions, and expressions of gratitude—really it's a bunch of personal stories from those who were part of the NOC in its early years, mostly up to about 1997, the first 25 years. The community created by this group remains strong and connected. When anniversaries of any kind are celebrated in Bryson City, North Carolina, or at the Chattooga River, it is not unusual for hundreds of former staff members to show up to reconnect, reminisce, and recapture the camaraderie and wonder that meant so much to them during their time at the NOC. For many of us, the magic continues.

 ## About the Contributor

John Burton was born in Evanston, Illinois, in 1947 and lived in the Chicago suburbs through high school. His first link to the North Carolina mountains came through Camp Mondamin, which his father had attended back in the 1920s and John attended in 1958. There he fell in love with paddling. As a frustrated competitive athlete, he found whitewater canoe racing very appealing. In 1965 he entered Dartmouth College, where the first two people he met on campus ended up being lifelong friends who were on the 1972 Olympic team with him. John had an uncooperative left elbow; he had dislocated it six times and had three operations on it before age 11, and it turns out that whitewater paddling was just about the best exercise for the arm. Contact sports were out, so it was also the best outlet for his competitive urges. With his many years of sound fundamental training at Mondamin before he got to college, he was a quick study and qualified for the 1967 US Whitewater Team. John competed on or coached every US team from 1967 to 1979 (except 1975), including the 1972 Olympic team in C-2 (canoe double), with Tom Southworth.

The main legacies of all the training and racing John did in the 1960s and 1970s were the communities and partnerships he was lucky enough to find. The cooperative yet competitive spirit that defined every US whitewater team was very compelling to John, and it kept him occupied in, actually immersed in—well, really to be truthful about it, compulsive about—his pursuit of competitive excellence. He had only two C-2 partners over the 12 years, and they have remained perhaps the two most important friends he has had in his long and lucky life: Tom Southworth and Gordon Grant. John discovered midway through his racing career that he enjoyed and got more out of competing with a partner than he did paddling his own boat by himself. He got incredibly lucky in having Tom and Gordon choose him as their partner.

The team nature of paddling competition morphed into John's role when he arrived at the NOC, first as a guest instructor (with Tom and Les Bechdel, the other 1973 US team coach) in the spring of 1974, and then when he moved to the NOC full-time in the fall of 1975. The community first envisioned by Payson and Aurelia was the perfect home for John, where his involvement in paddling, teaching, coaching, and business education came together in a perfect fit for him. John is one of the people for whom the people, principles, physical challenges, and community of the NOC were the perfect home at the right time.

He became president and served on the board of directors through 1991, when he and his wife, Jan Letendre, formed a group to purchase and run the Nantahala Village Resort, a 60-unit lodging and 100-seat restaurant operation nearby. The resort was sold in 2005, and after a brief stint in real estate, John returned to the NOC in 2008 as CFO. He left in 2013 to become a partner at Moonshadow Leadership Solutions, a coaching, facilitation, and team-building firm dedicated to "making the world a better place by making better leaders."

John has three children and lives with Jan in Bryson City, North Carolina. In addition to whitewater, he enjoys golf and stays in shape with bike riding and CrossFit.

How This Book Came About

By Payson Kennedy

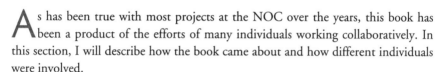

As has been true with most projects at the NOC over the years, this book has been a product of the efforts of many individuals working collaboratively. In this section, I will describe how the book came about and how different individuals were involved.

After my second retirement at the end of 2006, a number of individuals suggested that a history of the NOC was needed and that I was in the best position to write it because I had been involved in most decisions about the NOC since its beginning in 1972. I agreed strongly with the first point about the importance of an NOC history being written before all memories and records from the early years were lost. I agreed that the NOC had been unique in its philosophical principles, business practices, and emphasis on community. I agreed that it had had a major impact on the history of whitewater paddling in the United States and that these facts would make its history of interest to a wide audience of former staff members, NOC friends, and many others in the world of whitewater paddlers and businesses. I also agreed that I had knowledge of most events in the history of the NOC. I disagreed, however, that I was the best person to write this history, because throughout my life I have had great difficulty writing. I am not a natural storyteller like John Burton, Ray McLeod, or John Zubizarreta. I was confident that I could write down a lot of facts about the NOC but afraid that I would not be able to weave them into an interesting story.

This dilemma persisted with several individuals continuing to encourage me to undertake the project. Gordon Grant, who I thought would be one of the best persons to carry the project forward, was the most persistent in encouraging me to undertake it. I continued to think about the need for an NOC history and the possibility of undertaking it, but I didn't do anything to make it happen.

I was relieved and elated in 2011 when John Burton announced that he was going to write the history of the NOC. John and I had worked together in the leadership of the NOC from 1975 until 1991, when he formed a partnership to purchase and operate Nantahala Village just 3 miles down the road from the NOC. John remained a part of the NOC community throughout his time operating the village, and he often surprised me by knowing things that were going on at the center that I was unaware of. He came back to work at the NOC in 2008 after selling the village. I knew that John was an excellent choice, as he often remembered past events more than I did and he had detailed knowledge of most of what had happened at the NOC since 1975. I turned over to him much of the historical materials that I had collected over the years and spent several hours in interviews telling him about events of the first three years. John also conducted interviews with Horace and Aurelia about their memories from the beginnings of the NOC and began writing his history.

After the ownership of the NOC changed in 2012, John left to become a partner of Moonshadow Leadership Solutions, and the demands of the new job prevented him from continuing to work on the NOC history. I eventually decided that if the history was going to be written I would have to make it happen, but I still hoped to find a better writer, or a collaborator.

At this point I thought of John Lane, who is the most successful writer I know. John had worked at the NOC for about 10 years in the 1980s and 1990s, had done some writing while he was here, and had once expressed to me an interest in writing more about the NOC. John is now director of the Goodall Environmental Studies Center at Wofford College and has published numerous books of poetry, fiction, and nonfiction. I contacted John and asked whether he might be persuaded to write a history of the NOC or to collaborate with me on the project. John told me that his teaching and writing schedule wouldn't allow him to undertake the NOC history but that he would send me what he had previously written while at the NOC and would be willing to advise as I worked on the book. As we discussed the possibilities, we came up with the idea of inviting others to write down their memories of the NOC, rather than writing a traditional history.

Realizing that I didn't need to write the entire history but could invite others to share their recollections of life at the NOC, I felt great relief. I was confident that, because what was most distinctive about the NOC was the strength of the staff community that developed and the amazing abilities of the people it attracted, having some of them tell the story as they remembered it would reflect the unique character of the NOC story best. I also was confident that some good storytellers and writers would turn up among former NOC staff. At this point in the winter of 2015, I began talking with many others who had played a prominent role at the NOC in the early years.

Horace and Aurelia were the two obviously crucial people to tell the stories of their involvement in the beginnings of the NOC. I asked Horace and Aurelia about writing down their memories, especially recollections of how the center got started. Unfortunately, health issues prevented either of them from being actively involved. John Burton was the third crucial figure in the leadership from early years, and I knew he had already interviewed both Horace and Aurelia about their memories.

When I talked with John, he enthusiastically agreed to finish up his interviews with Horace, Aurelia, and me and to assist in completing the book. The next crucially important person was Bunny Johns. Bunny had begun working at the new NOC on weekends while she was still attending nursing school in 1974. After getting her nursing degree, she came to work full-time at the NOC and a few years later became manager of our instruction program. When John Burton left in 1991, she became president of the NOC; when I left in 1998, she became CEO. I asked Bunny to assist in the project and she agreed. Because the developments in the teaching of white-water skills had been such an important part of the history of the NOC and Bunny had been the leader of the instruction program throughout the years when most of these developments occurred, we agreed that she would focus on the history of our instruction program. We were now confident that with John, Bunny, and me all reviewing what each of us and other contributors submitted, we would feel confident that there would be no major errors, even though some erroneous details and dates would inevitably creep into the narrative. I was glad that even though we didn't have firsthand accounts from Aurelia and Horace, we would have their recollections of those years as told to John Burton (some of their recollections appear in Section VI: Early Leaders of the NOC).

Next I began contacting other leaders from the early years of the NOC to ask for their help in recording the NOC story. Les and Susan Bechdel quickly agreed to help, and Les's account of the early Chattooga years was the first contribution I received. Gordon Grant, Kent Ford, Dave Perrin, Ken Kastorff, John Barbour, and Janet Smith all agreed to send us some of their memories for inclusion. Ray McLeod, the great storyteller, didn't write down his stories, but he did recruit Susan White Hester and his children, Heather and Mike, to write down some of them. To make sure that we had stories from the perspective of some line staff, as well as formal leaders, I began to talk about the project to any former staff I encountered, and I opened a Facebook page and posted on my page and the NOC page that I was beginning this project and would welcome submissions from any former staff members and NOC friends.

Within days I received Mike Inman's account and soon others began to follow. I was especially pleased when several people who had worked during the first three hard years, when the NOC was struggling to survive, sent me stories. Tom Gonzalez, Florrie Funk, Allie Funk (Jones), and Sue Firmstone Goddard, all of whom worked during those years, sent their stories. Our daughter, Cathy Kennedy, who was here from the start, wrote down her memories of a great character of those years, Donnie Dunton. Charlie Walbridge, who worked here during our second summer, and Herb Barks, who began bringing Baylor School students to go down the Chattooga with the NOC about that same time, gave permission to use stories that they had already written about their experiences at the NOC. During the following year, I continued to receive stories from many more former staff members.

From the beginning, my two greatest encouragers in this project have been Gordon Grant and Cathy Kennedy. Gordon's encouragement was crucial in getting me to undertake it, and Cathy has continued to give me strong encouragement, support, and advice. She has transcribed or scanned many documents for me. Her greatest contribution to the project was in recruiting Greg Hlavaty as editor. Greg was assistant manager of the rentals operation at the Nantahala for several years in the new millennium, and he now teaches English at Elon University. In the spring of 2015, Greg agreed to collaborate, and since then he has done all the editing work on the stories, assembled and organized them, and submitted two stories of his own. Without Greg's gentle prodding, I'm afraid the project would have dragged on for another year or two and resulted in a less coherent final book.

The final person who gave valuable assistance in this project was Bob Sehlinger, an old friend from the 1970s who worked with me in the start-up of the Eastern Professional River Outfitters and who is now the publisher at Menasha Ridge Press. In the spring of 2016, when we had received lots of good stories and felt confident that they could become an interesting book, I contacted Bob to ask for his opinion and advice. Bob read the manuscript as it then existed and gave his encouragement and advice. In correspondence and on a visit to Wesser, he met with Greg, John, Bunny, and me to discuss his ideas. His advice was valuable in helping us form a more readable book.

When the manuscript was nearly complete, I asked several longtime members of the community to read it over and let me know of any errors they found. In addition to John and Bunny, Cathy Kennedy, Ray McLeod, Dave Perrin, and Villa Brewer reviewed the draft manuscript. Villa also agreed to search for photos to accompany the text and to serve as photo editor.

I hope this essay makes clear that *NOC Stories* is indeed the product of many individuals working collaboratively to keep alive memories of the first 45 years at the Nantahala Outdoor Center.

Payson Kennedy
Wesser, North Carolina
April 2018

SECTION 1
Life on the River

IN SERVICE By Gordon Grant

First, all recollections are fictions: We draw them from events that actually happened, but through years of recalling and burnishing selected facts, we turn the events into poetic truths that give an impression of what actually occurred at the time. Storytelling is an art form, one of the earliest, and there's much to be learned from sharing stories. So I believe that the storytellers are telling their truths, but that the facts have been slipping away quickly down the river of time.

So how should one remember what the NOC has meant to him or her? First, tell a story, small or grand, of an event that happened to you during your time at the center. Just tell it, brothers and sisters, tell it all. Second, reflect on that story: Why have you carried it with you all these years? What did you learn from that event and how have you used it in your life?

There's an argument that rages across the field of experiential education: Are these incredible experiences that occur out on the rivers and in the moun-

Gordon Grant geared up and ready to climb . . . and change lives (photographed by Mary Ellen Hammond)

tains generalizable? And do they really cause people to make changes in their lives? The field of outdoor education has lots of practitioners who deeply believe this but have a hard time proving it. Most of us who worked at the NOC for any period of time in the past 40 years—certainly those willing to put down their memories in writing here—would probably say, "Yes, my time at the NOC changed my life. I am different from what I would be had I not worked there for 1, 3, 5, or 15 years."

Is that so? Then you should be able to tell us what happened there and how it changed you.

Here's my recollection.

The Story: Chattooga, Section IV, late 1970s

I was coiling up the rope below Seven-Foot Falls when I noticed one of the rafts pulling over to the river's left shore. Everyone in the raft was looking down at someone on the floor, and the guide was motioning to me. Broken leg: A big male friend had fallen on a woman's extended leg, and it was clear that we would have to carry her out. So, using one of the ineffective inflatable splints of the time, we made her as comfortable as we could, rigged a stretcher out of cut poles and life jackets, and proceeded to thrash and carry her up the river's left side to Woodall Shoals, about 0.5 mile upstream.

I think it was the first trip I'd been on that required a carry-out. During the early years on the rivers, we all felt so indestructible, and our guests tended to be fit and tough adventure seekers, so we hadn't thought through all of the possibilities and consequences of injury to our guests or ourselves. None of us had the first aid and rescue training that is required of all guides today.

It quickly became apparent how tiring it was to carry the woman out; all of us were sweating in our wet suits, and the woman's friends—mostly big men, ex-football players now out of shape—were sweating and starting to hyperventilate. One man in particular concerned me: While he was helping carry the woman, his color had gone from red to pale, and I realized that it was possible we could have a cardiac event on our hands to vastly complicate and extend the day into a much more serious affair. I called a halt to the rescue, got everyone to rest, and sent some runners back to the trip to get more people to assist in the evacuation. I pulled the man aside and told him as diplomatically as I could that I was concerned about his health and that his friend would need him for support at the hospital. I asked him to wait on the trail while the guides finished the extraction, and, too tired to argue, he just nodded assent. The rescue proceeded, and we got the woman and her friends out at Woodall Shoals. I ran back and met the man on the trail, and we walked back together to continue the trip.

Two years later I was at the store counter at the Chattooga Outpost, selling one of Bobby Karls's ridiculous Chattooga Shark T-shirts to someone. A man walked up to the counter to introduce himself with the prefatory comment: "You don't remember me, but . . ."

He explained that he was the out-of-shape guy who had nearly had a heart attack two years before. He said the experience had shocked him into realizing that he had let his weight climb and his health decline, and after that trip, he'd decided to do something about it.

And he had: he looked great—trim and fit as the runner and triathlete he had become. But he also said that not only was he struck by the fitness of all of the guides, but also by the way we had treated him with concern and respect by getting him to step aside in a way that preserved his dignity.

He said: "So I waited to get really fit before I came back to tell you. Thanks."

The Reflection

At the time of this story, I was in my early 20s. It got me thinking, and I have kept thinking throughout my life, that we have no idea what unwitting agents of change we might be in other people's lives. It was amazing that a guy in his 40s—an old person to me at the time—could have a life-changing event on a trip that he had come on just for a good time. I resolved, and carried my resolve throughout my years at the NOC, to be open to being an agent for that kind of change—whether it be on the third Nanty raft trip of the day or with people wandering around the rentals parking lot. I was earnest about it, and I don't think too heavy-handed, and it animated me in my level of service at the NOC for the next 14 years. I never lost the feeling that each trip, each day, could reveal something extraordinary to me or through me to someone . . . and most days that feeling was justified.

Those were extraordinary years. I carried their purpose with me into my second career as a public educator. As a principal, where did I take my elementary students? Out on a river, of course.

About the Contributor

Gordon Grant came to work at the NOC as a 21-year-old in May 1976, though he had been hanging around training in the gates and running rivers with the crew there for a year. He remained for 16 years, until 1992, serving as raft guide on all rivers; instructor in canoe, kayak, river rescue, rock climbing, and cross-country skiing; Chattooga Outpost manager (the last one before Dave Perrin!); the head of the instruction program; Adventure Travel leader on the Grand Canyon and in Nepal; a member of the NOC Steering Committee; and the least-skilled laborer in the Raft Guide Construction Company (RGCC). Most important, the NOC is where he met his life's partner, Susan Sherrill Grant, and where they brought their daughters, Rachel and Glenna, into the world. It served as his true alma mater: the NOC is the bedrock of his education. Gordon picked up a few conventional degrees, including a doctorate, which allowed him to share what he had learned on the rivers and in the mountains in the following 24 years with Asheville City Schools. He now serves as the education director for the North Carolina Outward Bound School, and he has returned after all his exploring to where he began in experiential education, to know the place for the first time, grateful to those who taught him: Payson and Aurelia and the wonderfully talented community they assembled by the waters.

MARCH 1979: FIRST DAY ON THE JOB

By Dave Perrin

When I first arrived at the Chattooga Outpost in March 1979, Gordo (Gordon Grant) said, "The river is flooded and we're headed to Wesser to run the Upper Nantahala above the power plant. We've called our guests and told them to meet us there. It will be fun."

Wanting to make a good impression, I climbed in a van and we took off. Truthfully, I'd heard about this section of the Nantahala but had never considered running it, much less guiding guests through it, so I conveyed my trepidation to Gordo.

He replied with his typical irrepressible enthusiasm: "No worries! Payson and Burton have it under control." With Gordo, I came to realize his infectious grin and twinkling eye usually meant he knew something I didn't, which in this case turned out to be that they'd never run guests on the Upper Nanty either.

At Wesser, the widespread rain meant that all the regular Nanty trips would be fully guided with accompanying kayak guides. I kayaked, so with some relief I found out that John Burton had assigned me to one of those trips. I hadn't brought a boat and was told to head up to the fort and get one from instruction. I wandered around, trying to figure out where this so-called fort was located.

Walking toward the motel, I noticed a bunch of kayaks sitting on a well-tended grassy area, the only green grass to be found in March. It looked freshly seeded and

Dave Perrin, current Chattooga Outpost manager, in the Grand Canyon

tender beneath the jumble of boats. Nearby Silvermine Creek was a rushing torrent, carrying enough water to float a kayak.

I secured a Hollowform, which in those days had no outfitting, and headed back toward the Outfitter's Store, vaguely concerned about how the heck I would stay in the kayak should I roll over. Suddenly, a group of guides rushed by, shouting and pointing, in a mad dash toward the river.

I looked back and noticed that the grassy spot was now empty of kayaks. Out past the highway, people were scrambling down the riverbank and lunging into the swollen stream. What was going on?

It turned out that the grassy area I'd noticed was the center's first attempt at landscaping and had been carefully cultivated and tended by Payson. NOC had few hard and fast rules in those days, but one rule was that no kayaks should be stored on that grassy area—a rule that had been ignored with some apparent regularity. It seems Payson had seen the pile of boats that morning and had had enough. He'd tossed all those kayaks into Silvermine Creek to drive home the point. The boats were barreling down Silvermine, headed for the swollen Nantahala.

What a way to start off my career! When we finally ran the guided trip, I managed to waddle down the river in that kayak and even stayed upright in the enormous Nantahala Falls.

And Gordo was right; it *was* fun.

The camaraderie of the guests and guides at the end of the day was thrilling. Guests in those early days seemed as adventurous and hardy as the staff. Everyone was imbued with a shared sense of adventure. It typified what NOC came to mean to me.

Challenges were to be met and surmounted through skill, teamwork, and a can-do spirit. Indelible memories were made too, with the story of Payson tossing the kayaks into Silvermine Creek recounted around the picnic table to successive crops of wide-eyed new guides. Not quite sure what I'd gotten myself into, I felt it sink in on the drive home: this place was going to be different.

 ## *About the Contributor*

Dave Perrin is the current and longtime manager of the NOC's Chattooga Outpost. He's not sure there's anyone outside the Kennedy family whose life trajectory has been influenced more by Payson and Horace's creation of the NOC than his. Dave met and married his wife of 33 years at the NOC, built his home using skills learned from NOC's do-it-yourself philosophy, and then created a family to live in it. He and his wife raised three children, instilling many of the NOC core values into their upbringing, each loving the mountains and rivers they call home. The company has provided sustenance while influencing and shaping his life for 37 years and counting.

RUNNING DOWN THE
UPPER NANTAHALA By John Burton

One summer day sometime in the late 1970s, big rains caused the rivers to rise. The Nantahala, normally running at 700 cubic feet per second (cfs), was in flood, probably closer to 3,000 cfs that day. We had a trip of bigwigs from North Carolina Outward Bound School scheduled for the normal Section IV Chattooga trip, but with the high water, there was much consternation about what to do with the day's trips. Somehow we decided that this hearty group of kindred souls would be a good "canary in the coal mine" to gauge what a raft trip on the Upper Nantahala might be like. We had never done it before, not really studied it at high water. Most of the extra cfs in the Lower Nantahala was arriving from the Upper, which is faster, steeper, narrower, and much more demanding than the Lower.

So we took our best rafts up there and scouted as we drove up, all very excited about this new challenge. We had a guide in every boat! These days that seems normal; back then it was rare. We had our best guides: Payson, me, Les Bechdel, Dick Eustis, Kathy Bolyn, Ray McLeod, maybe a safety kayak or two, maybe other guides I don't remember. Anyway, we were ready. I don't remember what the OB folks were saying, much less thinking, as they saw the raging river next to the road, in some places lapping up onto the road, and heard us talking about how fast it was and how few eddies there were.

The fact that our rafts were small, soft, single-thwart bucket boats didn't weigh down our enthusiasm. There was no such thing as a self-bailing raft back then—all rafts had thin-fabric floors sewn or glued to the circular doughnut tubes, not the cross tubes. So when such a boat got full of water, the floor sagged and a rafter standing in the middle would be in thigh- or waist-deep water. And of course, such a boat was impossible to control or guide; it would have to be coaxed to shore somehow and either bailed or flipped to be emptied.

Payson was the senior citizen (in his early 40s), the boss, so the rest of us river "experts" deferred to his judgment. If he thought it was safe and smart to run this section, then we were in! We hadn't realized what a natural risk-taker he was—it's in his bones. (Note: In the summer of 2015, at the age of 82, he rowed a raft down the Colorado River through the Grand Canyon, until he flipped it and had a long cold swim.)

We found an eddy big enough for all the rafts to get in together, then looked at each other and peeled out as close together as possible on the assumption that we could provide safety for each other if someone were to fall out. No chance. Within 0.25 mile every boat was completely swamped, guides and crews were fighting to stay in the rafts—and losing. My memory is that half of the people were in the water and the boats were still right-side up. Complete, out-of-control chaos. Paddlers left in the boats full of water were gamely trying to maneuver toward shore, but it was tough. My lasting memory is of Payson sprinting down the road, paddle in hand, trying to get ahead of his raft so he could swim out to it and get back in. Not a sight you see every day.

Somehow we got all the people and boats to shore, into whatever eddies were available, in the next mile or two. No casualties, probably a few lost paddles, but we survived. We somehow got to the put-in at the powerhouse of the normal 8-mile run, with various shouts of exhilaration, exhaustion, fear, shock, relief, and joy. We were now in familiar territory, though at extremely high water levels most of us had not seen, much less rafted. We decided to continue on, and we had a fast, fun, boisterous ride to Nantahala Falls. I can't remember what we did there, whether we carried or ran it.

But my guess is we ran it.

 ## *About the Contributor*

See page 3 for more information about John Burton.

THE EARLY YEARS AT THE
CHATTOOGA OUTPOST By Les Bechdel

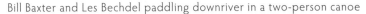

B ecause guides are social animals, their world in the early years of NOC revolved around what was happening in Wesser, North Carolina. The center offered comfortable housing, a delicious meal plan, and lots of social interaction. That wasn't the case at the Chattooga.

Guides assigned to the Chattooga for the weekend were often left there for days on end, waiting for the next trip to be booked. The meal plan was sketchy, the housing sucked, and the well often ran dry. The moniker *outpost* implied a remote posting, not unlike being in the French Foreign Legion. Undoubtedly, the river was beautiful and fun to run, but living at the outpost was not popular.

During the winter of 1975–1976, Payson Kennedy hired me to manage the Chattooga operations. I had plenty of whitewater kayaking under my belt, but I had never even stepped in a raft. I thought I was going to be trained on the relatively tame Nantahala, but instead, for my first experience, I was to go with Payson down Section IV of the Chattooga at relatively high water. With paying guests.

Bill Baxter and Les Bechdel paddling downriver in a two-person canoe

At an early staff training session, Bunny Johns, Dick Eustis, Kathy Bolyn (KB), and Payson Kennedy paddle a raft into the hole at Woodall Shoals on the Chattooga to see how sticky it really is.

Payson gave the orientation to our crew, gave me a steering pointer or two, and then had me immediately start guiding from the put-in. I am not sure what the guests thought as we pinballed down the river, but I liked coordinating the strokes of the guests and piloting the raft through the easy rapids. Thankfully, Payson took over at the hard drops. That day I fell in love with the concept of teaching a bunch of novices how to work together as a team to paddle through Class IV whitewater.

When we got back to the outpost, Payson gave me $100 in petty cash and told me to have a good summer. Wow, that was it? Fortunately, there were a couple of experienced trip leaders, Dick Eustis and Robert Harkness, to teach me the ins and outs of running raft trips on the Chattooga River.

Part of the Chattooga adventure was our transportation. We had a 2-ton, open flatbed truck to shuttle our guests to and from the river. We fondly called it the cattle truck. Two benches were fastened to either side of the stake body and it had no roof. On fair-weather days, it was a pleasant riding experience as we passed through the orchard country of Upstate South Carolina. When it rained, however, it was a cold, windy ride.

Our takeout road from Lake Tugalo had several miles of red clay, which we called gumbo when it became saturated. The truck did not have four-wheel drive, so to negotiate the hills, the driver had to keep up the momentum to make it up the next incline. Liquid mud would spray over the hood and the cab of the truck. The windshield wipers could not keep up with the mess, and one would have to steer by looking out the side windows. Of course, the guests would get splattered as well. When we returned to the outpost, we would spray everyone down with a garden hose, using cold water. But somehow, it was all fun.

The cattle truck was used to haul the inflated rafts to the put-in prior to transporting the guests. Four rafts were slid in on their side tubes and two were tied on top. One time, two of our intrepid guides, Gordon "Gordo" Grant and Fritz Orr, decided that the top raft would be a great place to enjoy the ride to the river. For some reason, the raft lashing failed and the speed was excessive enough to cause the raft to fly off the truck. Gordon got by with some minor scrapes, but Fritz hurt his back and it put him out of commission for some time. We were lucky the injuries weren't worse, but the days of raft riding on top of the cattle truck were over.

Because most of the guides arrived at the outpost via a company van, there was usually a dearth of private vehicles to go anywhere with. Come Saturday night, to relieve cabin fever, we would load the cattle truck with lawn chairs, pillows, and popcorn and head for the drive-in at Clayton. We would back the truck up toward the screen and lower the tailgate to enjoy truly terrible movies. Needless to say, more than one adult beverage was imbibed, but we did have a sober, designated driver named Sherry Spurlin, who was our outpost cook, driver, and mother hen. She proved to be the glue that held the place together and reversed the negative image that the outpost had previously held.

During the 1970s, interest in all aspects of whitewater was taking off. ABC was airing river descents on *Wide World of Sports*. All over the United States, outfitting companies were getting established. An immensely popular movie, *Deliverance*, had come out in 1972. In the making of that movie, Payson, along with Claude Terry and Doug Woodward, had worked as whitewater advisors, safety crew, and gofers. They doubled for Ned Beatty and Jon Voight with a dummy in the bottom of one canoe representing Burt Reynolds's character, as they canoed the rapids of the Five Falls, the most difficult rapids on the Chattooga River.

This movie inspired all kinds of people to try whitewater canoeing. The NOC decided to capitalize on this fad by renting canoes for Section III of the Chattooga. While reservations staff tried to ensure that users had prior whitewater experience, many would-be adventurers proved to have inadequate whitewater skills and would come back to the outpost with damaged canoes. We would estimate the damage and try to collect money for those repairs, but often the guests were inebriated and many of them argued about the cost of the work to be done. Sometimes they would come back empty-handed. It was usually dark when they returned and often they weren't able to describe very well where the canoe was left. Sometimes the canoe was left wrapped on a rock in the river. We would have to head out that night to retrieve the canoe so it could be rented the next day.

Most of the roads in the Chattooga backcountry were not maintained and required some serious four-wheel driving. Plus, to meet the standards of being labeled a Wild and Scenic River by Congress, most roads to the river terminated 0.25 mile from the water. Often, it would take several hiking forays to find the missing boat. When we did find it, we would have an uphill portage to get it back to our trusty Suburban. After that summer, we came to the realization that the canoe rental business was best served on the less difficult Nantahala River, which offered easy road access.

With the rental business behind us, Chattooga staff focused on the developing sport of paddle rafting. Payson and those early rafting guides worked hard to run safe trips. Part of the challenge was that the riverbed of the Chattooga had many undercuts and boulder sieves. Also, the difficulty of the rapids varied greatly depending on flows. Every tenth of a foot on the US 76 bridge gauge could change the nature of any specific drop and how we would run it.

Following each day's rafting, we would gather over dinner and analyze the day's rafting adventures: How could we have prevented that raft from flipping? How could we have effected a quicker rescue of the swimmers and the raft? We also started the honored tradition of having the guide who fell out of his or her raft do the dishes that night.

The Five Falls section of the river represented the greatest challenge to safety on Section IV. These were a series of abrupt drops, one right after another. As river levels rose, the current speed between the drops increased. We fine-tuned where to station our safety kayak and where to position throw ropes. In time, our trips became choreographed like an opera and rarely did we have a swimmer in the water for any length of time. Soon, the other river companies were emulating our safety protocols.

A few years later, one of our safety kayakers, Rick Bernard, became pinned underwater and drowned just above Soc-em-Dog rapid. Gallant efforts to rescue

Stewart Kennedy's raft flipping at Bull Sluice, proving that anyone can swim. According to Cathy Kennedy, Stewart said just before this flip, "I've never flipped a raft at the Bull."

Rick failed, and it took hours to recover his body. Later we debriefed what occurred, and to this day, I don't think any of the modern rescue methods could have saved his life.

Rick's death did, however, make us take a critical look at our accident prevention practices, as well as our rescue tools and techniques. That winter, a lot of us channeled our grief into developing innovative approaches to river safety. The NOC was incredibly supportive of these efforts.

We shared many of these rescue ideas in the *NOC Newsletter*, which had a huge circulation in the Southeast at the time. We started doing guide safety training sessions at the onset of each season. Private paddlers saw our training, and soon we began teaching river rescue classes to the public. Every rescue class experimented with different techniques, and we were constantly broadening and adapting our curriculum.

All of these efforts culminated in the publication of *River Rescue*, written by two NOC employees: Slim Ray and me. This was the first book to be written about river safety and rescue techniques, and it is still in print 30 years later. The NOC was instrumental in making that book happen.

John Kennedy pioneering a new line at Seven-Foot Falls. The route was considered radical at the time but ultimately drastically reduced injuries at this rapid.

 ## About the Contributor

Les Bechdel was first involved with the NOC by teaching kayak instructor classes in 1973 and 1974. He started working full-time in 1975 as the Chattooga Outpost manager and was there until 1978. He then became Nantahala River manager for a few years before becoming vice president in the late 1970s. As vice president he worked on a variety of tasks on an as-needed basis, but his primary job was supervising the NOC outposts. Les started the Bío-Bío River trips in Chile in 1981 and managed that program through 1983. Les was instrumental in developing river rescue techniques, which culminated in the writing of *River Rescue* with coauthor Slim Ray in 1985. During all of his years at the NOC, he taught canoeing, kayaking, river rescue, and rock climbing.

Les and his wife, Susan, left NOC in 1985 to start their own river business, Canyons Incorporated, in Idaho, which conducted extended wilderness whitewater river trips on the Middle and Main Forks of the Salmon River in the River of No Return Wilderness. The Bechdels sold their business in 2010, and for the last six years Les has worked as a seasonal river ranger on the Middle Fork for the U.S. Forest Service.

A YANKEE PADDLER GOES SOUTH:

A SUMMER WITH DONNIE DUNTON[1]

By Charlie Walbridge

In the winter of 1973, I found a help-wanted ad for NOC river guides and kayak instructors in the *American Whitewater Journal*. Being a Northern boy, I remember being apprehensive as I drove south the next spring for the job. I'd paddled in the Smokies on two previous occasions with Jack Wright, and the locals seemed friendly enough. I'd also met lots of likable Southern paddlers at races. But I'd seen the attacks on civil rights protesters on TV as a kid, and more recently watched the movie *Deliverance*. My dad, who watched the movie with me, couldn't understand why I wanted to go "down there." At a truck stop in East Tennessee, I passed a baseball cap that said, "Keep the South beautiful. Put a Yankee on a bus!" so I was worried about fitting in.

I shouldn't have been concerned. Once I got to the center, I quickly found myself among friends. But I also encountered two distinct types of Southern personalities. One was the strong, calm, thoughtful type exemplified by my boss, Payson Kennedy. A former university librarian, Payson had been paddling Southern rivers for decades. A tall man with an athletic build, he was a formidable open canoeist. He was also a savvy whitewater guide, an innovative instructor, and a fierce competitor.

The other type I met was the loud, aggressive, redneck kind personified by my coworker, Donnie Dunton. He stood about 5 feet, 4 inches tall and weighed nearly 260 pounds. He had a bushy brown beard, a huge folding belt knife, and a cowboy hat with a turkey feather in it. Although I never found out exactly where he came from, he spoke with the sharp twang of the Southern Appalachians.

At that time on Section IV of the Chattooga, guides would sit in their boats and wait for the guests to pick the one they wanted to ride with. Conservative customers who wanted a smooth, safe ride chose big, clean-shaven people . . . like me! Rowdies who wanted big excitement chose guides who looked like Donnie.

Our guests either loved him or hated him. Although he was the NOC's most-requested guide that summer, there were others who asked for "anybody but Donnie." One time my trip was approaching Seven-Foot Falls when we noticed that the trip ahead of us had pulled over below the drop. When we got into the eddy, their trip leader asked if I would switch places with Donnie. I did, and finished the run with a nice group from a North Georgia church. I later learned

---

[1] This essay is an excerpt from "A Yankee Paddler Goes South: Revisiting the Early Years of the Nantahala Outdoor Center," published in the May/June 2002 issue of *American Whitewater Journal*, 60–67.

Charlie Walbridge

that Donnie, at the lip of the drop, had screamed at them: "Paddle, you klutzy mother#^@%*&s, PADDLE!" The group had pulled over and refused to continue until they were given another guide.

Guiding Section IV is serious business, so I appreciated Donnie's frustration, but his fun didn't stop with the Chattooga. One time Donnie spent a long afternoon guiding the Nantahala with a group of guys who let him know in no uncertain terms that they were not impressed with the river. He put up with this smart talk for most of the run, then above Nantahala Falls he turned to his guests and smiled wickedly. "You boys want *the big ride?*" he asked. They did, and he delivered. He dropped his four-man sideways into the top hole of Nantahala Falls. Donnie bailed out the back as his raft began a lengthy surf. One by one the guests were thrown out, recirculated in the hole, trashed in the falls, and spat out. Donnie swam to an eddy and watched from shore, laughing.

Visiting Clayton, Georgia, today, it's hard to picture it the way it was in '74. Today it's a progressive, tourist-oriented place, but I remember a rough little hill town where some of its residents liked to get drunk and kick hippie paddlers around on Friday night. I remember a town so tough that guides who needed to buy beer went in groups so they wouldn't get beaten up at the Piggly Wiggly!

But Donnie soon became our unofficial ambassador to the local community. One day we were setting up our Chattooga trips under the US 76 bridge when a local guy tried to drive his Jeep CJ straight up a steep embankment under the bridge. After watching this foolishness for a while, Payson politely suggested that the man use the road located just downstream. The man was roaring drunk, and he staggered out of his car screaming and cursing. When our guides hustled over to see what was going on, the man got spooked, pulled out a pocketknife, and flashed its rusty blade.

"You oughtn't to press a man," he warned. "A fella could git cut."

Donnie moved smoothly up to the front of our group. He opened his huge folding knife and offered it gently to the man, handle first. "Long as we're talking about cuttin', I'd just like you to *feel* this blade."

Donnie was an expert woodcarver and the blade of his knife was razor sharp. The man slowly ran his finger down the blade. Suddenly, he let out a yelp as the honed edge drew blood. He dropped the knife to the ground. Donnie retrieved it quickly, then remarked in a friendly way, "Ooo, sharp little f^@%*&, isn't it? You'd better git on home now, before someone gets hurt!"

It's true that he was loud, outspoken, quick-tempered, and profane. But because he was competent, unpretentious, and hardworking, the folks at the center overlooked his rough side and found that behind his bluster was a good-hearted person on whom you could depend in tight situations.

Another Viewpoint

Payson also recalls that episode in Clayton, Georgia: "When the other guides gathered around armed with their paddles (the guides were then using much longer and heavier Norse paddles), I felt reassured but still afraid. I think our adversary was probably equally afraid because he was greatly outnumbered and there were some big guys in our group. He wasn't willing to lose face by backing down, though, and the situation could have easily resulted in one or more of us getting hurt. I think Donnie must have been in similar situations before, and I was greatly impressed at the skill he showed in defusing the tensions without anyone getting hurt or losing face."

About the Contributor

Charlie Walbridge first paddled whitewater at summer camp in 1962. He and Marty Pickands, his college roommate, founded the Bucknell Outing Club in 1966. After graduating he started Wildwater Designs, selling life vest, spray-skirt, and paddle-jacket kits through the mail. He ran this business from his bedroom in NOC's brick house in 1974. That summer Charlie primarily worked with Outward Bound canoeing groups, but he also guided on the Nantahala and Chattooga Rivers and helped out with whitewater kayaking clinics. He remembers learning a lot from Payson Kennedy by working alongside him on Section IV. After an unsuccessful attempt to make the 1975 US Whitewater Team, he worked as a Cheat River guide for the next eight seasons while continuing to run his business. He was safety chair of the American Canoe Association and one of the founders of their whitewater canoe and swift-water rescue programs. An American Whitewater board member, he is safety editor and manages its accident database. His publications include several whitewater accident anthologies, a river rescue text, guides to Mid-Atlantic states whitewater, and numerous magazine articles. He has worked as an expert consultant in 45 wrongful death cases involving fast-moving water. In 1996 he closed his business and began working as the eastern outfitter field rep for Northwest River Supplies, retiring in 2015. He and his wife, Sandy, now live in Bruceton Mills, West Virginia. He's currently on the board of Friends of the Cheat River, a local watershed group.

WALKABOUT BEGINNING[2]

By Herbert B. Barks

This story is a compilation of the first 10 trips I spent with Baylor School seniors on the Chattooga River.

In October of the first year, a group of students came to my office to ask me to take them on a camping trip. I agreed, and in April they returned ready for, in their words, "a weeklong camping trip."

"Guys, we're not going for a weeklong camping trip. You know that."

"Well, it was worth a try," they said.

So we decided on a one-night, one-day trip. The students were to choose our destination. They suggested that we should run a river called the Chattooga. I'd never heard of the river, but it was in Clayton, Georgia, not too far away. What I didn't know was that the movie *Deliverance* had been filmed on this river.

Larry Roberts, my colleague known for favoring off-the-charts adventures, said, "It's great, one of the best whitewater rivers ever." I had never run a whitewater river.

So our group, 10 students and myself, headed toward Clayton in a van. Now, this was an outstanding group of seniors; they'd been accepted at Stanford, Dartmouth, Virginia. So when we arrived at 9 p.m. at the Warwoman Dell campground on GA 28, outside of Clayton, I was confident of their camping skills. As I exited the van, I turned on my flashlight and began unrolling my sleeping bag on one of the concrete picnic tables. The guys wanted to borrow my flashlight.

"None of you brought a flashlight?"

"No, sir."

I hadn't suggested that they make a list of gear to bring, as I'd assumed that their camping skills were better than mine. Between the 10 of them, they had one tent, seven sleeping bags, clothes that were not warm enough, and no raingear.

When I finished setting up my campsite, I gave them the flashlight and sat to watch. They had built a fire. Apparently they had lighters. John had set his tent close to the fire. I pointed that out.

"It's OK, Dr. Barks."

His tent caught fire. They tried to stomp it out, but in doing so one of their pants legs caught fire. They ran to Warwoman Creek to put out the burning pants leg. Now a number of them were wet and cold.

It was one of the most miserable nights I've ever spent.

"Guys, can you keep it down?" I later asked. "We need to get some sleep."

"Sorry, we'll keep it down."

---

[2] This essay first appeared in *Walking the Hill: Memories, Dreams and Stories of Baylor* (Signal Mountain, TN: Waldenhouse Publishers, 2015), 99–107.

It was 4 o'clock in the morning before they finally dropped off, cold, wet, and exhausted.

At dawn they were up wanting to get the food and utensils out of the van to fix breakfast. There was no way I was going to let them have anything sharp in their hands.

"Guys, we'll find a place in Clayton to eat breakfast," I said.

We drove to the Clayton Motor Lodge. When we walked into the dining room, Mama Louise, all 300 pounds of mother love, met us.

"Oh, what have you done to these poor boys? You come over here through this line and get you some pancakes and some bacon and some grits and some biscuits." It was like Earth Mother had arrived. She went from table to table hugging them, asking if they had enough to eat, making sure they were happy. Happy?

She swept over to my table. "What are you guys doing?"

"We're from Baylor School in Chattanooga, and we're going down the Chattooga River."

She continued to wander around, and in a while a guy came in with a clipboard and a measuring tape. He began to take the boys' names and addresses and measure them.

I just watched and waited until it was my turn.

"Do you mind telling me what you're doing?"

The boys stopped eating to listen.

"Well," he said, "when we get bodies from the river, a lot of times they are bent up and it's hard to figure casket size. I'm the coroner, and so now when people are going down the river we try to get their measurements before they go."

It was quiet in Clayton.

As we were leaving, I said to the so-called coroner, "Louise put you up to that, didn't she?"

"Yep, we been wanting to do that for weeks. You guys were perfect."

Yeah, perfect. Now we were nervous.

We drove down US 76 to the bridge, where we met Payson Kennedy, our guide. He was inflating two huge black rubber rafts.

Our equipment was as follows: no helmets, life preservers that looked like they had been rescued from some World War II U-boat. They were square pieces of hard foam held together with canvas. There were big paddles, kind of square at the end.

Besides Payson, there was one other guide, Donnie Dunton. He weighed over 300 pounds and had the foulest mouth I have ever heard. Listening to him talk to the group, I thought, *Maybe I better get in there with them.* In his wrath he might kill one of them. He had already explained to them in graphic language how inept they were as they were trying to put on their life preservers.

Another Viewpoint

Payson's note on this event: "One of the most important skills a trip leader needed was the ability to guess who might find Donnie colorful and enjoy being with him rather than being offended by him. When Herb Barks began bringing Baylor students on trips with us, I was pleased that he seemed to form a bond with Donnie and always chose to go in Donnie's raft. I thought Herb really saw all the interesting things about Donnie and wasn't put off by his rough manners. It was only years later when Herb began telling the story of that first trip he took with us on the Chattooga that I learned he'd really chosen to go in Donnie's raft to be sure the students were safe from Donnie."

My first time on the river with Donnie, I assumed the first three rapids were named Mother#^@%*&. It took a while before we learned their names: Surfing, Screaming Left Turn, and Rock Jumble. On the first day, we finally made it to Seven-Foot Falls, inappropriately named because it ain't just 7 feet. The river actually narrows down to about 15 feet in width and turns 90 degrees left over about a 13-foot drop. We pulled out on the right side to scout the rapid. I was standing with Payson and listening carefully to his instructions, which he said were important, about this particular rapid.

"You see," he said, "the river narrows here and then turns left into that hole. The whole river flows right into that rock. It's a very tricky rapid. You have to set your angle as you come toward the rapid, because if we hit the top edge wrong, we will flip the raft down into the hole. Under the rock is a kind of depression or cave that you can wash into. If you do go into that depression, when you come up, you'll hit the ceiling and there's no air there. It's a little distressing. If you relax, normally you will wash out."

Normally?

"Guys!" I yelled.

The students were throwing rocks into the boiling hole beneath the rapid, not listening.

"Guys! Did you hear what Payson just said?"

"Yes, sir, we got it."

"I don't think you got it. Payson, would you tell them again what you just told me?"

Payson repeated the difficult nature of the strokes needed to navigate the rapid upright. Donnie, I noticed, was strangely quiet, smiling. He loved impending disaster.

I don't think the kids were listening. I think they were really thinking, *Let's run this baby.*

We flipped the entire raft, washing into the cave and panicking when there was no air. Normally, we washed out alive.

One year, a senior was caught in the cave a little longer than *normal.*

A rope was thrown to him and he was pulled to shore.

"Bob, are you OK?" I said. "Bob, you can let loose of the rope now. You're on shore. Bob . . ."

"Dr. Barks, I saw God!"

"It's OK. A lot of us have seen God down there."

My memory of the Five Falls on that day is blurry. We ran every rapid. I do remember turning over and swimming more than once and getting back in the boat to run the next rapid. Swimming a rapid changes your perspective about the next one. I remember that ropes were thrown, and I remember the rush of floating that little roller-coaster rapid into the lake at the conclusion of the fourth section of the Chattooga.

During the faculty meeting the week after we returned home, I told them, "In my opinion, we have done an outstanding job preparing the seniors for prestigious colleges, but they are going to get run over crossing the street trying to get to college. They don't listen to instructions well. They don't prepare for life situations well. Sometimes they cannot recognize danger when they see it. They are inept in uncomfortable life situations."

So, we continued to take students in groups of 10 down the fourth section of the Chattooga. We ate at the Clayton Motor Lodge and we paddled with Payson.

However, in the following trips we were prepared. Students paid attention. War stories were shared after each trip, so the next students were introduced to the possibilities and therefore were apprehensive and ready.

That was it, the first glimmer of the senior trip. And now, for more than 40 years, every senior at Baylor School has run that river.

 ## *About the Contributor*

Dr. Herbert B. Barks served as a Presbyterian minister in churches in Shreveport, Louisiana; Los Angeles; and Lynchburg, Virginia, for a total of 20 years. He was president and headmaster of Baylor School in Chattanooga, Tennessee, for 17 years, and headmaster of Hammond School in Columbia, South Carolina, for 17 years. He served on the NOC Board of Directors from 1989 through 1992. Dr. Barks and his wife live on Lookout Mountain in Georgia.

DONNIE DUNTON, AN NOC LEGEND: THE OTHER SIDE OF THE MAN

By Cathy Kennedy

The rough-and-tumble, loud, and sometimes foul-mouthed redneck Donnie Dunton was one side of the man I came to know. It's the side nearly everyone talks about, and it was the first side of Donnie I became familiar with. He was a bit frightening to me, as he was larger than life at 300 pounds or more, bushy haired, and a bit rough around the edges for sure. I'd never met anyone quite like Donnie in my city girl life growing up in Atlanta.

But I came to know another Donnie in the years before he died of cancer in 1976. That other Donnie I knew was a kind, sometimes playful, and occasionally eloquent man with a deep love of the land and of the rivers where we live. This is the Donnie that I remember most often, through fantastic stories that are mostly true but have occasionally been embellished with legendary status throughout the years. I remember him when I reread the last letter and poem he sent me . . . when I wear silver earrings Donnie purchased on a day-off trip to Cherokee.

Donnie Dunton gave this portrait to Robin Pilley.

31

My favorite Donnie story of all time involves a homemade river board thought up and crafted by Donnie and some of us "Kennedy kids" so we could surf the bottom hole of Nantahala Falls. I'd guess the idea for this game and most of the engineering of our river board was the brainchild of Donnie and my brother John, with a few suggestions here and there by the rest of us who played. This river board was a piece of plywood about 2 by 3 feet. In the short side, we drilled a hole in the middle to pull the end of one of our throw ropes through and attach a handle. I think that handle was a stick of good size for holding on to. We backed it up on the bottom of the board with a big knot so the handle wouldn't slip when we used the rest of the rope wrapped around a tree (vector pull) to tow each other upstream into the hole for a surf.

Donnie did all of the pulling upstream while the rest of us had our turns at trying to surf, but oh, when it was Donnie's turn to surf, it took all the rest of us pulling hard to move Donnie upstream into the hole for his turn. Remember, he was probably 300 pounds!

Now, the trick to a good surf of more than a second or two was twofold. First, you had to not get pulled too deep into the hole right off the bat; second, you had to keep the leading edge of the board up. If the leading edge dropped, the whole board with the rider would go straight to the bottom of the river and stay there until the rider turned loose and swam to shore. Donnie wasn't the best at keeping that edge up; in fact, he was terrible at it, and his surfs were notoriously short turns. This was OK with us but not always with Donnie, and we dreaded those times when he crawled out on the bank stating, "That just weren't much of a turn. I need to go again." We couldn't say no because Donnie did all of the pulling for the rest of us to surf, but we sure didn't look forward to pulling him up twice in a row!

We had good times and made good memories on the Nantahala. It was just as cold then as it is now, and I can't imagine how we stayed in the water at this game for the hours I recall. Maybe we all warmed up between surfs by towing Donnie upstream for his turn.

In 1974 when Jim Holcombe and I got married, I really wanted an outdoor wedding that people could walk to but also someplace a car could drive to so all my grandparents would come. I found the perfect spot in a field of wildflowers beside a pond about a mile from NOC on the Appalachian Trail. It was walkable but could also be accessed by car via a 45-minute drive, with the last portion being a poorly maintained dirt road to Watia Gap. Donnie volunteered to drive a van with my grandparents and a few others. He certainly got them there in one piece, but as I recall, my Grandmother Winnie thought she'd had the most exciting ride of her life and a near-death experience riding up that dirt road in an elderly van with Donnie.

Another of my favorite Donnie stories started at lunchtime in the original River's End Restaurant. While sitting in the restaurant, I saw a trout, and over time several trout, elevate out of the river and up the back wall of the Outfitter's

Store, where a window overhung the river, and into the store. Eventually I figured out someone inside the store was fishing out that window while they were working. Of course, it was Donnie.

In the early days of NOC, we all did everything: washing dishes in the restaurant, making beds in the hotel, working in the store pumping gas, raft guiding, cooking if you knew how, whatever needed doing. It was Donnie's day to work in the store and he'd decided he could get in a little fishing and get paid at the same time. I don't recall Dad (Payson Kennedy) having minded that Donnie was fishing while he was working, but when a wildlife officer at lunch saw a fish go in that window and went to the store to check out what was happening, it turned out that Donnie hadn't yet gotten a fishing license. That officer didn't fine Donnie for not having a license. It was just too good a story. The officer just told Donnie to quit fishing out that window until he got a license.

Donnie died at the age of 29 in 1976 after a short fight with cancer. I saw him for the last time when he came to visit us in Dahlonega, Georgia, where Jim and I were living at the time. Donnie had lost most of his hair and was moving a bit slowly, but still he was in good spirits, planning to get well and telling tales of what a terror he had been to the nurses while he was in the hospital. He said he didn't much care for the hospital and just wanted to go home. Eventually the nursing staff resorted to strapping his legs and arms down after he removed his IVs and tried to leave a few times. The doctor had just removed a huge tumor weighing 1.5 pounds from his heart, and the hospital was no doubt where he needed to be, but Donnie didn't like it at all. The doctors also told Donnie that a tumor that big would have caused intermittent erratic behavior and mood swings and that this could have been happening for quite some time. Hmmm, we all know Donnie could have quite the temper at times!

After that last visit, I got one letter from Donnie in September of 1975. I still have the letter and in it was a poem Donnie said for me to give a name to. I never gave the poem a name, but I did keep it. It was written on lined notebook paper in beautiful script . . . who knew?

I couldn't catch a butterfly
nor a pearl from the sea
so I send along this little poem
with love to you from me

Each night I make these wishes
wishes to the stars above
I wish you pretty rainbows
I wish you much love

I wish you all the happiness
that life can ever bring
I wish each day of life you live
to be as bright as spring

No I couldn't catch a butterfly
nor a pearl from the sea
so please accept this little poem
with love to you from me

For: Cathy &
Jim   Donnie
          you all can
          give this poem a name.

Final poem that Donnie sent to Cathy Kennedy and Jim Holcombe

This sign, memorializing Donnie Dunton at the rapid named in honor of him, reads:
IN MEMORY OF DONNIE DUNTON: Donnie loved/the "Land of the Noonday Sun,"/
friends who ventured on rivers & mountains,/nature &, most of all, life. He will be
missed. —Donnie's friends, July 1976

Donnie kayaking at Nantahala Falls. RIP, dear friend.

After Donnie died, his family and friends, led by Joe Cole, put up a memorial for Donnie on the banks of the Nantahala River. It stands at a rapid NOC guides still call Donnie Dunton's. The words on that sign say it all about the place Donnie chose to call home.

That sign is still there, a little bit weathered, but so are all of us who remember Donnie and the stories that have made him a legend at NOC.

 ## *About the Contributor*

Cathy Kennedy began working at the NOC in 1972 when her parents, Payson and Aurelia Kennedy, and Horace Holden started the company, and she remains at the NOC today. In 1972 she was 16 years old and the NOC paid her the princely sum of $25 per week; in 2016 she's somewhat older, somewhat grayer, and gets paid a bit more. There are two historical NOC records she can claim and is quite proud of both: first, the honor of being the NOC's first female river guide; and second, to have guided more trips and more people on the Nanty than anyone else in the known universe (originally calculated by Angus Morrison). During the 45 seasons she's worked at the NOC, she's performed jobs ranging from dishwasher, housekeeper, waitress, cook, raft guide, and trash collector to river manager and director of rafting operations. Currently her job title is director of operations.

Along the way at the NOC, she met and was married for 18 years to Jimmy Holcombe; together they raised two wonderful children, Andrew and Jennifer, both of whom started working at the NOC when they were 14 years old and continued through college and beyond. Today Andrew is the director of French Broad River Academy, an experiential middle school in Asheville, North Carolina, and Jennifer completed her MBA in 2017 at Illinois State University. Both use their skills to pursue their passions in the outdoor industry.

DODGING A BULLET AT THE FIVE FALLS

By Bob Tolford

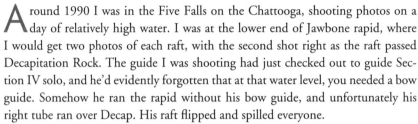

Around 1990 I was in the Five Falls on the Chattooga, shooting photos on a day of relatively high water. I was at the lower end of Jawbone rapid, where I would get two photos of each raft, with the second shot right as the raft passed Decapitation Rock. The guide I was shooting had just checked out to guide Section IV solo, and he'd evidently forgotten that at that water level, you needed a bow guide. Somehow he ran the rapid without his bow guide, and unfortunately his right tube ran over Decap. His raft flipped and spilled everyone.

Our safety boater was on a guest right away. All safety ropes were out, hitting guests perfectly. I watched as one guest, a lady, headed right for Hydroelectric Rock, where she got sucked in, feet first. I stood, somewhat horrified. Knowing how strainers were often caught in the hole, I prayed she would come out on the downstream side. It seemed about 15 seconds to me before I finally saw her surface just downstream. (A couple of guides said it was probably only about 4 or 5 seconds later that she popped up; time seemed to stand still.)

As she floated toward Soc-em-Dog, the safety rope thrower (Guide #1), positioned on river right above the Dog, had just thrown a rope to another guest and was hauling him/her in. Another guide (Guide #2), who had the day off and was kayaking along with the trip, was standing just above the Dog with Guide #1, who was hauling in the guest. The rest of the guests were safely being brought to shore at this point, so Guide #2 gathered up slack from Guide #1's rope and threw the slack end of the rope to the lady as she approached the Dog.

But there just wasn't *quite* enough slack, and the end of the rope fell about a foot and a half short. She washed over Soc-em-Dog as we watched pretty much filled with dread.

Somehow, the guest came up in Dead Man's Pool, laughing uproariously.

It was all good. Whew!

About the Contributor

Bob Tolford worked at the Chattooga Outpost for four or five seasons after marrying Jackie Willard. Jackie had been hired for photography by Ellie Feinroth after the two of them had worked at a food catering company (Proof of the Pudding) in Atlanta during the winter of 1986–1987. Jackie and Bob started dating about the same time she started working at the outpost. They got married the following year, and Jackie shot photos on weekends while Bob hung out and learned whitewater kayaking from guide friends. Later, Bob started shooting photos and Jackie cooked for the staff. During the week Bob worked for a contractor that did hazardous waste site investigations for the EPA. Since then he has shifted to working for the Georgia Environmental Protection Division's Water Quality Section-Intensive Surveys Unit, monitoring the water quality of rivers, streams, and lakes around the state of Georgia.

A QUIET FIGHTER[3]

By Greg Hlavaty

E arly in the season, the NOC organized staff trips to introduce new hires to other Southeastern rivers. Our veteran leader, Cathy Kennedy, chose Section IV of the Chattooga River, a difficult stretch of water known for its beauty and its long list of drowning victims. All of us said yes—some for the fun, some for the experience, and some for the Chattooga's mythology.

When we arrived at the Chattooga's put-in, Cathy was the first to exit the car and get us moving. Leaning on pumps, we pressed down and the forced air burrowed inward and raised slow-growing tunnels in the yellow rafts. The sun burned in the cloudless sky, and even at midmorning, my bare shoulders quickly warmed.

While the huge raft swelled, Ben Lawson squatted beside me and smoothed duct tape over our company logo. Bold silver lines streaked across the yellow rubber while Ben's hairy hand pressed air bubbles from beneath the tape.

He wiped sweat from his beard and looked at me. "How you feel?"

I shrugged, but inside I felt nauseated. My girlfriend, Jenn, who worked in River's End and was completely new to whitewater, seemed a little scared as well. The truth? I feared big whitewater. I'd been working in Raft Rentals for a month, so I knew my river features and had often performed basic rescues, but I spent far more time lifting rafts than guiding them. Still, I told myself I'd come to the mountains for a life change, a chance to do things I'd never done before.

But the Chattooga was well beyond my skill level. The other two Chattooga guides who'd agreed to help us had canceled that morning, leaving Cathy as the only person who'd ever guided Section IV. We depended on her to teach us the lines on this river, and on our safety kayaker, Mark, to follow the rafts and save any swimmers.

"I don't know, man." Ben tore a piece of tape with his teeth. "Never paddled Class V before."

"Me neither."

"Tell you the truth, I'm a little scared."

I nodded and stepped back from the pump. "Me too."

Switching places with me, Ben leaned on the pump and we both peered over the growing raft at the woods that hid the river from view. A dark trail curved between the trees and disappeared in shadow. I imagined I could hear the water hiss, the kind of sound that some boaters personify as the river's voice. But this voice's existence I always doubted until the day I heard big water break on rock.

---

[3] This essay first appeared in *Mayday Magazine,* Issue 8, Summer 2014.

The other guides laughed and sorted gear while Cathy, adrift on decades of river experience, walked between the busy crews. Testing each boat's hardness, she pressed a knee on each tube and bounced lightly.

"Look how calm she is." Ben nodded at Cathy, her long gray hair blowing in a slight breeze. "Makes me feel better just looking at her."

"Yeah. Wish someone hadn't just drowned here."

"That was a fluke and you know it." Ben stopped pumping and straightened. He was tall and broad shouldered, thick and hairy around his blue personal flotation device (PFD). He looked down at me. "That guy was out there alone."

"Still."

Ben motioned to our group. "Hell, we got three boats, lots of people, first aid kits. We're prepared."

I stared past him into thick, summer woods. Oak and tulip poplar leaves cut green swaths across gray trunks, their branches masking the water.

Ben hunched over the pump again, and its rhythmic squeaking cut the water-thickened air. Relentless heat quieted the birds, and even the main road was silent as if all traffic had rerouted itself for this one day when we would brave a river far older than our untested selves. For a long time we didn't speak, just forced air into growing tubes until the gray-haired woman nodded. We lifted our rafts and trekked the 0.25 mile to the water.

In 1974 Congress declared the Chattooga a Wild and Scenic River. It seems largely unpolluted and looks pretty much like it was shown in the 1972 wilderness thriller *Deliverance*. River, stone, and forest. No houses or businesses mar the landscape. The hand of man, though all around and slowly closing, has not been fully felt by this place. You can really feel that it's just you and your group gripped in some ancient rite that, at times, has instigated death.

With three rafts beached on river left, our group scouted our first major drop: Seven-Foot Falls. So far Cathy had chosen to read-and-run, picking out the lines from her boat and running the drop without stopping to scout the rapid, but Seven-Foot required more complex maneuvers. Cathy perched on the shore's edge and traced the line. "Ferry over to river right, then turn downstream and angle back to river left." Her finger followed an obvious swift chute of water. "The river will dump you over the falls, but you've got to keep the boat straight."

Jenn looked at the falls pouring over the ledge. "What happens after we go over?"

"Make a hard right turn into shore. If you're slow, your boat will hit the rock wall and fold in half." Cathy pushed her two hands together to mime the boat's folding. "Just ride it out and you'll be fine." She held Jenn's eyes and smiled.

Jenn, usually quick to return a smile, focused intently on the rapid. "What if we fall out?"

"You might get recirculated against the rock, but you'll wash out."

Jenn glanced at me and I slipped an arm around her waist. Seeing the river disappear over the drop, I felt as nervous as she did, but I couldn't bring myself to admit it.

"Can I guide?" Little Corey pushed his way through the group. The shortest among us, he had to look up to address Cathy. But even in this posture, he seemed no supplicant. Curly hair pulled beneath a custom helmet, he gripped his red PFD at the shoulders and smirked. "Doesn't look too hard."

Cathy looked at him a moment, shrugged, and walked toward her raft.

Ben looked at Cathy's crew of two, leaned, and spat. "Hell, Cathy. Take some more strong paddlers with you."

"Two's enough. Could probably do it alone if I had to." Cathy smiled and nodded, and her two chosen crew members slid into the front of the boat and tucked their feet under the tubes. As we watched from shore, her boat, nose angled upstream, ferried from river left to right, caught a swift diagonal line back to river left, and dropped perfectly over the falls. With practiced ease she ran the exact line she'd indicated.

With Little Corey guiding, we copied Cathy's ferry, and our entrance looked perfect. I'd only just met him, but Corey seemed to be learning as the river demanded; such moments of growth accentuated why Cathy had brought us on big water. Corey even smiled when I glanced back, but when we neared the falls, his small face tensed and he rose up off the rear tube.

Jenn looked at him. "Why is he standing?"

"Relax," Ben said. "He's just checking the line."

She turned and gripped her paddle harder, shoving her right foot deeper beneath the front tube to hold herself in the boat.

Corey held our line to just above the falls; then without warning, the boat twisted sideways.

"Oh, shit!" Corey tucked his foot beneath the rear thwart and leaned back, twisted his abdomen and pried hard to straighten us, but the current was too strong.

"Straighten us up!" Ben yelled.

"Hold on." Corey aimed the stern toward the lip of the falls. "We're going backward."

His voice submerged beneath the roar of falling water. Sitting in the bow, I looked back toward Corey, but the stern had disappeared first over the ledge, and for a moment I could look over the lip at falling water. Then the whole raft tilted over the falls. When we hit the water below, the stern slammed into the rock face, and Corey dove forward and landed belly down on the center thwart. The boat folded in half, rebounded, and whipped back into its oval shape. We spun, eyes wide, to the beach.

As our crew pulled the raft onto the beach, Mark, our safety boater in a kayak, ran sweep. Just like us, Mark's entrance to Seven-Foot Falls seemed perfect, but at the edge of the falls, his bow nosed into a wave and he flipped, shot over the drop, and landed upside down at the bottom. As the current pushed him toward us, he rolled up and drifted, his face slack and staring. His paddle hung loose in one hand, and he bunched his left shoulder against his body. When he neared shore, he said, "I think my shoulder's out."

While Jenn and I stood back, Ben helped Mark from his boat and held him steady at the waist. Cathy bent Mark's arm at the elbow so his hand pointed out in front of him, and then she pulled his upper arm away from his body. With the ball free, she rotated his arm in a half circle so his hand traced an arc from the treeline before him to point directly at the sky. The ball eased back into the shoulder socket.

"That's got it." Cathy smiled and stepped back. Little more than a minute had passed since Mark's injury, and already she had taken control.

Mark rubbed his shoulder. "Thanks."

"Should we tie it up?" I said.

Cathy shook her head. "No. Could get caught in the sling if he swims. He'll just have to support it with his other hand while we paddle him out."

Mark held his injured arm and watched Cathy. "Never seen anyone reset a shoulder that quickly."

"Can't believe it worked," she said.

Ben stepped forward. "You've never reset a shoulder before?"

"Nope. But I've seen it done a lot." Cathy shrugged, returned to her boat, and unpacked our lunch from a red dry bag. She moved with easy grace, flowing like water around rock, and the rest of us stood stunned. Somehow her confidence eased her reaction to stressful situations and allowed her to take effective action. Ball slides into socket. Dusted hands. No doubt. No mistake. It was the confidence I had hoped to find.

Since I'd first arrived at the NOC, I'd often wondered if the calm the experienced displayed under pressure, like Cathy's easy resetting of Mark's shoulder, was a hard-won asset found through years of working outside of their comfort zone, that liminal area where fear tests those who enter. The only way to pass that test is through effective action. As a 16-year-old Nantahala guide, Cathy had come upon a man who'd had a heart attack while paddling. She pulled him from the water and administered CPR, even though, as she admits now, he was long past saving. She recalls crying on the ride home, and when I asked how she could hold her emotion in check during traumatic experiences, she only said, "I deal with it and fall apart later."

Maybe this is a philosophy formed in fire, a part of the self that the experienced have faced and made peace with. Engulfed in Class V whitewater, an adventure-seeker's eyes go wide and she finds that the feeling she's been skirting all these years is nothing more than the age-old fear that life will halt. And when she's faced her fear and comes up breathing, she learns that positive action is the antidote to self-doubt. Face these situations with openness and the comfort zone expands. It's the positive side of being an adrenaline junkie, I suppose: a growth beyond the selfish desire for thrills.

But I'd also heard stories in which the daring went big and failed, where the boat flipped and eyes got one last look at the breathing world. For Cathy, who nearly drowned on the Ocoee River, that moment narrowed her focus until breathing became her only sought-for action. As she recalls: "If I could have spoken, I'd have been saying *breathe*." It's so hard for us to let go of the only gift whose value requires imminent death to fully appreciate.

≋

After our embarrassing run at Seven-Foot, we'd switched guides and done well, but Jawbone, the fourth rapid of a harrowing stretch of river called Five Falls, had a more difficult entry and posed much greater consequences if we made a mistake. Here the river broke into a long white pour that crashed against and split around a giant, half-submerged boulder called Hydro.

We huddled onshore just above Jawbone, and when Cathy asked for volunteers to guide, only one raised his hand. Blake, sluggish and with belly hanging from beneath his PFD, hitched his swimsuit and smiled. "I'll try not to mess it up."

"This is no joke," Cathy said.

"Course not." When she turned away, Blake grinned.

Cathy pointed out the line just to the left of Hydro. "Skirt the rock, then pull off fast at river left before the next drop."

"Looks hard," Blake said.

Cathy nodded. "It is. But you can do it."

Jenn stepped forward and studied the river with the guides. Usually she was quiet and standing in back, playing the role of passenger, much as I was. This was the first time she'd physically put herself on par with those doing the guiding, and others noticed and fell silent. Finally, she looked at Cathy. "What if we miss the pull-off?"

"You'd have to run Soc-em-Dog. At this water level, you'd flip and get recirculated until we got you a rope."

Though Jenn was renowned for her constant smile and easygoing nature, her face had pulled to a tight, concentrated stare that fixed on Soc-em-Dog. It forced the rest of us to look too. We stood on tiptoe and eyed the roiling hydraulic on river right. It spanned half the river and whipped a brownish froth like a tornado laid sideways in water.

"Soc-em-Dog," Jenn said. "That's where that guy just drowned, right?"

Cathy narrowed her eyes. "We're not thinking like that. You can do this."

Just then I regretted encouraging Jenn to get into whitewater sports. Even though she had come on this trip of her own accord, I still felt responsible because coming to the NOC was first my dream, and she had followed. As the sheer force of water at Jawbone rapid swept the last of my courage away, it seemed laughable that

I'd ever expected to inhabit the riparian world as comfortably as Cathy did. Now I just wanted to make it to the takeout.

Cathy stood very still, like she was listening to some minute sound beneath the water's roar, that riparian voice that only the experienced could hear. She pointed again to Hydro. "There's a submerged hole running through that rock. Sometimes it gets clogged with branches, and if you go in, you're pinned and that's it." She turned from the river and looked at each of us. "We don't want to find out if it's clogged."

When she finished talking, she turned away, and again her small crew paddled smoothly through the rapid, perfectly executing the line she'd identified.

Blake smirked. "Makes it look easy."

"It ain't." Ben turned and growled into his face. "Don't say it is."

"I'm not."

"Don't even think it."

"OK, dude." Blake stepped away from us. "OK."

Ben took the front. Jenn and I sat in back, and though she kept looking at me, I stared at the rapid ahead. I felt she wanted some reassurance I could not offer; we'd come this far and would have to finish. All any of us could do was paddle.

Blake braced himself on the rear tube, and we ferried into the current. "All forward!"

In rhythm with each other, we leaned forward and cut dark water with white blades. Then gritting our teeth, we flexed our abs and rotated, pulling hard against the water.

"Dig it in!"

Knuckles white, we attacked the rapid. Paddles jammed in subsurface current, and their red shafts rose from the water. We were headed for the chute just left of Hydro and what seemed a perfect line. Then just upstream of the rock, the current forced the boat sideways and slammed us broadside into Hydro. In seconds, the water turned the raft on its side, and its bottom slapped flat on Hydro and wrapped around the huge rock. Blake and I grabbed the side ropes, now running horizontally above us, and scrambled up the raft and on top of Hydro. Jenn clung to the bottom tube, her lower body hidden in white froth pulling her toward Hydro's submerged hole.

Though an experienced raft guide would have stayed on the high side of the raft, I acted on instinct and climbed Hydro. I lay belly down on the rock and reached for Jenn. "Grab my hand!"

She looked right at me. Her face was as white as the water that broke around her. I stretched but could not reach her without falling off the rock. All she'd have had to do was reach up, just a little, and I'd have her. I knew I could pull her up. I had the strength. If she'd offer her hand, I would not let her go.

"Grab my hand!"

Still she ignored me and clung to the bottom ropes as the water pounded the raft. When the raft finally shot off the rock, Jenn screamed and plunged beneath the water. That fast. I saw her open mouth; I heard her scream. And then there was only white froth where her face should have been.

She was gone.

I perched on Hydro and screamed at Cathy, but my voice was lost in the water's hard crush against stone. I waved my arms, and when Cathy saw me, I pointed to Hydro and then to the spot where Jenn should have resurfaced. Downstream from where I stood, green water rushed for the roiling hydraulic, and for the first time, I saw the last victim's drowning as more than a news story. I really understood how he had become trapped in Soc-em-Dog.

Stranded on the rock, I could only watch and point, so I scanned the downstream current for some sign of Jenn. Finally, she popped up, looked quickly at both shores, then turned on her belly and swam to the nearest shore, away from Cathy and her crew.

Three people threw ropes. The orange bags soared over the water and the ropes uncoiled smoothly, but the ropes all fell short.

Cathy stood on her tiptoes and screamed at Jenn. "Swim, girl! Swim!" It was the only time I've ever seen Cathy lose her composure.

Jenn swam hard to river right, where a rocky crag jutted upward to form the shore. Swift green current flushed her closer to the hydraulic, and she grabbed the rock wall, hung there a second, then slid off.

The current whisked her downstream and again she swam hard. Just upstream of the hydraulic, she grabbed the rock, and even as her body whipped in the current, she held on and slowly dragged herself up the wall. She rolled onto the flat top of the rock and lay there, face turned to sky, her body a living shape rising and falling against a jagged green treeline.

≈≈≈

After Blake and I swam off of Hydro, Cathy's crew ferried across to retrieve Jenn, and we ran the rest of the river with little talk.

Only once did Blake, still guiding, flash a smile and joke: "You guys want to run Jawbone again?"

Ben turned and flexed a big hand on his paddle. Then there was silence.

At dusk we paddled across Chattooga Lake with Mark, his injured arm pressed to his chest, riding on the bow. Our paddle blades cut the water in a steady, even rhythm, and everyone stared ahead at the rows of pines as if in some river-induced trance. We didn't talk for some time, and even at the takeout, only a few people muttered terse instructions to deflate, pack up, and drive home.

If the river silenced us by taking away our self-assurance, then civilization, with its comfort and ease, brought our voices back. We sat at a long table in a

Mexican restaurant and sipped beer from frosty glasses. Hesitantly, the guides started telling the day's stories, which revolved around their newfound skills and the belief that they'd somehow faced down big water and won. Jenn and I sat silently at the end of the table, and Ben would look at her, shake his head, and look away. Usually loud and boisterous, he barely spoke that night.

No one mentioned the event at Jawbone, that place that signaled so clearly that we had passed the point of our experience. Jenn could have drowned, a nearly fatal mistake due to poor judgment on everyone's part, including hers and mine for joining a trip without enough experienced guides. Then again, many of us had wanted a test, and having experienced guides would preclude our being wholly challenged, so the river had only granted this wish. Maybe I've no right to complain.

In later years Cathy would reference that trip as the time she tried to drown my girlfriend, and I would look for some trace of fulfillment or regret, but her face was inscrutable. Whatever lesson Cathy hoped the Chattooga might teach us, Jenn and I at least learned that our hearts would never beat as hard as when their next beat was not assured.

It took a long time for me to ask Jenn what she was feeling when she was swept through the rock. She recalls touching the rock as she passed through the tunnel and wondering if she would be pinned. When she surfaced, the thought of "that one didn't kill me but the next one might" drove her to take responsibility for her own fate and swim hard rather than give herself up to the current. She'd always been a quiet fighter, and when she pulled herself up to shore, she'd passed a harrowing test.

Maybe it sounds strange, but I think I can hear it now, the river's voice. I feel its syllabic pulse whenever I approach whitewater. For many people, it seems to tell them to let go and live, to not fight the current within and without. That's the popular Zen message I wanted to hear, the one that would have made me confident like Cathy, but what the water tells me is something darker. That's why my head is always half-turned, anticipating what the river will say next. It might be the sound of my beloved going under. It's a sound no roar can drown.

 ## *About the Contributor*

Greg Hlavaty studied writing at Western Carolina University, and his essays have appeared in various magazines and literary journals, including *Arts and Letters, Barrelhouse, Yale Anglers' Journal,* and *Bird Watcher's Digest.* He teaches writing and literature at Elon University, where he blends eco-literature with hands-on wilderness survival skills. He has taught survival skills classes and led outdoor trips in North Carolina and Alaska. He lives in Graham, North Carolina, with his family.

STARING INTO THE EYE OF GOD

By Eric Nies

M y first year guiding I remember a night of ungodly rain at the Chattooga. Sleeping in the flat-roofed Tin House didn't help. The next day I went from a 10-trip rookie who checked out at a water level of 1.3 feet to a high-water guide running Section III for the first time ever, with the river at 4 feet and rising.

Buzz Williams was leading the trip, and I stayed right on his tail, my eyes getting wider as we picked our way down to Sandy Ford. Here we gathered and Buzz reiterated to all the rafts—really, to me—the one rule of high-water Section III: Do *not* go left at the bottom of the Narrows. This had been a topic of much discussion at breakfast in the guide house. I'd been told that I would see the Eye of God, the fabled 10-foot twister wave at the bottom of the Narrows, and that this was the one place I did not ever want to be. So of course, I chased Buzz through the Narrows. And of course, for no good reason, my middle left passenger fell in and got away. I had no choice; I had to chase him. It happened quickly, maybe 15 seconds, and I had him back in the raft and paddling. But the river was bending right, bending right, and I had slid to the outside of the bend. My fate was set. I set our angle back to salvation, and we paddled hard. As the bottom of the rapid came into view, I saw two things. First, I saw that we were not making the right exit *at all*. No chance.

Then, I saw the Eye of God. My memory is vague, but I remember a giant corkscrew thing, breaking hard right, and mist coming up like the edge of the world. It was a tornado on its side. I have been waiting 30 years to see that wave again, and if I never do, my recollection will mostly be a thought of amazement that water could do such a thing. I do remember, clear as day, that I had a choice: I could try to go right and fail, or I could square up *now* and take my best shot. Phyllis J. was in my raft that day, bow left, and I also remember so clearly the look she gave me when I yelled out, "Left draw! Left draw!"

We locked eyes and she gave me the tiniest nod; somehow in a half-second she acknowledged the entirety of the moment. Then we squared up and charged. Chaos, noise, the boat seemingly airborne and totally submerged at the same time, then on its right tube, me deep in a vortex of mystery, Phyllis somewhere in the sky. And then calm. We were upright, floating away, and then somehow we were sitting in an ordinary eddy, looking back at the Narrows. The sound of the rapid was soft, even soothing. Luck had brought us through and we were totally, completely fine.

Later that day, in the seemingly endless Class II below Keyhole, Buzz stood in his raft like a gondolier. In the raft behind him, I stood up and guided like Buzz because it just seemed the perfect thing to do. Little pry strokes and pushes, just enough to keep us in the current. A moment of bliss and beauty. No need to work. We let the river bear us on its back.

 About the Contributor

Eric Nies worked at the NOC 1981–1990, mostly guiding rafts and teaching kayaking. He has logged thousands of river miles guiding, paddling, and contracting unpleasant illnesses in Asia and in Central and South America. Eric is currently an ER doctor in New York. He continues to believe that he can boat Class V.

APPLE-EATING EDDY

By Joe Huggins

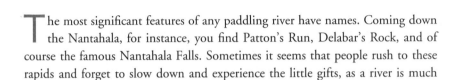

The most significant features of any paddling river have names. Coming down the Nantahala, for instance, you find Patton's Run, Delabar's Rock, and of course the famous Nantahala Falls. Sometimes it seems that people rush to these rapids and forget to slow down and experience the little gifts, as a river is much more than a succession of paddling highlights.

According to German author Hermann Hesse, a man named Siddhartha could hear a thousand voices in his river without moving from a single spot, but actually the sound and sights and moods of a river are too mixed and too moving to ever be counted. John McPhee wrote that "rivers are the ultimate metaphors of existence," and I must agree. Where else is the infinite intricacy and interconnectedness of the universe more physically and visually evident? Where is determinism more magical than in the leapings and duckings and swirlings and sparklings of tiny water droplets tossed about and controlled by forces too complex to predict? There is so much to see and hear and learn from moving water.

I have to warn you: this kind of thinking will make you the last one down the river every time, and probably late for supper too. I know. I've been there.

But it's worth it. The moods of a river must be honored or else you will find *only* what you go looking for, and you will miss the unexpected discoveries that can turn an ordinary day into a very special one.

A case in point: Pip Coe and I once set out as a tandem open boat team down the Nantahala. It was soon evident that the "push to paddle" was not in us. The river seemed to be singing a lullaby and we quickly succumbed to the mood. We were truly laid-back—figuratively and physically.

"Do you think we'll have to paddle through this next rapid?"

"I hope not."

"Maybe you should at least be prepared to put out a low brace for that hole at the bottom."

"OK, I'll brace if you'll turn around and get your feet back in the boat."

"OK."

It was that kind of run. We were making it through on river knowledge, an occasional brace, and appropriate downstream leans.

Now and then we would get charged up to reassert our paddling expertise and we would proceed to bend our blades toward the execution of a sharp eddy turn or two. It went like this: First, eddy left (stop here to stare at wildflowers and ferns).

Joe Huggins bakes at Relia's Garden and leaves a legacy of careful and artful recipes.

Then, peel out and paddle hard across the current to the eddy on the right. Oops! This one was already occupied—by floating apples.

Some tree or overturned basket upstream was feeling benevolent and we were feeling receptive. We remained in the eddy, bobbing for apples until our bailer was full. With paddles shipped, we continued downstream, collecting fruit on every side until, ankle-deep in apples, we ran aground on a rock and swung around facing upstream into the sunset. Stuck on the rock, we began lightening the load by eating apples and tossing the cores overboard. Meanwhile, the sun was busy working up a light show in the sky. We soon became enchanted with the beauty of it all and dangerously engorged on apples. It was nice to be on the river yet so far away from the push of paddling.

We decided to call this place Apple-Eating Eddy—not so much a still place in the river as a quiet place in time, a feature of us and the river together, which would disappear when we paddled on. Which we did.

And it did disappear. I haven't seen Apple-Eating Eddy since then. I haven't really looked for it. It belongs, I think, to a day gone by and to the memories of that day. But, I do continue to look and to see, and each time I run the river I find new features and fresh beauty, for the river promises continuing discovery for those who look and are receptive.

About the Contributor

Joe Huggins was born in the Smokies in 1950 and returned to the mountains of Western North Carolina in 1979 to try being a part of the company and community of the Nantahala Outdoor Center. Intervening years had been spent learning and growing through diverse pursuits and settings: classrooms, shrimp boats, oil rigs, construction sites, forest trails, and more (a degree in physics, chemistry, English, and math was in there somewhere). Then a chance encounter with a copy of the *NOC Newsletter* led Joe to consider spending a summer back in the Smokies. That first season expanded into decades of involvement as Joe discovered at the NOC a special blend of friendships, adventures, work, and play. Joe has worked at all of the NOC's restaurants and was the creator of the original Slow Joe's Café. Attracted by elements of variety and change, Joe shifted to working at various NOC outposts in the 1990s and has since worked many jobs, including outpost assistant manager, store manager, photographer, bus driver, repair and maintenance guy, resource assistant, general gofer guy, and more, mostly at the Nolichucky and Pigeon Rivers.

CHATTOOGA:
RACING DOWN SECTION IV

By Kent Ford

A side effect of the Olympic- and world-caliber guide crew at the NOC in the early 1980s was perhaps most distinctly felt at the Chattooga Outpost. Part of the magic was the classy leaders there: Gordon Grant, Dave Perrin, Buzz Williams, Scott Kolb, Ellen Feinroth, Tracy Chapple, and so on. But the other part was the racer community that rotated through there and brought with them a competitive attitude (John Burton, Gordon, Angus Morrison, Payson Kennedy, Mark Wiggins, and a bunch of world-class guides in the early 1980s). For extra exercise, guides ran home from the takeout, and after work went up to the pond for slalom training or an evening paddle at Woodall.

The result was that the NOC rafts simply went faster than those from the other companies. Perhaps this was due to guide skill and precision mentality. Or it could have been that NOC simply had the smaller rafts to borrow (from the center at Wesser) for low water, an option less available to the smaller companies. Whatever the reason, the NOC trip leaders juggled the awkward task of passing other companies as they were stuck on rocks, and sorting out other minor troubles.

Kent Ford on the Ocoee River at the US team trials in 1990. Ford is racing C-1, a decked boat that is a smaller, higher-performance version of a canoe. (photographed by Villa Brewer)

Friendly NOC competitiveness at the Great Raft Race (1985). John Kennedy's raft passes Jim Holcombe's raft at The Ledges on the Nantahala. In the first raft are Eileen Ash, Stephen U'Ren, John Kennedy, and Dan Dixon. (photographed by Villa Brewer)

One issue all companies dealt with was the cluster of raft trips at the Five Falls. The U.S. Forest Service identified this as a problem and squelched it when the service instituted launch times and time windows at rapids. While we complained at the time, this clearly improved the experience for everyone, regardless of which company they worked for. Nonetheless, a reputation of mild elitism surrounded the NOC guide crowd, and looking back, I can't help but wonder if our competitive mindset and pride sometimes impaired our appreciation of the natural wonders of the area.

About the Contributor

Kent Ford worked at the NOC from 1979 to 1992 as a guide, instructor, and head of instruction. His years at the NOC were formative, providing him a well-rounded background in teaching and coaching paddling. Thanks to the many talented folks he worked with, he was able to coach slalom at a high level, train instructors at paddle schools worldwide, and help inspire many boaters through his instructional video company Performance Video (performancevideo.com). Readers will enjoy his film on the history of whitewater paddling, *The Call of the River.* You can find him in Durango, Colorado, or on the rivers of the Southwest in a canoe, kayak, stand-up paddleboard, or dory.

NOC PRIDE

By Dave Perrin

Pride has typified my experience at the NOC. Everyone seemed to possess it, which drove staff to meet or exceed the abilities of those around them. This resulted in a subtle but intense competition for excellence. The reputation of the company spread throughout the country, and for a time, all roads led to the NOC if you wanted to rub shoulders with some of the best minds and skills in the expanding world of whitewater sports.

The flip side of pride is hubris, and I demonstrated that on the Grand Canyon in 1990, on a trip for NOC's adventure travel program. The trip included Kent Ford and Bob Powell as guides in hard boats, with me guiding a paddle raft.

We'd developed into a tightly meshed rafting crew, hitting our lines and cruising through the big rapids of the canyon with relative ease. At Lava Falls Rapid, we took a leisurely scout, letting all the other kayaks and rafts run ahead of us.

Humbled by the Grand Canyon: Dave Perrin's raft just before the flip at Lava Falls Rapid

Unfortunately, all that scouting didn't ensure success. We flipped in the big crashing wave at the bottom of the rapid. Our raft contained several older ladies, including Bob's mom. As I flew headlong into the roiling water, I was almost overcome with worry for the grandmothers in my crew.

After the deepest, longest swim of my life, I surfaced behind my upside-down raft, gasping, feeling more like a drowned rat than a rescuer. With relief, I spotted Kent and Bob already acting to save the crew. Kent had gotten out of his boat onto the upside-down raft, and he began pulling guests on it while Bob was rescuing others on the back of his kayak. I swam to the raft, heaved myself up, and collapsed, thoroughly chilled and shaken. Unflustered, Kent and Bob had already pulled half the crew onto the raft. I myself was thrilled to be there.

Bob made a head count and calmly announced, "We're missing three."

Kent, sizing up the situation, replied, "They must be under the raft," and dove into the water to look for them.

I reluctantly followed, overcoming a strong urge to never get in the Colorado River again. Underneath the raft, we emerged into a dark, cold air pocket formed by the floor of the inverted raft and searched the individual compartments for the missing guests.

I croaked out the name of one of the errant crew members.

A voice answered quietly, "I'm here."

I grabbed her hand and we swam out from under the boat. Scrambling back on the raft, I helped pull her up and then collapsed again.

Kent also had found someone and pulled her onto the raft. Lower Lava, a small rapid that now seemed huge, given the state of our craft, was closing in. Our sorry group sped out of control toward it on the upturned raft bottom.

Bob, who'd been keeping track of the crew, announced, "We're still missing one."

Kent jumped into the water immediately as I gasped, whimpered, and followed. After my own fruitless effort, I surfaced to hear Bob say, "Kent's got her." Climbing back onto the boat, I started pulling the guest's personal flotation device (PFD) while Kent pushed from below. It was tough going. The woman was stunned by the experience, in shock, and helpless from fear.

By now we were entering Lower Lava. I desperately heaved on her PFD, as Kent pushed her bottom from the water. It was a race between the river and us. Every time I pulled, the PFD slipped a little farther over the woman's shoulders, threatening to come completely off. I was frantic at the thought of losing her to the river if the PFD slipped farther. With one monumental push from Kent, she flopped up on the raft, her head engulfed by the PFD, arms limply protruding toward the sky.

The raft bucked through the standing waves, now headed for a sheer canyon wall at the base of the rapid. Another flip seemed imminent if we brushed the wall with our waterlogged heap.

Pausing for an instant on the recoiling boil line next to the wall, we whooshed downstream, the river hissing and pulsing as we passed. A feeling of euphoria came over me, which further clouded my already addled state.

This is where NOC pride got the best of me. We got the crew paddling, aiming for an enormous eddy and beach. A motor rig swung up to us and asked if we wanted a tow. I waved them off, saying confidently, "We've got this." Bob and Kent had calmly and effectively contained my mishap, and I pridefully thought we could finish the job on our own.

The eddy line was powerful and sheer, preventing us from breaking through with our bargelike, inverted raft. We bounced off the eddy and recoiled upriver, circulating toward the dreaded rock wall once more. The motor rig circled back and called out, "Are you sure?"

I hollered for the rope.

Mindful of getting the rope tangled in his prop, the boatmen gunned the engine as soon as I caught it. Watching the rope hiss through my frantic grip, I leapt over the end of the raft in a desperate attempt to belay through a d-ring before it completely slipped my hand.

I clung desperately to the last bit of rope as the boat bulldozed us toward shore. Sputtering and flailing, the river drowned the remaining pride out of me as the end of the raft submerged in response to the tow. We porpoised toward shore, the rope slowly slipping my grip. Suddenly, the line slackened as we neared the beach. Thoroughly spent, I stumbled onto the sand and collapsed.

Lying there, chest heaving, a shadow crossed my closed eyes. Outlined in the desert sun stood a grizzled canyon boatman who'd witnessed my undoing. Looking down, almost like an apparition, he quietly said, with some pity, "Looks like you could use a drink," as he handed me a bottle of whiskey. Nothing before or since has ever tasted so good.

So much for pride. The crew was OK, thanks to Kent's and Bob's actions. I, with no small amount of chagrin, strangely never felt better. The furnacelike air and warm embrace of the desert sand was good enough.

 ## *About the Contributor*

See page 14 for more information about Dave Perrin.

ADVENTURE IS MADE OF ADVERSITY[4]

By Kevin "Taz" Riggs

It seemed like just another Chattooga trip until leaves, branches, bits of dirt, and bark fell from the sky from no discernible direction. The underside of the clouds was like a low but mobile ceiling of giant cotton balls coated with coal dust, rolling, bounding, and marching in waves. Then the trees bowed, whipped, and twisted this way and that. They screamed and cried to the ground and the boulders that held them as their limbs were ripped from their torsos and carried out of sight. Then came a light, a dark and eerie electric green. The kind of light that didn't give comfort or ease. But just like that, the light changed to a pale green, to yellow and then to bright white. The clouds became white sheets and soft blankets. The calm and stillness came so suddenly that it felt almost as violent as what had just passed.

There had been no place to hide. The woods were no option and there were no rocks or overhangs to crawl under. We had pressed our guests against a low ledge in a tight sort of huddle and hopelessly guarded them with our own bodies. Maybe only seconds had passed, a minute at the most. We all stood up, staggered and stunned by what we had just witnessed, then stumbled down to the rafts; they had stayed dutifully where we had abandoned them, untethered. We brushed off the leaves, pine needles, and bits of dirt and bark, then lifted the two limbs that had fallen across the length of Paul's boat. He had been tying a cooler in place when he left it and ran to the group; the big end of those branches took the place where he had been standing.

Obviously we were shaken, but in spite of the white scars on the tree trunks, the twigs swirling in the water with the greenery still attached, among the bark and brown bits of leaves like a liberal dose of salt and pepper, everyone began to relax a bit. We loaded up and floated out into the pool (Dead Man's Pool, but I don't think anybody mentioned that). Because we had just finished portaging Soc-em-Dog, Shoulder Bone was no more than a float at that level. My memory isn't perfect, but I'm pretty sure that we did not stop to play at Ambush Rock or I would have remembered it as somewhat inappropriate. So we probably drifted on in our posttraumatic daze.

A quarter mile on, the river made a dogleg to the right, just below Class III Possum Drop. The rapid was not difficult, but it did demand some attention. There in the pool below the last drop, we looked up to the single ridge that backdrops the river in a line that runs out into the lake. That was what it had once been. Every tree

---

[4] This essay first appeared November 28, 2014, in *Dirt Bag Paddlers* (dbpmagazineonline.com/2014/11/28/adventure-is-made-of-adversity-by-kevin-taz-riggs).

was now slapped and stomped to the ground, chucked and piled into each other. Huge oaks were splintered and shredded. Never-before-seen rocks and outcrops were visible. The damage went up the creekbed that defined the crook in the river and out into the lake as far as we could see, from the top of the ridge to the water.

Just above the last rapid of the day, someone suggested that we scout first, but I for one felt too lucky and stupefied to worry. This was a short, minor Class III, after all.

We didn't see the danger until we'd committed. Though almost all of the wreck was on river left, two trees from opposite banks met in the middle of the river and tangled on the rocks and each other, right at or just above the surface. What a scramble! I rear-loaded my crew, slid up on the trunk, shifted my people to the front, and teeter-tottered over cleanly. One or two boats followed my lead, some broadsided and high-sided into the mess; one or two found refuge at a shallow rock, unloaded, and manhandled their boats over.

There are two things that still amaze me to this day. First, no one and nothing with us was hurt—not a scratch nor a broken fingernail, not a raft punctured in the wind with the flying limbs or against the trees crossing the river, not even a lost paddle. The other thing, I don't remember much of any rain. There were a few of those big splatting drops when the wind picked up. There was a kind of mist as everything calmed down. But we were not wet to the point of dripping.

Several years passed and I was at a trade show, promoting the Chattooga River and the three companies that ran trips on it. I was off to the side with some brochures in front of me; a raft and inflatable kayak behind me; some paddles, personal flotation devices (PFDs), and helmets on display; and a few large action and scenic photos mounted on the partition wall. The arena was filled with flashy motorboats, shiny decked out pontoon boats, electric fish-finders, collapsible kitchens, and stainless steel propane grills. Everything one might need for getting back to nature. For some reason I got little attention, but I did my best to engage people as they walked by. Some would just shake their heads and keep moving; some would take a brochure and then keep moving, leaving me gaping midsentence.

By day two I was really bored. I put on a PFD and helmet to get attention. I waved a paddle at people, balanced it on my chin in the aisle. Nothing. Dejected and near the end of the day, I just sat there. Finally some guy walked over and was looking through the literature. No eye contact.

I'll go for the soft sell approach, I thought. So I gave him a little time, trying to gauge his interest.

Still no eye contact.

Then I casually asked, "Ever been rafting?"

"Yeah," he said gruffly.

I paused. "Where'd you go?"

He tapped the brochure in his hand against the ones on the table and said in a slightly elevated voice, "Chattooga." Still no eye contact. Then in a matter-of-fact way he said, "Nearly got hit by a tornado."

By the time he looked up to gauge my reaction, I already had a sly grin and wide eyes.

When he met my gaze, he exclaimed, "You . . . You were there!"

We jabbered and gestured nonstop for more than a half hour, like long-lost friends who had seen the same miracle.

People started picking up brochures, but we didn't let up; maybe they thought they had missed something.

They had.

When the man had to leave, I asked him one last thing, "Did it rain?"

"Not much, no," he said.

To this day, I still tell my rafting guests, "Life is an adventure, and true adventure is made of adversity." That day on the Chattooga, the effect it had on that man and me proved it. So I remind folks, even as the rain soaks us: "We never tell stories about the vacation that went perfectly; there's no adventure in it."

 ## *About the Contributor*

Kevin Riggs, known to all as "Taz," first came to the NOC as a client on a five-day beginning canoe clinic in 1982. Hired the following year as a baker at River's End Restaurant, he became a river guide and canoe instructor in 1986, working as a guide and trip leader on all of the NOC's rivers, serving as a head guide on the Chattooga for seven years. He also worked five years as a boatman and logistical coordinator for adventure travel trips on the Bío-Bío River. Taz continues to work as a guide on the river he still considers the birthplace of his passion for whitewater: the Chattooga River.

PROJECT RAFT AND NANTAHALA '90

By Bunny Johns

I n 1988 Payson learned about Project RAFT (Russians and Americans for Team-work), which was led by Donnie Dove and Jib Ellison. Donnie and Jib were working with paddlers in the Soviet Union to bring paddling teams from around the world to Siberia for a rafting/paddling rendezvous and competition. In the spring of 1989, Team NOC and 49 other teams ended up in Moscow as the Cold War neared its end. We then flew to Barnaul in Siberia and traveled by bus to a small town in the middle of nowhere where the Siberian State Symphony Orchestra played for us. A magnificent performance! Another full day of travel brought us to the frozen banks of the Chuya River. Each team was provided with a language-appropriate interpreter (Team NOC was assigned to Olya Godlevskaya, who not only got us to all the events on time but was a wonderful companion), a bag full of

Bunny Johns at her desk

Nantahala '90 participants in St. Patrick's Day parade, Atlanta, Georgia
(photographed by Villa Brewer)

canned food labeled in Russian, and enough vodka to ward off the cold. There were racing events during the day and singing, dancing, and other activities at night. Team NOC did well in the competition. In fact, we should have won, but there was a rule that was reinterpreted—not in our favor. At the awards ceremony, Payson stunned everyone (including Team NOC) by inviting the world to the NOC for Nantahala '90, the next iteration of Project RAFT. He also invited Olya to be the official Russian interpreter for this event.

Back in North Carolina, the NOC staff began frantically trying to get ready for the competition, but at the NOC we were ready for the challenge and ready to make impromptu decisions. Fortunately for Project RAFT and rafting teams around the world, the NOC had Ellen Babers, Sherry Spurlin, Olya Godlevskaya, and a lot of excited NOC staff to host the world in far Western North Carolina.

The March dates were selected to coincide with the high-water season. And, high water we got! When the teams arrived in Atlanta, the Nantahala River was at 9 feet, with 3 feet of water in the Raft Room parking area and water lapping at the porch of the raft room building. Tsali Campground, where all the teams were to camp, was under water. Fortunately the rain did slow down and then stop. The families in Atlanta that were hosting the teams overnight were asked to keep them another day.

NOC staff and locals cleaned out the NOC parking areas. The sun eventually returned, and the Nantahala River remained at around 6 feet for most of the race events—a great level. The Chattooga River, the site of one of the downriver races, held at over 3 feet. The locals and the teams loved it. Ellen Babers and the NOC staff coped magnificently. It was perfect for river rats of the world! And our friend Olya remained in the United States for several years, first at NOC and subsequently with the North Carolina Outward Bound School. A tale of international travel, friendship, and goodwill.

About the Contributor

Bunny Johns worked with the NOC from 1975 to 2002. From 2002 to 2013, she worked for Nantahala Power and Light and subsequently Duke Energy on the recreational aspects of the hydropower relicensing of their hydropower projects on the Nantahala, Tuckasegee, and Catawba Rivers. Currently retired!

ROCKED BY THE CHEOAH

By Ken Kastorff

Looking back at my time at the NOC, from 1975 to 1993, I see that there was a drive to push the limits of whitewater adventure. That drive still exists, but the biggest difference in that earlier time was that there were still a lot of rivers and creeks that had never been run, or at best had never been attempted without a lot of portaging. It seemed that every year, new and harder rivers were being explored. It was a time when the Green River; the Pigeon River in Great Smoky Mountains National Park; Overflow Creek, a tributary of the Chattooga River; and the Cascades section of the Upper Nantahala all started getting popular. When they weren't taking people down Section IV of the Chattooga or teaching canoe or kayak clinics, just about all of the guides were always looking for new rivers. Here is a story of one of those new rivers, which we had a chance to explore for a couple of weeks back in the early 1980s.

The Cheoah River in Graham County, North Carolina, is only about a 40-minute drive from the Nantahala River. After spilling out of Lake Santeetlah, the Cheoah flows along US 129 for about 8 miles before becoming part of the Little Tennessee River system, where it eventually enters Calderwood Reservoir. The river flows through a beautiful forested canyon in the Nantahala National Forest with little or no development along its banks.

The Cheoah had been a dry riverbed since 1916, when construction was begun on the dam. When I drove past the dry riverbed in the 1970s, I always wondered what all the brush and trees growing in the river were hiding. No one I knew had ever talked about running Cheoah. While driving over to Knoxville one day, I was surprised to see that all the trees had been cut out of the riverbed. It appeared that the powers that be (also known as the Alcoa Corporation) were planning to spill water from the lake and down the riverbed. I asked around and found that my suspicions were correct. Alcoa was indeed going to be doing some repairs to the powerhouse and consequently needed to dump water from the lake. Hearing that, I made a beeline back to the NOC to let folks know that we were going to finally get to see what the Cheoah was all about.

A country store near the put-in is one of the few signs of development along the Cheoah, and I'd given the store owner my phone number, asking him to please call me if he ever saw water running in the river. Two days later I got the call! That call initiated a mad dash to see who could get off of work to go paddle. Three of us succeeded: Homer King, who like myself was teaching kayaking for the NOC; Joe Huggins of Slow Joe's Café; and myself. We loaded our boats and were at the put-in an hour after that phone call.

Standing at the put-in, we were amazed at the amount of water flowing down the river. And although it was a beautiful day, the water was steaming. When we went down to check it out, we found it was, like the Nantahala, *cold!* We decided to do a quick car scout of the river to make sure there weren't any unexpected problems that we needed to know about. We did not scout far before we realized that this was going to be not only one of the most beautiful runs we had ever done, but also a busy, busy run to say the least.

It was good that we looked at all that scenery before getting on the river because we wouldn't have much time to enjoy it once we were on the water. We noted that the riverbed was just a little bit bigger than the Nantahala, but that was where the similarity ended. We guesstimated the gradient to be somewhere between 60 and 100 feet per mile with steep boulder-choked rapids.

The first thing we encountered on our scout were the ledges—a series of meaty drops ending with a 6-foot ledge situated just below the flume that crossed the river and highway (that drop is now called Wilma's Ledge). We slowed the vehicle down enough to see that we should be able to punch the holes at the bottom of the drops without too much trouble. Below the ledges, the river moved away from the road for several hundred yards before becoming visible again—that almost always spells trouble. We all agreed that on the way back to the put-in, we should take a closer look at the river where it disappeared from the road. Downstream, the river came back to join the road, and it looked like it was going to be a high-water Ocoee-type run. It was steep and fast down to the bridge across the Cheoah, where the forest service road goes up to Big Fat Gap (which by the way, takes you to the put-in for Slick Rock Creek, another great run in the area).

From that bridge down to the takeout on Calderwood Reservoir, the gradient increased and the rapids became much more continuous. There was one big ledge drop that had a complicated approach. We all agreed that it would be ugly if someone came out of the boat above that one or got shoved off line and ended up going off the middle of the 12-foot ledge drop. And down below, there wouldn't be much opportunity to stop and regroup. We named this one the Big Drop, which is the name it still goes by. Just below that rapid, the river just got more complicated with one ledge after another of pour-overs. After 200 yards of mayhem, the river settled down just before going under the highway bridge at Tapoco Lodge. After going under the highway bridge, the river continued into a steep canyon.

Well, to say the least, we were impressed. This was a section of river that was not to be taken lightly, but with some care we felt that we could make the run. We turned around and drove back to the top. On the way back, we came to that one spot where the river and the road parted, and this time we noticed some white through the trees.

Homer said, "Hey, let's have a look at what's going on here!"

So we pulled over and took a quick look, and as we'd suspected, the moment the river got out of sight of the road, it started doing some nasty stuff. It turned into a teenager left home alone for the first time, deciding to have a party that gets all out of hand. Here the Cheoah dropped like the downhill side of a mad roller coaster through a boulder-choked maelstrom of holes and blind drops. The worst of it was all the way down the river-left side of the rapid. The right side wasn't looking good either. And if that weren't bad enough, the granddaddy of all holes was in the middle of the river just as you entered the rapid. It looked like at whichever side of the hole at the top you entered, your fate was pretty much sealed as to where you were going down the rest of the rapid. (Interestingly, people still refer to this rapid as Joe's Demise, in honor of Joe Huggins, though it depends who you talk to).

Right then and there I made up my mind where I was going in this rapid—right and right some more. But when I heard Homer telling us he was going left of the first hole, saying something about "I think I'm going to go for the big stuff!" I had to look again to make sure I wasn't missing something.

But Homer going left into the big stuff wasn't what really surprised me; it was Joe agreeing and saying, "Me too." Had to wonder what Joe was thinking.

Joe Huggins sharing his legendary enthusiasm (photographed by Villa Brewer)

Well, I wasn't changing my mind. I figured that both of my buddies were big boys and capable of making decisions for themselves. But I was going to start out right, and if it looked any better after I entered, I figured I could always bite off a little more.

So back at the put-in we dressed for the cold water. Forever the fashion-conscious paddler, Homer wore an old wool sweater, with a paddle jacket, holey paddling pants, a life jacket that was marginal at best, and a helmet that had been repainted but looked as if it did some time in the Great War. Not World War I—I'm talking about one of the Roman conquests!

I usually would give Homer grief about his attire, but after checking out Joe's wardrobe, Homer looked like he was going to a formal. Joe always looked like he got most of his paddling gear from the lost-and-found box. Today he was exceptionally attired, complete with white long underwear and high-top tennis shoes. He looked more like a drunken cowboy caught somewhere he shouldn't have been. God knows what he had on under his paddle jacket. Nonetheless, what might have been missing in style was more than made up for in enthusiasm.

We finally put in and quickly drifted downstream in a fast-moving pool, enjoying the absolute beauty of the river. But shortly, the pace picked up and we found ourselves a bit too occupied to watch any more scenery. About the only thing the trees onshore told us now was how fast we were flying downstream.

We stopped above the ledges under the flume and one by one dropped over them without mishap. At the bottom of Wilma's Ledge, Homer took the lead from me and Joe was in the third position. It seemed like it was only a few moments before the river pulled away from the road and I could see that we were heading for a horizon line. I turned and shouted to Joe that this was the rapid we had stopped to look at.

As planned, Homer eased toward the left side of the river and disappeared over the lip of the drop. As we got closer to the edge of the rapid, I could see that Homer had apparently changed his mind and somehow managed to do a close-to-impossible move and get back more toward the center of the river, rather than staying along the left side. I went flying by the right side of the hole at the top and was shocked at how big it was. Then for several seconds the rapid below had my undivided attention.

As soon as I could, I looked over my shoulder to see how Joe was faring. At first I couldn't understand where he was. But all of a sudden I saw one end of his boat go flying by in the center hole. Then another end and another and so on—I guess in the confusion of Homer going one way and me going another, he had gotten lost and ended up dropping in for the surf of a lifetime!

These days everyone looks for that short boat so they can do easy multiple ends and hot rodeo moves. I've said for a long time it doesn't matter what length boat you have as long as you find the right hole. And if the number of ends I saw zinging by was any indication, Joe had found just the right size hole for his 13-foot boat.

As soon as I could, I caught an eddy. I'm using the term *eddy* loosely here, as it was pretty much nonexistent, but it was enough to hold my position in the rapid long enough so that I could help Joe. This was one of those "not *if* he swam, but *when* he swam" situations. Nobody was coming out of that hole in one piece. Joe finally surfaced about 20 feet below the hole and about 10 feet off of the left shore. Looking at his face, I was pretty sure that he had seen God.

I got Joe on the back of my boat and it was "let the games begin." We were on the left side of the rapid in the big stuff that Homer had referred to. We had gone about 50 feet when Joe suddenly let go of my boat. I was horrified! I hollered at him not to let go, but it was too late. Turned out he had let go of my boat to grab a limb sticking off of shore.

When I turned around, I had only enough time to think, *Oh, no!* While I'd been watching Joe, I had failed to notice that there was another hole at the bottom of the rapid and I was zeroed in on it like a well-placed shot out of a rifle. I don't know exactly what rodeo moves I invented but luckily it washed me out pretty quick.

Homer was chasing Joe's boat and finally caught it several hundred yards downstream, where he was waiting for me. I got out of the river and walked up the road to see where Joe was. Our shuttle driver had spotted him and we were all now watching him walk downstream to the spot where Homer had stashed his boat.

Our shuttle driver asked me, "Hey, wasn't Joe wearing long johns and high-top tennis shoes?" I looked and she was right; the long johns and high-tops were gone. In fact, Joe had lost everything from the spray skirt down!

We finally got Joe and his boat to the roadside of the river. He opted to see the rest of the run from the shuttle vehicle. I have to say that I could hardly blame him. He told me that seeing my boat next to him in that rapid was the best sight he had ever seen in his life.

Homer and I continued downstream and had a great run. The section from the road to Big Fat Gap down to the takeout was some of the best water he and I ever had the chance to run. We returned every day to run the Cheoah until they finally turned the water off.

On rare occasions over the years, we have had other opportunities to get back on the Cheoah, but it was always a hit-or-miss situation at best. This is just one small example of the early years of paddling with great friends. It was a special time when some of the best paddlers in the world, like Jimmy Holcomb, Carrie Ashton, Arlo Kleinrath, Bunny Johns, Dan Dixon, Kathy Bolyn, Dick Eustis, Chris Spelius, and countless others all found themselves in the same place at the same time. The sport of kayaking certainly took a giant step forward in those days. I doubt that would have happened without the popularity of the Nantahala Outdoor Center.

About the Contributor

Ken Kastorff worked at the NOC from 1975 to 1991 and was assistant head of instruction from 1976 through 1987. He was born in Austria, grew up in Wisconsin, and started whitewater canoeing in 1962 and kayaking in 1972. He trained NOC instructors; led kayaking trips in Chile, Costa Rica, and Ecuador; and started Endless River Adventures with Juliet Jacobsen Kastorff in 1992. He now can be found guiding fly-fishing trips on the rivers near Nantahala Gorge.

SECTION II
History of a Southeastern Paddling Culture

A BRIEF HISTORY OF THE NANTAHALA OUTDOOR CENTER:

THE GROWTH OF A SOUTHEASTERN PADDLING HUB

By Payson Kennedy

Editor's Note: The information in this chapter is based on the memories of Payson Kennedy, Bunny Johns, John Burton, and Kent Ford and is supplemented from the minutes of NOC Board meetings. The authors do not claim that this history is comprehensive or entirely reliable and welcome suggested revisions from readers.

Introduction

The story of the Nantahala Outdoor Center (NOC) is also the story of the growth of paddle sports in the Southeast and of innovation in paddling instruction. It would be impossible to discuss one without the others, as the NOC and paddle sports in general fed each other. With this in mind, this section attempts to weave these elements together, discussing the growth of the NOC as a company, the cohesion of paddle sports as an industry, and the influence the center had on paddling instruction.

The Story of the NOC

In the fall of 1971, Horace Holden reached an agreement with Vincent and Dorothy Gassaway to purchase The Tote 'N' Tarry, a complex that included a 14-unit motel, a small restaurant, a gas station, and a souvenir shop, where the Appalachian Trail crossed the Nantahala River. The complex had been built and operated over a period of years by the Gassaways, whose clientele were mostly

Horace Holden, who purchased the Tote 'N' Tarry in 1971 and asked Aurelia and Payson to manage an outdoor recreation center there for the 1972 summer season

tourists visiting the Great Smoky Mountains National Park, the Cherokee Indian Reservation, and the Nantahala National Forest, as well as fly fishermen enjoying the Nantahala River. A small but increasing number of their patrons were Appalachian Trail hikers and river runners.

In the winter of 1971–1972, Horace recruited Payson and Aurelia Kennedy to manage his operation at the Nantahala the following summer, and they began making preparations to operate a recreational facility at what had been the Tote 'N' Tarry Motel complex. The three agreed that they would call it the Nantahala Outdoor Center and that the new facility would serve the general public, as well as groups from Horace's camp and family club. Services would include food, lodging, shuttles, equipment, and instruction for people enjoying various recreational activities in the area. Payson suggested that offering raft trips might be the best source of revenue for earning the profits needed to meet the annual mortgage payments, but the three of them also agreed that they wanted it to be an outdoor center with a wide variety of activities, rather than just a rafting or whitewater center.

Jim Holcombe poling a canoe

The NOC's first brochure emphasized rafting on the Nantahala, but it also offered specially arranged group trips on the Chattooga, Chattahoochee, Hiwassee, Little Tennessee, and other area rivers. Nantahala trips were $10 and included lunch; Chattooga trips were $20. The company purchased four Rubber Fabricator 12-foot, single-thwart rafts and recruited about 20 staff, largely from Explorer Scout Post 49, which specialized in whitewater kayaking and for which Payson, Claude Terry, and Doug Woodward were advisors. Crucially, Jim Holcombe, a veterinary medicine student at the University of Georgia, also agreed to come work at the new NOC.

A member of the Canoe Cruisers Association from the Washington, D.C., area, Jim was the only person on the initial NOC staff who had ever been on a commercial rafting trip, having worked a previous summer for Wilderness Voyagers on the Youghiogheny River in Pennsylvania. At that time the only commercial rafting in the eastern United States was carried on by four companies operating on the Youghiogheny River, John Dragon's company operating on the New River in West Virginia, and Jim and Jeannette Greiner's newly established rafting operation on the Chattooga River. That summer Payson was granted a leave of absence for the summer from his job at Georgia Tech, and Aurelia, as a public school teacher, had her summers free. They planned to give the NOC a trial during the summer and return to their regular jobs in the fall.

All staff did whatever jobs needed to be done, whether it was guiding a raft, cooking, waiting tables, washing dishes, cleaning motel rooms, or driving a shuttle. The Kennedys (including their four children) and almost all the staff slept at the brick house up Gassaway Road near Wesser Creek, which Horace had also purchased from Vincent Gassaway. The Kennedys and female staff lived in the house, and the garage was converted to a bunk room for the other male guides.

That first summer in 1972, the NOC took about 800 guests on guided rafting trips on the Nantahala and 400 on Chattooga trips. Though the company operated at a loss, the Kennedys loved life at the new NOC and believed that it could eventually prove successful.

During the following fall, the Kennedys struggled to decide whether to risk committing their future to the new and unprofitable company and a life in the mountains, even as they continued to drive to the mountains most weekends to run Chattooga River raft trips, which were quite popular at the time because of *Deliverance*. Because all four of the Kennedy children would soon be of college age and Payson and Aurelia wanted to be sure that they were able to attend college if they wished, it was a difficult decision. They eventually decided that if they sold their house in Atlanta and collected their retirement funds, they would be able to invest $25,000 to become partners with Horace in the new venture. They decided that if they could recruit another couple to assist them in supervising and overseeing all the young employees of the company and to also invest $25,000, they would commit to moving to the mountains to run the venture. The $50,000 of additional capital would be used to do necessary maintenance on the facilities, to enlarge the raft fleet so that simultaneous trips could be run on the Nantahala and the Chattooga, to purchase canoes and kayaks for instructional use, and to provide inventory for an outfitter's store.

As soon as they made this decision, the Kennedys devoted all of their available time to working with Horace on the first issue of a newsletter, inviting others to join in the venture, designing a new brochure, and recruiting an older and more experienced staff for the following summer. That spring they resigned from their jobs, sold their house, and prepared for the big move, fully committed both psychologically and financially. They hoped to recruit another couple to join them in the venture and raise another $25,000 of capital but proceeded without the additional capital when no other investors were found.

The final piece in solidifying the new company was incorporating it. One Saturday of the previous summer, two kayakers had turned up at the Chattooga put-in as NOC staff members were preparing to launch a trip. They asked if they might paddle along since they weren't familiar with the Chattooga. Payson replied that the guides' first priority would be to look after the NOC guests, but they would be glad to have the two kayakers paddle along. The kayakers both turned over and rolled several times during the trip but were able to take care of themselves. After the trip, Payson learned that this was actually the kayakers' first whitewater river and that they had learned to roll on flatwater. They returned to paddle with the NOC frequently during the following weeks of the summer and fall of 1972 and became close friends of Payson's.

During the winter of 1972–73, Horace and Payson had been meeting with a lawyer from a large Atlanta law firm who was tasked with incorporating the new company. He described numerous options and asked all kinds of questions about plans and preferences, to which Horace and Payson didn't have good answers. The meetings dragged on throughout the summer of 1973, with a large bill accruing and the incorporation not happening. Finally, in frustration, Payson asked Jim Shannonhouse, a Charlotte lawyer and one of the two kayakers mentioned above who had been accompanying NOC trips, whether the process had to be so complex. Jim replied that it did not and that he would do the required work for $1,500 worth of stock in the new company. So, on March 1, 1974, Jim Shannonhouse incorporated the Nantahala Outdoor Center in North Carolina. The initial shares were valued at $10. The first board of directors was made up of Horace, Aurelia, Payson, Jim Shannonhouse, and Scott Price, with Horace serving as chairman. Jim Shannonhouse remained one of the NOC's best friends and most valuable directors for 20 years.

Over the years, summer camps and university outing clubs would become a prime source of exemplary NOC staff. Cathy Potts was the first of many employees from the outing club at Sewanee: The University of the South. The faculty advisor for the outing club was Hugh Caldwell, an occasional racing partner of Payson's. Hugh became the director of Camp Merrie-Woode and over the years directed many good staff to the NOC from both Sewanee and Merrie-Woode. Camp Mondamin was another source of strong paddlers who came to work at the NOC. Such key staff members as John Burton, Gordon Grant, Steve Holmes, and Lecky and Fritz Haller all got their start as river runners at Mondamin.

By 1975 the NOC was beginning to be seen as a cultural hub in the whitewater world. Eastern outfitters were invited to send representatives to an organizational meeting for a new confederation of outfitters. The first meeting of what was to become the Eastern Professional River Outfitters was held in the living room of the Stone House in November, and Payson was elected to serve as the first president of the organization.

For the most part, the NOC operated without competition on the Nantahala until 1976. That year, Mason's and Brookside were the first companies to rent rafts on the Nantahala, with the NOC following with rentals in 1977. The initial NOC Rentals operation was run from the garage located at the downstream end of the old

NOC Grand Canyon trip in 1978, with the 4-meter kayaks everyone used at that time

Esso gas station. The NOC's first guided trip competitor on the Nantahala River, Nantahala Rafts, also began running raft trips in 1977. It was owned by Keith Maddox and operated out of the old Gorgarama Rock Shop located 1 mile upstream of the NOC. Soon afterward, Gary Duven, who had been an NOC guide, started Rolling Thunder River Company. Other companies followed, and by 1983 13 companies were offering raft trips on the Nantahala.

Extending its success with rafting, the NOC began diversifying its offerings. In February of 1976, NOC ran its first Adventure Travel trip on the Usumacinta River in Guatemala and Mexico, and the following year added its first Grand Canyon trip for rafters and kayakers.

It also offered rock-climbing instruction under Les Bechdel's leadership starting in 1977, and with successive winters offering good snow, the NOC began leading cross-country skiing trips on the Blue Ridge Parkway and Clingmans Dome Road. Renting skis to students on winter weekends became a mainstay of business in the NOC outfitter's store in Cullowhee, North Carolina (site of Western Carolina University), which opened in 1978 under the management of Robert Harkness and James Jackson.

The NOC made major acquisitions of property in 1980. Most important, it purchased the Flint Ridge property of 50 acres on river left extending from Nantahala Falls downstream to Wesser Falls. The company also bought riverfront property on river right, extending from Nantahala Falls downstream to the original NOC property acquisition. This gave NOC ownership of both banks of the river from Nantahala Falls downstream to the mouth of Silvermine Creek.

NOC also began an extensive building program on its newly acquired river-left property. On Flint Flats, the NOC constructed a large parking lot (essentially the same then as it exists today), public changing rooms, and a large rafting facility. Southern Railway (later Norfolk Southern Railway) still operated trains on the railway through this property and maintained a siding (short railroad track) for loading rock from the quarries up Silvermine Creek in the area where the NOC trip-talk pavilion and gas tank are now located. The first two rental cabins, designed by Tim Mason and Chris Larsen, guides who had come to the NOC together after acquiring architecture degrees, were built at the edge of the Appalachian Trail right-of-way. The company also purchased property for an outpost near the Ocoee River.

After a decade of rapid growth, weather took its toll. The year 1981 was the first year of a severe drought, which lasted through most of the 1980s. The Nantahala and Ocoee were less affected because of their reservoirs, but summer water levels on the Chattooga were usually under 1 foot and went as low as 0.45 foot. NOC's growth in river numbers dropped to 9% after having been above 35% in the 1970s and about 30% in 1980.

Because of the drought and the resulting decrease in growth and profitability, the NOC experienced a cash-flow crisis in the winter of 1982. The company eventually decided that all winter staff (including company officers) would be cut back

Kathy "KB" Bolyn keeping it fun at Corkscrew during the drought in 1980

to a four-day workweek, a painful but equally shared experience. Many staff actually continued to work a full week, even though they were paid for only four days.

Taking further austerity measures, the company also closed its Cullowhee Outfitter's Store and ended its cross-country skiing program, which was struggling because of the recent years' inconsistency in snowfall. The company was still offering numerous whitewater paddling courses, as well as instruction in rock climbing, backpacking, wild food foraging, photography, and log cabin building.

Despite slowing business due to low water, the NOC still expanded in some areas. In 1982 the NOC purchased Smoky Mountains River Expeditions from Rich Wist and began offering French Broad River and Nolichucky River trips. In 1983 the NOC also invested in the start-up of the Rocky Mountain Outdoor Center on the Arkansas River in Colorado. Dick Eustis, who had managed the Ocoee Outpost, moved there as NOC's representative. Dick became president of the Rocky Mountain Outdoor Center a year later and eventually started his own company: Rios Honduras. And in 1985 the NOC purchased High Country's Nantahala River operations and renamed it the Great Smokies Rafting Company.

The mid- to late 1980s continued to see further acquisitions. In 1985 the NOC purchased Sunburst Adventures on the Ocoee River from Marc Hunt and Bill Chipley. Bunny Johns became president of Sunburst. Planning for Relia's Garden restaurant building was completed and work began in the fall.

During this time, the Norfolk Southern Railway announced that it was abandoning its railway from Dillsboro to the state line, including the portion along the Nantahala River that traversed NOC property. Payson was a member of the North Carolina Department of Transportation's Bicycle and Pedestrian Advisory Committee, and he lobbied hard to get the right-of-way converted to a bicycle trail. He was ultimately unsuccessful when the Great Smoky Mountains Railroad company was organized to offer tourist excursions and freight service over the abandoned railway instead. The state encouraged the formation of the Great Smoky Mountains Railroad and eventually granted them favorable terms for acquiring the railway.

In 1988 the Great Smoky Mountains Railroad began operating excursions from Bryson City to the vicinity of NOC staff housing about a mile downstream from the put-in on the Nantahala. At that point the locomotive used a siding to shuttle to the other end of the train and began the return trip to Bryson City, stopping for an hour at the NOC along the way.

The peak year for the total use on all rivers, at 150,000 river days, was 1995. This overall peak was driven by a total of over 55,000 rental users and 32,000 guided trip participants on the Nantahala, almost 17,000 on Chattooga trips, and more than 25,000 on Ocoee trips. The NOC's Wesser and Ocoee Outfitter's Stores set sales records. Since 1996, the NOC has experienced minor ups and downs in river numbers but never the relatively steady growth of the prior years, and it has generally seen a slow decline in rafting numbers.

Seeking an International Paddling Community

The NOC was founded on a dream of building community, and eventually this spirit expanded beyond the borders of the United States. In the spring of 1989, a team from the NOC went to the Chuya River in Siberia for a Project RAFT–sponsored week of competition with teams from about 15 countries (RAFT stands for Russians and Americans for Teamwork). The Russians traditionally gathered to paddle there over the May Day holidays, which usually came soon after the breakup of the ice on the rivers and the beginning of the paddling season. Events included slalom, downriver races, orienteering along the river, and river rescue, mostly in rafts but with some kayaking competition. The Russians used mostly homemade equipment, including catarafts and plot boats, which were new to most US paddlers.

Teams camped along the river and the Russians provided food to be cooked by the teams. At the completion of the competition, the NOC invited participants to come to the NOC the following year for a similar competition in the United States.

That same year, at the request of the Jammu and Kashmir Ministry of Tourism in India, the NOC agreed to send guides to Kashmir to train a dozen Kashmiris to be whitewater guides. The government had purchased a great variety of rafts, kayaks, canoes, and auxiliary equipment to start a water-sports center at Manasbal Lake. The equipment included slalom, downriver and touring boats, and even such unusual craft as a K-4. Nick Williams and Payson each spent a month there training the Kashmiris, and they traveled to several different rivers, including the Indus and the Ganges for training trips.

Russian team paddling a cataraft at Nantahala '90 (photographed by Villa Brewer)

Payson tries paddling a local watercraft while in Kashmir to train locals to be river guides in the fall of 1989.

Unfortunately, the breakout of hostilities between Pakistan and India in Kashmir prevented the program from succeeding, as tourists were afraid to go to Kashmir for water sports and rafting. During these years, many Nepali and Indians as well as paddlers from various European countries came to the NOC to train and work as whitewater guides.

In March, Nantahala '90, sponsored by Project RAFT, was held. On the day that participants were to travel to the NOC from Atlanta, where they had marched in the St. Patrick's Day Parade, the river flooded and rose to 9.5 feet. (The normal reading on the old gauge when the power plant was operating was 3.2–3.4 feet.) At 5 a.m. Payson, who was in Atlanta with the participants, received a call saying that participants would have to stay in Atlanta for an additional day because many of the NOC facilities and the campground where foreign teams were to camp were under water.

While Payson frantically made arrangements to have the host families

Pemba Sherpa—one of the NOC's earliest international raft guides (photographed by Ciro Pena)

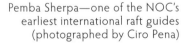

Flooded Nantahala

house, feed, and entertain the participants for an extra day, folks at the NOC began bulldozing and shoveling mud from Flint Flats as the water receded. Twenty-four hours later, when participants arrived at Wesser, a large tent in this area had been erected for serving lunch each day.

Greatest extent of the flood of March 1990—rocks under this wave are the big rocks on river right at Nantahala Falls.

Competitions were held on the Nantahala, Chattooga, and Nolichucky Rivers, and the high water created exciting conditions. The course for the giant slalom on the Nantahala included Wesser Falls, where the dangerous rocks were well padded by the high water. The orienteering competition took place on the Chattooga, and a few teams spent some time becoming well acquainted with the hole at Bull Sluice. The downriver race was held on the Nolichucky River.

In 1991 the NOC sent a team to Costa Rica '91, another Project RAFT international rafting competition. The NOC team won two events and placed second in four events, third in one event, and fourth overall. Payson notes that NOC would have been first overall if he had not missed the first checkpoint in the orienteering event, from which the team never recovered. They came in 40th of the 48 teams in that event.

NOC rafting team: Cathy Kennedy and Donna Holcombe in the bow

Employee Ownership: Dream vs. Reality

Though the NOC was often described as an employee-owned company, the dream of employee ownership was a slow-growing movement and not without its complications. It began in 1976, with the creation of NOC's first employee stock plan. Under its terms, each staff member who worked for at least 12 months was then granted the right to purchase four shares of stock for each additional month that they worked, at a price of $1 per share. In 1980 the NOC replaced the employee stock plan with a new employee stock ownership plan (ESOP), with the goal of eventually moving to full employee ownership of the company.

In 1987 Payson proposed that to further strengthen the sense of ownership and community among staff, the NOC should convert from a corporation to a staff-owned cooperative. He suggested as models the Scott Bader Company in England, as described by E. F. Schumacher in *Small Is Beautiful*, and the highly successful Mondragon cooperatives in the Basque region of Spain. George Snelling led an effort to study this proposed change, and in 1989 the board restructured the current ESOP "so as to include a 401(k) provision," known as a KSOP, which was less expensive and less risky than converting to a cooperative structure.

By 1996 board meetings were held much more frequently than in the past, and the board was taking a more active role in running the company. Minutes for board meetings for the first 6 years of the new board are approximately equal in number of pages to those of the previous 19 years of the old board. In the past, the board had only considered broader issues of long-range vision and policy and generally discussed them until a consensus was reached. By 1996, as many more immediate management decisions were being considered, there was more frequent disagreement and a number of five to four votes. The basic division on the board seemed to be between those who had been at the NOC for many years and believed in the values that had been agreed upon and included in its statements of purpose and newer employees and members of the board who espoused a change in priorities in favor of greater emphasis on profitability over other values.

The NOC statements of purpose included profitability as the last of four purposes and recognized that it was a necessary means of supporting the other purposes, rather than an end in itself. In the recent more competitive campaigns leading up to board elections, some candidates placed greater emphasis on higher profitability. They argued that this would enable NOC to pay higher salaries, improve working and living conditions more rapidly, and create more rapid growth in the value of employee's KSOP accounts. A few years later, the board actually voted on a proposal to make the fourth purpose regarding profit-making the company's number one priority. The proposal was defeated by a five-to-four vote of the directors. Payson (and he believes probably many others) began to have doubts as to the wisdom of having converted to employee ownership, which he had proposed and strongly supported.

 ## *About the Contributor*

John "Payson" Kennedy enjoyed a 15-year academic career at Longwood College, Hampden-Sydney College, the University of Illinois, and Georgia Tech. He worked at the new NOC in the summer of 1972 and then began year-round work at the NOC in June of 1973. He served at the NOC as president and later as CEO, chairman of the board, and CPO (chief philosophical officer) until his retirement from full-time work in 1998. He returned to full-time work at the NOC as CEO and CPO from 2004 through 2006. While working at the NOC, he also guided regularly on six rivers, taught canoeing and kayaking courses, worked as a ropes course instructor, and led extended trips in Central America, the Cayman Islands and Nepal. Since retiring from full-time work, he has continued to serve on the NOC board, usually guides about one trip per week on the Nantahala River, and especially enjoys regular bicycling, working in his pond, and continuing to do adventure travel trips.

THE BUSINESS OF WHITEWATER RAFTING:
GROWTH AND CONCERNS

By Payson Kennedy

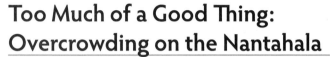

Too Much of a Good Thing: Overcrowding on the Nantahala

As early as 1977, with NOC rafting numbers growing, the complaints from private boaters about overcrowding on the river increased. In 1978 John Burton and Payson wrote an editorial for the *NOC Newsletter* about overcrowding on the Nantahala and stated that the NOC would limit its business on busy summer Saturdays to 800 rafters. Gary Duven, a former NOC guide, began operating Rolling Thunder River Company on the Nantahala. That summer, employees of Rolling Thunder and Nantahala Rafts reported that they could tell when the NOC had reached its limit and were declining additional reservations when their phones began ringing.

At the end of the season, John and Payson decided that their decision to limit business to reduce traffic on the Nantahala had been a dismal failure and simply diverted business to the other newly established rafting companies.

By the next year, the NOC was offering up to four trips per day on the Nantahala, three trips per day on the Chattooga, and two trips per day on the Ocoee. The NOC began trying to develop a voluntary agreement among outfitters to limit trip numbers on the Nantahala but met great resistance to the idea.

In 1980 the NOC tried another tactic to limit river crowding through its land acquisitions. Because the company had recently purchased land on both sides of the river from Nantahala Falls all the way down to Silvermine Creek, NOC leaders believed that this would give leverage to obtain an agreement with other outfitters to limit river numbers in exchange for allowing them to take out on NOC property. NOC leaders were mistaken in this supposition. One competitor went to court, arguing that a historical right had been established for the public to take out on that property. He was politically active and influential in the county and was able to have a sheriff's deputy, with lights flashing, serve a restraining order on a busy summer Saturday morning. This prevented NOC from excluding others from taking out on its river-right property until the case was resolved. The case was dropped a few years later when NOC agreed to trade its river-right property to the U.S. Forest

Service (USFS), which agreed to limit the number of outfitters and to limit their numbers on the busiest Saturdays.

In 1984 the USFS began a permitting system on the Nantahala. Permits were issued to commercial operators, including some summer camps and schools that had conducted trips in 1983. Numbers for each company were restricted on peak-use days to the average number that the company had taken on its highest-use days in 1983 plus 10%. These numbers were to be adjusted annually. Permits were issued to 13 outfitters with a total allotment of 2,295 rafters on peak-use days. On Saturday, July 30, the USFS counted a total of 3,491 paddlers, including private boaters, on the river. This was a day that they hadn't designated as a peak-use day for that year. Total commercial use for the year was 102,618, and estimated total use, including private paddlers, was 130,000.

In 1989 the land exchange that the NOC had been negotiating with the USFS for several years finally closed. The USFS acquired 35 acres on the river right below Nantahala Falls for use as a takeout area for other rafting companies. The NOC received a small sliver of land along Silvermine Creek, where the original store and front office buildings encroached on USFS land; a few acres adjacent to staff housing at Hellard's; as well as a few acres surrounded by the oxbow of the old riverbed adjacent to Wesser Falls. At the same time, the Tennessee Valley Authority (TVA) also gave the NOC a permit to use their land lying below 1,710 feet within the oxbow. This land within the oxbow was usually dry but flooded any time Fontana Lake filled to the spillway level of 1,710 feet. The land within the oxbow became the location of the NOC ropes course, Alpine Tower, and eventually the Zip Line Adventure Park.

Growth of NOC Rafting on the Ocoee River (1977–1996)

On Labor Day, 1976, the old flume on the Ocoee River was shut down and water began running regularly in the old riverbed. Paddlers began running the Ocoee on a regular basis, and the following summer several companies began offering guided rafting trips. One of the most prominent, Sunburst Adventures, was run by Marc Hunt and Bill Chipley, two Baylor School graduates who had rafted with the NOC, bought three used NOC rafts, and begun their own operation. The next year, the NOC began operating on the Ocoee River with Dick Eustis as the outpost manager. This made a total of seven rafting businesses on the Ocoee at that time.

David Brown began coordinating lobbying efforts to ensure regular recreational water releases on the Ocoee after the renovation of the flume was completed. In 1984 Brown's work to save the Ocoee for paddling was rewarded. Congress made an appropriation to the TVA to assure regularly scheduled water releases on the Ocoee River.

Olympic venue on the Upper Ocoee, 1996 (photographed by Villa Brewer)

In 1986 the NOC purchased Sunburst Adventures on the Ocoee River from Marc Hunt and Bill Chipley. Bunny Johns became president of Sunburst.

Like the other rivers, interest in NOC Ocoee trips grew throughout the early 1990s, culminating in a boom in 1995, with NOC Ocoee guests topping 25,000. The boom in river numbers is attributed to the release of *The River Wild*, a white-water adventure film starring Meryl Streep and Kevin Bacon, and anticipation for the 1996 Olympics, with competition to be held on the Ocoee River.

For the 1996 Atlanta Olympics, the whitewater slalom event was held on an artificial course constructed in the normally dry section of the Ocoee above the section where rafting had taken place since 1976. The Ocoee River was closed to commercial traffic during the days of competition, and for the remainder of the season, folks seemed to be scared of crowding and high prices in the vicinity. NOC use there declined from a peak of 25,000 in 1995 to 20,500 in 1996, and this decline marked the end of peak rafting numbers on the river.

Growth of NOC Rafting on the Chattooga (1972–1996)

The NOC's first brochure in 1972 stated that the head guides were Payson Kennedy, Claude Terry, and Doug Woodward, but by this time Claude and Doug were making plans for their own rafting company on the Chattooga River, which would later evolve into the creation of Southeastern Expeditions. Either Jim Holcombe or Payson led all the NOC trips that first summer, and usually both of them came along.

On 1972 Chattooga trips (costing $20 and including lunch), guides met guests at the US 76 bridge, and a shuttle was run so that guest cars were waiting at the Lake Tugalo landing when the trips ended. While drivers made the shuttle, some guides pumped up the rafts with foot pumps, gave instruction on paddling technique, and often took the guests up to Bull Sluice rapids for a few practice runs. When trips were scheduled on successive days, the guides camped overnight near Thrift's Ferry Road.

During that summer the NOC took an estimated 400 guests on the Chattooga. In the fall, demand for raft trips on the Chattooga continued. This was partially due to two serendipitous factors: Whitewater slalom competition was included in the Olympics for the first time, and the movie *Deliverance* was released in August. Payson made a trip to Atlanta to see the movie and hand out NOC brochures featuring trips on the river where the movie was filmed.

In 1974 Congress designated the Chattooga as a Wild and Scenic River. At this time, the NOC had run several three-day trips on the Chattooga. They started the first day at Burrells Ford on the section of the river that was later closed to paddling and went as far as Long Bottom Ford, where they camped the first night. On the second day, they traveled most of Sections II and III and camped the second night at Thrift's Ferry. On the third day they continued on to the Lake Tugalo takeout.

The following year the U.S. Forest Service (USFS) began regulating trips on the Chattooga River. Because the USFS regulations limited companies to six rafts and 30 guests per trip, the NOC switched from four-person rafts to larger rafts that could take five or six guests. While the excitement decreased, safety improved; the larger rafts, while less maneuverable, proved far more stable. The number of flipped rafts and swims at Seven-Foot Falls and the Five Falls decreased drastically.

In 1976 Les Bechdel became NOC Chattooga Outpost manager and began many improvements to the organization and trip safety. Les also began renting canoes for Section III of the Chattooga River. After a season of frequently having to search for paddlers and equipment into the night, he decided that the river was too remote and difficult for rentals to be safe or practical.

In 1979 the NOC suffered a tragedy when Rick Bernard, an NOC staff member, drowned on a Chattooga trip. The stern of his kayak became wedged in a rock crevice at Jawbone rapid and the kayak folded in half, trapping him in the cockpit. This accident inspired Les Bechdel and Slim Ray to begin developing rescue techniques for use in whitewater, and this eventually resulted in the publication of their book, *River Rescue: A Manual for Whitewater Safety*, which continues as an admired text and is now in its fourth edition.

During a severe drought, which lasted through most of the 1980s, the Chattooga staff, dealing with water levels as low as 0.45 foot, showed great imagination in finding low-water routes and techniques and learning to make the trips fun, even when there was little water.

They began such activities as swimming through the pothole at Raven's Rock, surfing at the ledge hole near Blind Drop and bodysurfing at the first rapids below Long Creek.

As with the other rivers, Chattooga numbers peaked in 1995, at nearly 17,000 guests.

 ## *About the Contributor*

See page 81 for more information about Payson Kennedy.

A LEGACY OF GROUNDBREAKING PADDLING INSTRUCTION

By Kent Ford and Bunny Johns

Before the founding of the NOC, whitewater paddling in the Southeastern United States was practiced primarily in the many private camps of the mountainous areas. Camps Merrie-Woode (for girls), Green Cove (for girls), and Mondamin (for boys) taught extensive flatwater, whitewater, and canoe-camping skills and were running the rivers of Western North Carolina in the 1930s in wood-and-canvas canoes and after World War II in aluminum Grumman canoes. The rivers included the Green, Tuckasegee, Nantahala, Keowee, and the Chattooga.

These camps had a connection with the American Red Cross and its paddling and safety programs through Ramon Eaton (water safety director and later executive director), who had paddled extensively in the region. Ramon, Frank Bell (founder of Camp Mondamin), Pat Bell (his daughter), Fritz Orr (founder of Camp Merrie-Woode), John Delabar (Mondamin waterfront director), and Billy Pratt made the first known descent of the Nantahala in 1945 in wood-and-canvas canoes. On a later trip, John infamously wrapped a canoe around a rock in the river that is still named for him (Delabar's Rock).[1]

Some of the earliest NOC staff members got their start at these camps as well. Aurelia Kennedy paddled Nantahala Falls with Ramon in 1954, when she was a counselor and canoeing instructor at Camp Merrie-Woode. On a trip in the early 1960s, Bunny Johns arrived at the Nantahala Put-In (a short trail through trees) with Ramon, Fritz Orr Sr. (camp owner), and Hugh Caldwell (the camp's resident philosopher, river expert, and University of the South philosophy professor). There were 10 canoes and 15 campers. There was no water flowing that afternoon. Ramon walked over to the powerhouse and asked for water in the river. Soon they were paddling down the gorgeous Nantahala River in aluminum canoes with no flotation, no personal flotation devices (PFDs), and a towel for kneepads—consumed in the intricate dance with the river. There were no unplanned swims, and they watched Ramon and Hugh run all the canoes through Nantahala Falls. This was late July and there was no one else on the river! There was a restaurant and gas station where River's End and

---

[1] Will Leverette's book, A *History of Whitewater Paddling in Western North Carolina: Water Wise* (Charleston, SC: The History Press, 2008), gives more detailed information about early trips on the Nantahala and the canoeing programs at Western North Carolina summer camps, especially Camp Mondamin. Kent Ford's video *The Call of the River: A Hundred Years of Whitewater Adventure* (Durango, CO: Performance Video, 2009) includes footage from more than 100 sources, including scenes from some of these camps, as well as interviews with many whitewater pioneers. The most comprehensive source on the history of whitewater paddling is Susan L. Taft's *The River Chasers: A History of American Whitewater Paddling* (Mukilteo, WA: Flowing Water Press and Alpen Books Press, 2001). Taft covers all aspects of whitewater paddling in all regions of the United States from 1945 through the remainder of the 20th century.

the Outfitter's Store stand today. Everyone slept well on the way back to camp in the back of that big truck pulling a trailer with 10 Grumman canoes.

In the late 1960s, canoe clubs began forming in the southeastern states—Georgia Canoeing Association (GCA), East Tennessee Whitewater Club (ETWC), and the Carolina Canoe Club (CCC), to name a few. These clubs helped many people, including the founders of the NOC, learn about and enjoy whitewater paddling. Payson, Aurelia, and Horace Holden were active members of the GCA. The CCC, GCA, and other clubs started building fiberglass kayaks, as there were few kayak companies at the time and plastic kayaks did not exist. The clubs also had scheduled trips in which more experienced paddlers helped the less experienced paddlers get safely down the river.

Later, NOC worked with Tom Foster from New England Outdoor Center, Bob Benner of the CCC, and others to develop the American Canoe Association Instructor Training Program. This involved developing the curriculum, designating the first instructor trainers and conducting instructor training workshops. Many canoe clubs from around the southeast sent their experienced paddlers to these workshops, the long-term effect being that most canoe clubs now conduct kayak and canoe clinics to teach the general public not only how to paddle but also how to be safe while doing so.

A Legacy of Olympic Athletes and Groundbreaking Paddling Instruction

When Payson, Aurelia Kennedy, and Horace Holden founded the NOC, their vision was to provide instruction in outdoor skills and activities that would teach people about the great outdoors, how to enjoy it safely, and how to care for it. This vision gave birth to the NOC's instruction program, which attracted excellent teachers and significantly advanced current-day paddling techniques, such as the C-to-C roll, forward stroke technique, and water reading, as well as boat outfitting ergonomics and river rescue. The NOC became a national focal point for incredible advancements in whitewater sports.

But why would the Nantahala Gorge become the hub for all this? The simple answer was the unusual mixing bowl between people dedicated to understanding and teaching whitewater boating and Olympic-level slalom racers. It might seem an obvious match now, but in the 1970s, paddle sports in the United States were in their relative infancy, and there was no central place where knowledge was brought together. In 1972 whitewater slalom competition was included in the Olympics for the first time and was held on an artificial course constructed in Augsburg, Germany, on the Augsburg Eiskanal, a diversion of the Lech River. The United States brought a full team:

C-1 (canoe single)—Jamie McEwan (earned an Olympic bronze medal), Angus Morrison, and Wick Walker

K-1 (kayak single) Men—Eric Evans, John Holland, and Sandy Campbell

K-1 (kayak single) Women—Carrie Ashton, Louise Holcombe, and Cindy Goodwin

C-2 (canoe double)—John Burton/Tom Southworth and John Evans/Russ Nichols. Over the next several years, seven of the paddlers on that US team came to work at the NOC, and thus the connection between Olympic-level racing and whitewater instruction was made.

In March 1973 the NOC's first whitewater instructional clinic was conducted at Camp Chattahoochee near Roswell, Georgia, and on the Nantahala. The instructors were members of the Ledyard Canoe Club of Dartmouth, including Eric Evans, who was on the US Olympic Team the previous summer and US national champion in slalom kayaking for many years. The clinic attracted more than seventy participants, mostly from the Georgia Canoeing Association, which Horace had founded a few years earlier and for which Payson was the immediate past president.

Louise Holcombe and Carrie Ashton, both of whom were kayakers on the US Olympic Team the previous summer, came to work at the NOC in the summer of 1973 and played an important role in getting the instruction program off to a strong start and in attracting other Olympic paddlers to work at the NOC.

Carrie Ashton at Nantahala Falls, early 1980s. Carrie was the first woman to paddle the Niagara Gorge. (photographed by Villa Brewer)

Ray McLeod teaching canoeing (note: non-eco-friendly foam block we used for flotation back in the old, unenlightened days)

Initially there was much demand for whitewater canoe instruction—primarily tandem. Many guests brought their 16-, 17-, or even 18-foot Grumman or wood-and-canvas tandem canoes to the clinic. This worked well for the lake but often not so well on the river—even the Class I Little Tennessee. Many either left with a Blue Hole canoe or had one the next time they were at the Nantahala.

However, the emphasis gradually changed to kayaking. As it became a new and popular adventure sport, open canoeists were switching to kayaks, and new paddlers wanted to be in kayaks. This came from seeing kayaks in the 1972 Olympics, fiberglass kayaks becoming available through canoe clubs and retail outlets, and the commercial development of responsive playable plastic kayaks.

In 1974 Louise Holcombe's fiancé, Russ Nichols, who had been a C-2 paddler on the US Olympic Team in 1972, began working at the NOC and later made documentary films, including a series of very popular whitewater safety films for the Coast Guard. These included *The Uncalculated Risk, Margin for Error,* and *Whitewater Primer.* He also made a promotional film for the NOC called *Center Magic,* which did an excellent job of capturing the spirit that made the NOC successful. Other prominent paddlers who worked during those early years were Al Harris, a top C-2 competitor, and Charlie Walbridge, who became the national expert on whitewater safety for many years.

It was at this point that racing culture started to form around the NOC. Claude Grizzard, a GCA member from Atlanta, had won the C-1 class at the open canoe whitewater nationals in Maine the previous year and suggested that the GCA would

Les Bechdel at Nantahala Falls (photographed by Villa Brewer)

be willing to sponsor the nationals on the Nantahala in 1974. It would be the first time the whitewater open canoe nationals were held in the South. Taking place at Delabar's Rock rapids, NOC staff members won many of the slalom events. The team of Miki Piras and Carrie Ashton won the women's tandem class in both slalom and wildwater, while Bunny Johns and Jeannie Bracket were second in both events. Charlie Walbridge won the men's slalom class, and Les Bechdel was second.

John Kennedy, at age 14, paddling with Payson, won the junior-senior class and had the best time corrected for penalties of the boats in all slalom classes. There were 76 entries in the slalom classes and 70 entries in the downriver classes.

John and Payson Kennedy at Open Canoe Nationals in 1984, 10 years after their first win at the Open Canoe Nationals in 1974

John Kennedy and Linda Aponte—racing C-2 at Nantahala Falls
(photographed by Eve Burton)

This event was also significant because Mad River Canoe introduced a Kevlar open canoe at this race. Soon after, Hollowform introduced the first roto-molded plastic kayak at a price of $129, ordered directly from the factory, and in 1976 Bill Master's company Fiberglass Technology introduced the HD1, a solo open canoe for whitewater paddling.

Throughout the 1970s, the Olympic talent continued to flow. In 1975 John Burton, who was another member of the 1972 US Olympic Team, came in as assistant director and eventually became president. Cindy Goodwin, the third K-1 Women's paddler on the 1972 Olympic Team, also joined her teammates Louise Holcombe and Carrie Ashton at the NOC. Other staff who began that year were Linda Aponte (who became C-2 [canoe double] Men's national champion with John Kennedy in slalom) and Mike Beesch.

Closing out the decade, the 1979 World Championships were held at Jonquière, Québec. US paddlers Jon Lugbill, David Hearn, and Bob Robison swept the C-1 class, and Cathy Hearn won the K-1 Women's class in slalom and wildwater.

Even with all the new attention and innovation, this was a relatively new sport. Even 10 years earlier, in the early 1970s, kayaking was dwarfed by open canoe participation and was in the quick transition from aluminum canoes to fiberglass kayaks (dominant throughout the 1970s) to plastic, which took a while to gain dominance. Olympian Chris Spelius, NOC instructor and guide, was fond of saying that he would never paddle plastic, and "plastic keeps turkeys fresh." The next closest kayak school was probably the Hampshire College program in New England.

Sue Magness and Phil Watford on the Nantahala at Five-Eddy Rapid (photographed by Villa Brewer)

The NOC had gotten the moniker of the Harvard of Kayak Schools. So Olympians like John Burton ('72 Olympics and NOC assistant director); world-class racers like Les Bechdel (1967 US National Champion in K-1 Slalom and NOC Chattooga manager); and Olympians Angus Morrison and Carrie Ashton had a huge impact on attracting the next generation of world-class racers turned guides and instructors.

Some incredibly gifted and analytical teachers were also doing a substantial part of the instruction: Ken Kastorff, Kathy Bolyn, Eric Nies, Mary (Hayes) DeRiemer, David Dauphine, Dick Eustis, Homer King, Arnie Kleinrath, and Sue Magness.

In later years, many others contributed to the shared body of teaching pedagogy as well. At the time, Bunny Johns was running the NOC instruction program, while in her free time dedicating tremendous energy to starting the American Canoe Association instruction certification program, which became the de facto worldwide standard. She had transferred her scientific (biology) mindset to replicating a quality instructional experience.

Soon the NOC, with its Harvard-esque reputation, had consistent and large enough classes that most clinics had two instructors sharing ideas. As context, few other schools even existed at the time, so having two-instructor clinics enabled the exchange of powerful ideas. Led by Ken Kastorff, who became NOC's lead instructor, it was common for them to experiment with different teaching techniques always in search of a new, better, and safer way for students to learn to kayak. So the mix of top racer technique was shared through co-teaching and, importantly, through endless mealtime discussions. Breakthroughs in teaching progressions happened quickly and were disseminated through lively discussion at the staff meal plan. Over many long evening discussions and much time on the water, they came up with techniques like the Stern Draw Ferry, Head Dink, Paddling in the Box, and ways of teaching the kayak roll that emphasized safe shoulder position.

Arnie Kleinrath and Chris Spelius also brought freestyle kayak techniques to the program. Arnie won one of the first rodeos on the Arkansas River in Colorado.

Playing the River became as common in clinics and in canoe/kayak clubs as Running the River, and clinic participants could learn to do both.

Pure skills such as stroke technique were advanced through specific staff development clinics by the Olympians. These were influenced particularly by Angus Morrison (who raced slalom in '72 and narrowly missed the 1976 Olympic Team in flatwater sprint racing). While he was too shy to speak to a crowd, his one-on-one lessons were quickly shared and adopted as common knowledge. Others shared techniques in a remarkable atmosphere that truly seemed dedicated to raising all skills. Instructors would join burgeoning paddlers (guides, cooks, and waitstaff) on the water after work. It was all so fresh and exciting that the exchange itself was motivating.

Certainly the largest contribution to kayaking methods of today was the development of the kayak rolling technique. Until the early 1980s, most people in the sport had learned to roll through a tedious trial and error process, often from one page of illustrations in a book or pamphlet. A Russ Nichols film at NOC, *Whitewater Primer,* captured instruction of the early 1970s. But by the early 1980s, NOC instructor Ken Kastorff had figured out the C-to-C roll. This novel concept proved to provide the perfect cookbook for reliable instruction to NOC clients. Even if they didn't leave a clinic with the roll, they left with the cookbook, the step-by-step method of how to do it.

This was popularized even further by the video *Grace Under Pressure,* produced by Tom DeCuir and a crew from the NOC. The humor and clear explanations now were suddenly available worldwide, via the distribution of videotapes.

This was a time when relatively few paddlers traveled, and without the Internet there was little information exchange, so info-thirsty communities gobbled up the

Chris Spelius teaching a kayaker to roll (photographed by Villa Brewer)

Mike Hipsher and Bunny Johns racing downriver C-2 (photographed by Ciro Pena)

C-to-C roll instruction (which is still prevalent worldwide today, particularly in sea-kayaking communities).

NOC instructor Chris Spelius was one of the few who traveled across the United States with an instructional mindset. Legend has him at Otter Bar Lodge Kayak School in California and Sundance Kayak School in Oregon, bragging that he could teach rolling with the C-to-C faster than they could teach a sweep. They accepted the challenge, and to their amazement, he chose a nimble woman as his demo student. This was a shock, because flexible people were thought to be the toughest candidates for the sweep roll taught in the West. Whoever won the contest was lost in the lore, but the idea that different rolls suited different body types was born. Most paddlers knew only one roll technique, and they roundly criticized any other style as being dangerous for the shoulders.

Spelius, despite a show of braggadocio, was also keen to learn the "western" sweep roll being taught. Before 1990 he arranged for Phil DeRiemer to visit NOC instructor staff training to tutor the NOC staff on what came to be known as the twisting sweep roll. This took a while to be fully adopted, but by 1995 wide-planing hull play boats hampered the C-to-C, and this opened many minds to the twisting sweep that Spelius/DeRiemer had brought East in the late 1980s. Kent Ford's video *The Kayak Roll,* featuring Mary and Phil DeRiemer, accelerated the spread of that technique worldwide.

And throughout this time period, the marriage between the NOC and Olympic-caliber athletes continued. Some highlights are as follows:

Adam Clawson training in C-1 (photographed by Villa Brewer)

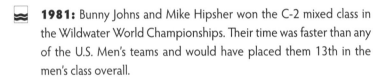

1981: Bunny Johns and Mike Hipsher won the C-2 mixed class in the Wildwater World Championships. Their time was faster than any of the U.S. Men's teams and would have placed them 13th in the men's class overall.

1990: The US Olympic Committee designated the Nantahala Racing Club as a center of excellence for training in slalom competition.

1992: Three paddlers from the NOC—Joe Jacobi and Scott Strausbaugh in C-2 and Adam Clawson, a C-1 paddler who had grown up and learned to paddle at the NOC—went to the Barcelona Olympic Games as members of the US Whitewater Slalom Team. In the C-2 event, Joe and Scott won the only gold medal the United States has ever won in Olympic slalom competition.

1996: For the 1996 Atlanta Olympics, the whitewater slalom event was held on an artificial course constructed in the normally dry section of the Ocoee River above the section where rafting had been taking place since 1977. Four Nantahala Racing Club members made the US team. They were Adam Clawson, Scott Shipley in K-1, a student at Georgia Tech who trained primarily at the Nantahala, and Wayne Dickert and Horace Holden Jr. paddling together in C-2.

Boat Design and Outfitting

Most of the boat outfitting of today was largely created in the NOC test tank. Outfitting in the plastic kayaks of the early 1980s was poor, due to the knees being forced down and close together. NOC instructors saw firsthand the trouble people experienced fitting themselves in the boats comfortably, not to mention how the outfitting inhibited control and stability. For a few years, there were elaborate aftermarket outfitting companies, but most people simply had to carve their own knee space and heel space with serrated knives "borrowed" from someone's kitchen.

In 1984 along came Vladimir Vanha, a Czech who had escaped to the West while in Paris as a manager of the Czech paddling team and had started work at the NOC as a dishwasher. He produced short play kayaks under the name Noah Boats and later teamed with Ken Kastorff (who now owns Endless River Adventures) to create a boat called the Jeti, which had comfortable outfitting and was based on the understanding that comfort and control came from the heels together/knees splayed position. This was a major advancement in the sport, mimicked today by all manufacturers of kayaks.

Later, Chris Spelius had a big influence on the beginning of Dagger Kayaks. According to Kent Ford, when the first boats showed up for testing, Chris and Joe Pulliam tried to keep them a secret, but soon Dagger kayaks was the industry leader, with multicolored boats in complex swirled patterns. By then, the NOC Outfitter's Store was flooded with people coming to choose boats with unique color schemes.

To some extent, even the stand-up paddleboard (SUP), today's rage in paddle sports, has some strong heritage from back when Rand Perkins, Payson, and Bill Baxter pioneered the standing technique for the fall triathlon.

 ## *About the Contributors*

See page 52 for more information about Kent Ford and page 61 for more about Bunny Johns.

SECTION III
Life Beyond
the River

WILD IN WINTER WOOD

By Cathy Kennedy

Author's Note: I wrote this haiku for an assignment in high school. When I wrote it, I was thinking of the Nantahala and Chattooga National Forests and the lichen-covered rocks on the riverbanks and just how long they have been there compared to me.

wild in winter wood
pattern etched ancient stone
how brief is man's time

About the Contributor

See page 35 for more information about Cathy Kennedy.

WELCOMING: TWO SISTERS REMEMBER THE LOCAL COMMUNITY

By Florrie Funk

There was an old man named Roy Dills who lived in the gorge. He was one of the first of the local people to befriend us strange outsiders who had moved into their community. We all loved him. I have a clear memory of him wearing denim overalls and sitting in front of the store whittling. I still have a ring that he made for me, carved from a peach stone. He gave it to me with the understanding that it was not a proposal of marriage. He often talked about the old days when he worked building the railroad through the gorge.

Sometimes he would take my sister, Allie, and me on walks in the woods and talk about the different plants—which ones were poison, edible, or medicinal. He said you could eat creasy greens and branch lettuce and Indian cucumber-root. Doll's eyes (baneberry) can kill you. There was one plant that Roy said a fellow "from off the mountain" ate (against Roy's advice) because he thought it was a wild carrot. The man almost died. I believe it was hemlock parsley; numerous plants in that family are poisonous. American Indians used to eat Jack-in-the-pulpit roots, but Roy said that they knew how to dry them and cook them right. If you don't, they are poison. The juice from jewelweed will stop the itch from poison ivy and the sting from stinging nettles. You can make a spring tonic from sweet birch, sassafras twigs, and pine needles that will help you get your strength back after the winter. Slippery elm bark can cause a woman to lose a baby, but that's not something you should talk about.

Roy showed me how to find hellgrammites in the river for fish bait. He helped Allie lay out trails for the horseback trips she led at NOC. He sometimes said people might think it unseemly for him to be out walking in the woods with young women, but he didn't care what other people thought.

Roy often invited us to come to his church on Sunday. So one Sunday Allie and I got up, dressed modestly, and went to the little church up Wesser Creek. Most of the congregation was already seated. We didn't know anyone there except Roy, so we went and sat next to him. People nodded at us. Nobody said anything. Partway through the service, we noticed that we had seated ourselves on the men's side of the church. All the other women were seated on the other side of the aisle. After the service, people told us they were glad we had come and they hoped we would come back. No one said anything about us sitting on the men's side, and Roy never mentioned it either.

About the Contributor

Florrie Funk worked at the NOC during the summers of 1973–75. She worked as a waitress and occasionally helped in the stables, caring for the horses and taking customers on trail rides. After traveling with other NOC staff members in Mexico, Guatemala, and Belize, she participated in what became the first NOC international expedition on the Usumacinta River in February 1976. Having survived that, she returned to the United States and the following July she married Tom Gonzalez, another NOC staff and expedition member. Over the years Tom and Florrie have lived in Spain, Puerto Rico, Canada, California, Florida, Missouri, Illinois, Massachusetts, and Georgia. They raised two beautiful children, Candler and Emma. Florrie has done volunteer work in nature centers and botanical gardens. She now lives in Asheville and pursues miscellaneous artistic and botanical interests.

By Allie Funk (Jones)

Roy Dills and I spent a good deal of time together in the woods cutting trail for the horseback rides. I enjoyed his use of language. What I called laurel he called ivy and what I called rhododendron he called laurel. We skirted the places where the horses might get mired down and we swamped our way through the hillside laurel thickets. Once, he made a wide detour around a bush, rather than cutting it, and smiled, asking if I knew why he did not cut that one?

"Cause that one is a rhododendron!" Roy smiled. "Wait until you see it bloom." (It was a red Catawba rhododendron, rather than a white rhododendron maximum.)

One time he complimented me by saying that there weren't much to me but I was stout as a man. He worried that all the time we spent together alone in the woods would cause people to talk and ruin my reputation. He said that he would marry me but that he was an old man and it would not be right to leave a young woman a widow.

I thanked him for his concern.

Roy Dills was always the gentleman, but I think perhaps he enjoyed the reputation he got among his Baptist neighbors for what they considered his scandalous association with the young women of the NOC.

Another neighbor who lived up the road from the brick house was Harv Clampitt, who spoke in a thick Appalachian dialect. As he walked past my little vegetable garden, he commented that it was "a right nice garden even if ya do work in it on Sundays."

Once I asked him about a bug, and he answered, "That there is a tater bug. Put it on the ground and tread on it. Get shed of it."

Another time he brought me a tan squash the size and shape of a watermelon. He called it a custard squash. When I asked how to cook it, he said, "Ya just put it in a pot and boil it."

Another day he walked by with a puppy. I asked what breed it was and he replied, "A pot licker." Harv Clampitt was a nice man, but I think he was probably one of those who wondered what Roy Dills and I were doing in the woods. He often invited me to church.

Tomas was a young man who sometimes helped me at the barn. He was big and strong for a 15-year-old and a quick learner. He owned a quarter horse stud colt that was his pride and joy and wanted to learn everything about how to take care of horses. I taught him what I could and loaned him my British Pony Club manual on horse care. He studied it diligently.

One day when Tomas came to the barn, he was beaming. The next day would be his 16th birthday, and he told me with pride that now he could drop out of school.

"Oh, Tomas," I said, "you don't want to do that. Think of your future."

"Yes, I do," he replied. "I have been waiting for this 'cause now I can go to work at the sawmill and earn money to buy indoor plumbing for my mom."

I argued that he needed a high school diploma to get a good job, but he countered that he did not ever want to leave Wesser Creek, and the only good job in Wesser Creek was at the sawmill. They did not care if he had a diploma. He could work there now. Besides, he argued, he had missed some school, and though he was almost 16, he was still only in the eighth grade. He would be 21 before he ever graduated, and they hassled him about chewing gum in class.

Really he wasn't chewing gum. He was chewing tobacco and he was fed up enough that he might spit it at them. He figured it was better to go on and drop out of school than be kicked out.

His decision was rational, but I grieved the loss of his potential. The next summer he married his 15-year-old sweetheart.

About the Contributor

Allie Funk (Jones) worked at the NOC from the summer of 1972 through the summer of 1976. She primarily set up and ran the horseback riding program, but she also occasionally helped out at the restaurant, cleaned a few motel rooms, and in lieu of taking a day off, guided some raft trips, mostly on the Nantahala. She lived at the brick house up Wesser Creek because it was near the barn. She was part of the (in) famous Usumacinta trip, the NOC's first international trip to Belize and Guatemala in 1976. Having been a professor of sociology at Appalachian State University for 35 years, Allie is now retired and raises sheep in Ashe County, North Carolina. Of course, she still has and rides horses.

GUESTS IN THE OLD DAYS

By Allie Funk (Jones)

Some of our early NOC guests were amazing, inspirational people. I remember one elderly man, perhaps in his late 70s, who stopped by to reprovision as he walked the Appalachian Trail. He had planned to walk the entire trail that summer but had fallen and broken some ribs, so now he decided to take it easy and rest a few days with us. Having just discovered the NOC, he was interested in the trips we had to offer. The first day he chose a Nantahala raft trip. The next day he went on an all-day horseback ride. The following day he did Section IV of the Chattooga. Then, apparently feeling well rested, he headed on up the trail.

Some guests, however, were a challenge. One day two separate families showed up for a 1-hour horseback ride, a routine trip that I led several times a day. One family was a couple with a 5-year-old girl. I put her on the little pony on a lead line. The other family was a couple from New York City with a boy of about 11. The boy's father was irate that I was not lead-lining his child like I was the other family's little girl.

Still, I put the boy on dependable Barney, his father on my own placid mare, and off we went. His wife was delighted. She thought the forest and wildflowers beautiful. Even prettier than Central Park, she said!

All the other riders were having a good time, but the man from New York was grumbling. About halfway through the ride, Barney was stung by a bee and jumped, but he did not buck or bolt as another horse might have. Nevertheless, the boy slid off of Barney, but he was unharmed. I got off my pony, tied up the little pony with the 5-year-old girl, and went to help the boy get back on.

His father got off his horse and ran to his son, hugged him and said surely he was too injured to get back on that wild beast. The boy assured him that he was fine and climbed back on. At this point the bottom dropped out of the skies and it rained so hard that one's underwear was wet in a minute. The father refused to get back on his horse, saying she would surely slip and fall on the steep wet trail. I assured him that she had four feet on the ground and was much less likely to fall than he was. She did this trail several times a day with no problem. He refused again, so I told him I would take the others on to the barn and come back to get him. He heroically said yes, save the women and children first.

When I came back for him, the sun had come out, and the man finally tripped and slipped his way on foot back to the barn. There he hugged his embarrassed son and wife and got down on his knees and prayed to God for deliverance from the wilderness.

About the Contributor

See previous page for more information about Allie Funk (Jones).

By Bunny Johns

One time two open-canoe instruction clinics traveled over to Section III of the Chattooga. It was one of those beautiful Chattooga days—warm weather, great water level, enthusiastic paddlers who even enjoyed the river while swimming with their boat and, of course, their paddle. As usual we were in a hurry at the takeout so we could get to dinner at the Dillard Motor Lodge in Clayton, Georgia, hosted by bigger-than-life cook, Louise (I don't think I ever knew her last name). So, the call went out: "Canoes all tied down? Gear in the gearbox? OK, get you and your stuff in the van!" We sure didn't want to miss dinner at Louise's.

Everyone hopped in the vans and off we went to Clayton. We filled up two or three big tables and ordered dinner. About that time, I sensed something amiss so I counted us all. There appeared to be one person missing. Anyone in the restroom? What about the other tables? What about the porch? Then I realized the obvious— we'd just left a guest at the takeout.

After a hurried drive, I reached the takeout at late, very late, dusk. A very patient man waited for me at the bridge. After my profuse apology, he simply said, "I knew you would be back for me eventually, but I was starting to think about a night in the woods." We returned to Clayton, where he got a standing ovation, and we never heard another word from him about that lapse in accounting for all our guests.

Like I said, guests were really tough in those big ol' open canoe days.

About the Contributor

See page 61 for more information about Bunny Johns.

SNAPSHOTS FROM RIVER'S END RESTAURANT

By Florrie Funk

I started working at the NOC in the summer of 1973, after my sophomore year at Duke. Mostly I worked as a waitress in the restaurant. The restaurant had been in operation before Horace bought it, and the clientele was still largely people from the surrounding area, as well as truck drivers passing through the Nantahala Gorge.

The short-order cook at that time was a Greek guy, I think, named Pete, who was from somewhere in the Northeast. He was in the habit of using colorful language. Early one morning, a truck driver came in and ordered French toast. When I brought him his plate, the truck driver looked at it and said, "Hey, this ain't right. There's a dry spot. There's not enough egg on this piece!"

So I took the plate back to the kitchen and told Pete that the customer had complained that his French toast had a dry spot.

Pete raised his eyebrows and said, "Hand it back here. I'll piss on it for you."

Aurelia had bought some bright flowered material and made ruffled, ankle-length aprons and matching triangle head scarves for the waitresses to wear. One hot summer day, I was working a busy lunch shift, feeling very feminine in my flowery apron over cutoff jeans, hiking boots, and a sleeveless shirt. I wore my hair

Maggie Parkes in early River's End uniform (photographed by Ciro Pena)

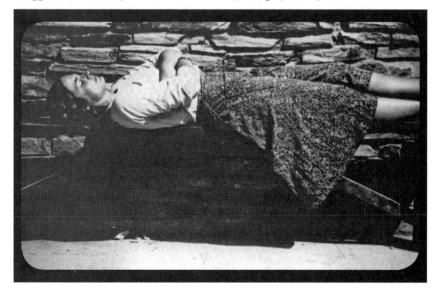

in long braids. I was a skinny little thing back then, and being a liberated young woman, I had quit shaving my legs and armpits. Going unshaven was not a widely accepted practice at that time, but I assumed that all women would come to their senses in the coming years because shaving was an obviously unnatural and unnecessary thing to do.

As I moved around the dining room, I noticed two men who kept looking at me funny and talking quietly to each other. Finally, one of them motioned me to come over to their table. He said in a serious tone, "Hey. Me and him have a bet going. Are you a boy or a girl?"

About the Contributor

See page 102 for more information about Florrie Funk.

By Payson Kennedy

Aurelia loves to tell the story from that first summer of a time when John Stevenson, one of the Explorer Scouts, was the breakfast cook. Aurelia told him to multiply amounts in the recipe from *The Joy of Cooking* to make pancakes. John added 2 cups of baking powder, rather than the specified 2 teaspoons, and the batter was soon overflowing like a volcano onto the stove and floor.

On another occasion, when the air-conditioning repairman asked whether little people were running the restaurant, Aurelia found that, in a sense, he was correct: our children were running the restaurant. Cathy was cooking, Frances was waiting tables, and John and Stewart were standing on Coca-Cola crates to wash dishes at the big double sinks. Cathy remembers that she always wanted to be guiding rather than working in the restaurant that first summer. She often was able to talk Jim Holcombe into delaying the afternoon raft trip until she finished her shift in the restaurant and was able to join.

About the Contributor

See page 81 for more information about Payson Kennedy.

MAINTENANCE

By Sue Firmstone Goddard

In the early 1970s, NOC employees weren't hired as raft guides; they were hired to do whatever was needed. Women were expected to double as waitresses, and men were on maintenance. I wasn't afraid to work, but I just couldn't picture myself as a waitress and so I asked Payson if I could be on the maintenance crew instead. Somehow he agreed, though I spent my first three days shoveling gravel, and I have always believed that was a test of sorts. I must have passed, because I never did find myself serving food.

Like much of the staff, I lived at Hellard's. One of my first jobs was to help install the gas heaters for the winter. I had aspirations, later realized, of being a carpenter and was pretty handy with tools, but I had no real training. I was often paired with Bob Bouknight, who had legitimate skills as an electrician, and somehow we got things done whether we knew what we were doing or not. Bob's dog, Big Dog, kept us company, and Bob let me drive his blue and white Land Cruiser, to the consternation of his wife, Laurie, who was not afforded that privilege.

When guides weren't on the river, there was plenty of other work to keep them busy. We needed to clean the motel rooms, take care of all maintenance needs, cut foam blocks for the Blue Holes, drive hiker and other shuttles, and take garbage to the dump. One of my proudest moments was when Payson commended me at a staff meeting for the quality of my dump runs!

For the privilege of working, I was paid $80/week plus room and board. I've never been happier. I had to be told to take my mandatory days off, or I would just keep guiding. The food was good and plentiful. We had to take turns cleaning the kitchen at night after the restaurant closed, cleaning the pots and pans and mopping the floors. It wasn't so bad with the right partner. My favorite was Scott Price, who lived up along the Appalachian Trail.

I had been a bus driver in Pennsylvania prior to arrival, so I was often asked to drive the bus or Big Truck. Joe Cole kept the vehicles running. The bus had no key—a screwdriver in the key slot got it running. Driving to a staff ballgame one night, it blew a rod and we all had to wait for rescue.

On one assignment I had to walk to each end of the center with a posthole digger and a 4-by-4-inch post with a WESSER sign affixed and officially designate the boundaries. That gave me a sense of ownership. Later I got put in charge of the Wesser water system, which consisted of a couple of springs high up the ridge of land between the motel and the highway. There were small dams that we built with concrete block and water cement, and we ran black plastic pipe down to a holding tank; from there gravity fed it to the motel, restaurant, and store. I had to periodically check for leaks or washouts. One morning before leaving for the river, the restaurant folk complained that the water was intermittent. I hiked up the hill and found a crawdad with its head stuck in the pipe. When its body blocked the flow sufficiently, it started backing out, which allowed the water to resume its flow but sucked the crawdad back in. That was an easy fix.

As the demand on the systems grew, the septic system needed to be updated. I worked with Allan Quant to hand-dig trenches on the downstream side of the maintenance garage. The trenches were head-high, and they periodically caved in and needed to be dug out again, but we got the pipes in. I can't remember anyone suggesting a need for an engineer or permit.

At that time, the center facilities consisted of several motel rooms, an office, and the restaurant/store/gas station/maintenance room. Betsy Quant ran the office, which meant she handled virtually everything—reservations (river, horse, and motel), payroll, scheduling, and no doubt much more over one phone line. There was a pay phone outside the office (by the elephant ear tree) that was the only phone for most of the staff.

It's shocking to me to realize I only worked at the NOC for one year, and not even through the winter. I still think of it as the best year of my life, and I remember it with a clarity that, even after 40 years, astounds me.

 ## *About the Contributor*

Sue Firmstone Goddard worked at the NOC 1974–1975 as a Chattooga guide, Outward Bound canoe instructor, bus driver, water system wizard, gravel spreader, garbage hauler, and plumber/electrician/carpenter, as required. After leaving the NOC, she spent several years instructing in Outward Bound programs and outdoor programs for adjudicated or otherwise special youth. When she tired of the nomadic life, she returned to her home state of Pennsylvania and found work as a carpenter. Of late, she administers grants to repair homes of low-income folks. She has raised three young adults who take to water and boats as though they were meant to do so.

THE OLD STORE

By John Barbour

In the spring of 1974, the store was a far cry from what it would eventually become. It was a combination grocery store, gas station, and souvenir shop. We sold Esso gas, Coca-Cola in the bottle, and Skoal (yep Skoal!). The old building was rundown, hot in the summer and cold in the winter. We dealt with the heat by adopting a somewhat relaxed dress code (that is, bathing suits and bare feet, top optional, depending on gender!). A quick dip in the river and then back to work, no problem. Heat in the winter was provided by an old potbellied stove that burned wood at an insatiable rate and only heated within a 10-foot radius. Still, it was cozy and a favorite spot for the locals to hang out. I have fond memories of two old men, Roy Dills and Jim Breedlove, teaching me how to play Fox & Geese, a board game similar to Parcheesi. Our first cash register was an antique with a large lever that made the classic *ka-ching* sound when it opened. We also had an antique cheese cutter and sold slices of hoop cheese. The old building housed not only the store but the rafting and rentals operations as well. Hard to imagine that now.

The store was a popular hangout for river rats—real rats that would periodically devastate our candy bar stock. One of these critters became famously known as Chunky Rat, due to his fondness for Chunky chocolate candy bars. We finally caught Chunky, but in one last great act of defiance, he managed to drag the trap through a hole in the wall and down into the crawl space under the store where he died. We couldn't reach him, so for the next few weeks the store smelled like dead rat. The revenge of Chunky!

Many changes came about quickly over the next few years. We dropped the Esso gas after the Exxon Valdez oil spill; the Skoal went, as did the soft drinks in the bottle. We were the last store in Western

John Barbour watching the destruction of the old Outfitter's Store (photographed by Villa Brewer)

New Outfitter's Store

North Carolina to sell bottled drinks, recycling before it became ubiquitous. The antique cash register was replaced with an electric one, and soon another was added. The old store began to fill with kayaks, canoes, and outdoor gear. It quickly gained a reputation as the best whitewater boating store in the South, and later the nation.

As the outdoor industry grew, so did the NOC, and we soon outgrew the old store. When the day arrived to tear down the original building, I took the first wall down with a backhoe.

As I watched the building begin to collapse, I knew whatever we built would be OK. The building itself was never what made the NOC store a special place; it was the people inside, and that hopefully would never change.

About the Contributor

John Barbour came to the NOC in 1974 from Western Carolina University, where he was majoring in Parks and Recreation, and was active in the Outing Club. He was hired initially to repair rafts and rental equipment but ended up guiding rafts and working in the rental department. He took over managing the store in 1976 and ran it until 1991, at which time he took over as vice president of retail. John left the NOC in 1998 for Florida, where he currently resides, enjoying semiretirement. John is currently working part-time at Wild Birds Unlimited in Gainesville, Florida.

NOC STORE TALK

By John Lane

With only a couple thousand feet of display space, the NOC store had the feel of an old mountain store. Goods were piled to the ceiling in a few places. (Maybe there *was* a real cracker barrel somewhere under all those T-shirts.) Some items moved fast, like current issues of *Outside* and Snickers candy bars, while others, like a pink wet suit, collected dust in a corner for an entire season until the fall sale. But, like most old stores, one thing moved fast 12 months a year: store talk.

Store talk was never bought or sold. It was given and received by the staff with a common purpose and spirit: to have fun, to inform, to tell guests about our work and life. Store talk was not a trivial pursuit, or blabber. It was conversation. An exchange of opinions, ideas, and observations. Sometimes serious, sometimes not.

On a summer day in Wesser, you might walk away from the store with much more than you'd expected for the price of a T-shirt. Some lingered at the back window watching the river, or paused at the bookshelf and listened closely to the clerks talking at the counter when the rush was over. They caught river talk—crash-and-burn stories and river levels—which they might have come to Wesser to hear. But river stories were not all they heard.

Someone usually wandered in and asked how far it was to Franklin or Cherokee; if there was water on the Appalachian Trail between the store and Fontana; or if we knew some isolated camping spot, gravel road for mountain biking, or put-in or takeout to a hundred Southeastern rivers. We never tired of the answers. Stocking T-shirts and punching two cash registers kept our hands busy, but most people John Barbour hired loved to talk, and answering questions kept our mouths working.

In an 8-hour day, there were hundreds of stories about camp kids to tell; Steely Dan lyrics to recite; and bits of

John Lane reading Barry Lopez
(photographed by Villa Brewer)

knowledge to dispense about weaving and mountain bikes and the important differences between gummy bears and grunch pads. You may even have heard a dissertation or two on target shooting, a discussion concerning the poetic traditions of Emily Dickinson and Walt Whitman, an introduction to the geology of Utah, a critique of the latest movie playing in Andrews, or a verbal demonstration of the perfect paddle stroke from one of many almost-perfect store paddlers.

Although store staff loved to sell, we liked giving just as much. Store talk was our gift.

About the Contributor

John Lane worked from the mid-1980s to early 1990s in the Outfitter's Store. Since leaving the NOC, he has taught at Wofford College, combining writing with environmental studies, and is director of Goodall Environmental Studies Center. His poetry and prose have made their marks in both academic and popular circles. He recently received the Water Conservationist Award from the South Carolina Wildlife Federation and an induction into the South Carolina Academy of Authors. His books include *Chattooga: Descending into the Myth of Deliverance River* and *My Paddle to the Sea*, where he used his 200-mile kayak trip from his South Carolina backyard to the Atlantic Ocean to highlight critical water issues in the southeast. In 2015 *Blue Ridge Magazine* named him both a cultural and conservation outdoor pioneer.

SCENES FROM WESSER CREEK

By Allie Funk (Jones)

The second summer that NOC was open, almost all of the staff (18 of us) lived in the brick house up Wesser Creek. There was only one bathroom for all of us to share, so when the line was too long, males often went to the woodpile behind the house.

One morning Jim Karwisch returned from the woodpile white as a sheet, stammering that he had pissed on a copperhead. While Karwisch seemed terrified, Jim Shelander was distressed only about the poor snake.

In those days I ran the horseback riding trips. We had not built the best fencing system and there was no way to keep the horses out of the hallway of the barn. One little fat bay horse, Barney, was persistently greedy about food. This particular morning there was a copperhead on a bale of hay in the hallway, and Barney did not have on a halter, so I could not tie him up. He was determined to try to eat the hay out from beneath the snake. I struggled to keep the horse off the snake and called for help.

Shelander arrived and as usual was more concerned for the welfare of the snake. The horse had hurt the poor copperhead, and so he insisted we transport it to the top of the mountain, where it would be safe. Shelander held the snake and I drove him way up the road in my 1956 Willis Jeep, Blue Goose.

Shelander just wanted a place where the snake would be safe from humans; I just wanted it not to get loose and make its new home in my jeep.

 About the Contributor

See page 104 for more information about Allie Funk (Jones).

ABOVE BONE RING LAKE:

FOR JOHN DOLBEARE (1957–1989)

By John Lane

Author's Note: John Dolbeare, known far and wide as Dolby, worked in the NOC store as a shift manager and climbing consultant throughout the 1980s. He died in a paddling accident in West Virginia.

Dolby, I thought of you as I worked up over
weather-split stone here in the Bighorns.
Thunderstorm brought you back above Bone
Ring Lake, cross-country bushwhacking.

You'd be headed higher for the ridgetop too,
goat-jumping, stone to stone. I'd like to climb
fast as you, but I breathe hard, a summer of talk
instead of paddling water, walking ragged land.

I've learned to love the way the mind eats
at the body, sets stiff muscles on brittle edge,
makes me want to give out just as windflowers
spring up among standing snags of an old burn.

The living sure as hell are with us, but you
dead are too, lying around like fallen silver trunks,
brittle bones, stacked against lodgepole pines.
Your presence never left me, mountain-spirit,
scree-in-the-hills, home on this distant range.

Stone, wind, and water-born, this place
called you out of my backcountry silence,
out of the oracle gurgle of hidden streams.

I slow down, search the boulder field for you,
and the light above—strange conjunction of ridge,
trail, and memory: your ashes, moving still,
somewhere near the sea by now, dropped in
the Nantahala, mixed with windflowers
and the true mourning song of forty friends.

John Dolbeare paddling the Cascades on the Upper Nantahala
(photographed by Villa Brewer)

Are you hiding in this godless scrabble of down logs,
left by weather, fire, or age for me to kick or straddle?
You laugh—a jay, crow?—as I break through my lungs'
summer-off-the-mountain pain and push on up,
through the pine's brittle branches, the stones'
cracked orbits, the slick moss slime.

Your dead voice is the wind pounding my mortal ears—
"Don't hang back. Climb, John, Goddamn it, climb."

 About the Contributor

See page 114 for more information about John Lane.

AUTHENTIC LEADERSHIP

By Betsey Lewis Upchurch

Leaders at the NOC were not afraid to critique, coach, and even tease people into doing their best work. At times, this was hard for me to take, but today, in a busy consulting practice that I run with ex-NOC staffer Ellen Babers, I often tell this story to clients to show the value of honest feedback or to illustrate how telling the truth is often the best thing you can do for someone.

At the NOC, I was the manager of custom programs. It had grown exponentially for several years and was never an easy program to pull off. Guests came to us in groups, using many different services of the center, with time frames that didn't always work with the schedules of the other departments. For instance, if we were discussing something critical to meeting their goals, our group would be late to dinner, which threw the whole restaurant off and made instruction groups show up to tables that were still full when they should have been ready for them. Lodging needed to have people out on time so they could clean for the next group, but we often needed late checkouts. Instructors needed full weeks of work, and if custom programs used them for only three days, the rest of their week was filled with odd jobs instead of river work.

While our guests paid well, they could be demanding and they didn't always conform to their schedules. Dates changed frequently, which made planning across many different departments difficult and annoying. And, the truth is, I didn't manage details well and often forgot to tell people about important changes. This program was a difficult fit into the center's routines, and I made it a lot tougher. I always felt on the defensive, especially when I was the one who was making the situation worse.

One day, Janet Smith, who was the vice president of custom programs, called me into her office. She looked at me and said, "People like you, but they don't like working with you." She went on to tell me a list of the critical things that I was doing that made everyone else's lives difficult. And then she said, "I know we can make this department go from having the worst reputation at the center to having the best. I want to meet with you every week, and within six months to a year I think you will have turned this around. I believe in you."

That wasn't easy to hear, but she was right. It turned around. We did very well over the next year. We stabilized staff, we had the other departments working with us, we worked much better with them, and we were giving even better programs and service to our guests. None of that would have been possible had she not had the courage to tell the truth, the vision to see how to play to my strengths as a leader, the skill in coaching to help me get there, and the willingness to believe in me when others were calling for my head on a stick.

One of the many gifts of working at the NOC was the example that Janet and many others lived every day as authentic leaders.

About the Contributor

Betsey Lewis Upchurch joined the river staff at the NOC in the spring of 1987. In 1988, she took the reins of the custom programs department, working with schools and corporate groups. She remained there until 1994, moving to New Hampshire to teach wilderness emergency medicine. It didn't take long before she realized the world needs more compassionate organizations. She has since worked in almost every industry doing culture change and leadership development. The contacts she made with other consultants while at the NOC remain collaborators to this day. The children she writes about in this book are grown with wild and crazy children of their own. She lives in Fort Mill, South Carolina, and still goes paddling when she isn't traveling.

OFFICE SPACE

By Susan Bechdel

When I came to work at the NOC in 1978, I was between a master's and a PhD program. Weary from years in academia, I knew I had landed my dream job. Working outdoors would be just the break I needed. But what about the office hours that came with it? I just hoped I could tolerate the nine-to-five tedium in exchange for those soul-saving days on the river.

Today, companies like Google and Facebook alleviate office boredom with perks like free food and video arcades, but back in the 1970s, office employees tucked their shirts into high-waisted slacks and their rear ends into rolling office chairs for 8 long hours every day. It was not something I was looking forward to, even at an outdoor company. Fortunately, as it turned out, that was not something that happened at the NOC.

Having a desk job at the NOC in the 1970s meant being surrounded by dynamic people and exposed to a plethora of experiences. It came with high-quality professional development like Outward Bound clinics and self-awareness work-shops. There were slalom gates to run and waves to surf during lunch. Scheduling was flexible and staff could join a rock climbing clinic, or an international adventure. There were classes on timber frame building and informal music jam sessions.

Comprehensive health care and meal plans supported the culture of a healthy lifestyle. Not only did we have childcare available, but many of our kids had once-in-a-lifetime experiences before they were even born. Our second child, Max, took an in utero bike trip in England, and another NOC baby-to-be, Josh Burton, sloshed around in his mom's belly as she rafted the Bío-Bío.

Unlike the barbershops and massage rooms at Facebook and Google, none of these experiences were contrived. This is just what happens when like-minded people share their love of work and life. This authentic environment didn't come from sticky notes on white boards and strategic planning sessions. It came from

Susan Bechdel with her son, Max
(photographed by Villa Brewer)

an administration that treated employees with deep respect and shared a mutual love of the outdoors.

I remember one day when I stayed late to finish some office work. I was planning to take the next day off to ride my bike from the Nantahala to the Chattooga. A lot of factors had to coalesce for this to happen. My husband would have to pick up our kids from day care. I'd arranged a ride back in the NOC shuttle van, and I had my snacks packed and tires pumped up. Just as I was wrapping up work late that afternoon, CEO Payson Kennedy came into my office and asked if I would meet with him the next day. My heart sank as I realized the next day's bike trip would now be dashed, but I took a chance and nervously mentioned it anyway. Payson hesitated for a brief and painful second. Then he smiled and asked if he could join me.

 ### *About the Contributor*

Susan Warner Bechdel began work at the NOC as a Chattooga guide in 1978. She married Les Bechdel the next year and the two of them stayed at the NOC until 1985. During those years she guided on the Nantahala, Ocoee, Chattooga, and Nolichucky Rivers and taught canoe clinics and Outward Bound courses. She guided rafting trips in Chile, Mexico, and Guatemala as well as assisted on bicycle trips in England and trekking trips in Nepal. With this Adventure Travel experience under her belt and a baby in her belly, Susan joined Payson in the Adventure Travel office for her last couple of years at the center before she, Les, and their two children packed up and headed west. They started their own business on the Middle Fork and Main Salmon Rivers in Idaho, enjoying frequent trips, booked cooperatively with NOC, and a continuing relationship with their NOC friends and colleagues.

"HELLO, JEROME"

By Susan Hester with Ray McLeod

In September of 1996, I was the manager of the NOC Rafting Reservation Office and Ray McLeod was heading up NOC-owned Great Smokies Mountain Rafting, which was located just up the Nantahala Gorge. While we had separate reservationists at each location, all the staff knew each other well.

One of our "bookies" was Rodney Millspaugh, who was friends with one of the Great Smokies bookies, Jason. Jason had mentioned to Rodney that, due to a toll-free number mix-up, Great Smokies had been getting a lot of calls for a cable TV company. Rodney mulled this over and later made an elaborate hoax call to Jason at Great Smokies claiming to be an outraged customer named Jerome. It was truly a masterful performance, and we were all laughing so hard we cried.

Almost immediately afterward, my office phone rang. It was Ray McLeod, who was heading up Great Smokies Mountain Rafting. He filled me in on how "Jerome" had just called their reservation line. After hearing a spirited rendition of the conversation, I decided we had better come clean. If you've met Ray, you know he has a great sense of humor, so I immediately thought he'd appreciate Rodney's performance, but after I explained the joke, the silence on the other end of the line was deafening. I should have known then that what Rodney had done was the equivalent of waving a red rag in front of a bull. Basically, he'd challenged a practical joke master, and revenge was now in the air. All Ray said to me before he hung up was, "We're going to get him back, and you better help."

To set Rodney up, Jason and Ray scanned a piece of North Carolina Health and Environmental Services letterhead and wrote a letter to Rodney. The letter explained that during routine water testing, "several of the 14 chemicals banned by the Todd Keppenheimer Act"—this was totally made up—"[had] been detected in the Little Tennessee River." The letter continued, "Further investigation has tracked the chemicals back to the drain field of the Millspaugh cabin of residence." Jason had done a great job crafting the letter. It looked completely official and was full of long "chemical" names (which were incidentally obtained from the back of a NAB cracker package). Though these "chemicals" were actually the cracker ingredients, Ray knew that Rodney wasn't a chemist, so they were probably safe. They set up the letter so that it was delivered through the NOC mail system (helped along by my post-dating the envelope so it looked authentic). The letter demanded Rodney meet health department officials at his cabin that very day, and at a time that was only 20 minutes after he first opened it. The letter threatened, "This issue needs to be *immediately* addressed," and "your absence at this meeting, Mr. Millspaugh, *will not be viewed with favor*." Needless to say, Rodney, somewhat freaked out, left work immediately to meet the health department officials. For moral support, he took along a fellow bookie, Mike Canata.

When Rodney arrived at his cabin, he was shocked to see the black and silver of a North Carolina Highway Patrol car, and his cabin was completely surrounded by streams of yellow crime-scene tape. Unknown to Rodney, the highway patrolman was Ray's son, Mike McLeod, who, like his father, is always up for a good practical joke. Mike walked up to the car and in his sternest state trooper voice said, "Which one of you is Rodney Millspaugh?"

When Rodney identified himself, Mike continued, "Get out of the car *now* and come with me." He then pointed to Rodney's passenger, Mike Canata, and said, "You! Stay in the car!"

During this time, just to set a little atmosphere, Ray had Jason, dressed in a black jumpsuit with an ATF cap pulled low over his face, pacing around Rodney's front porch with a beeping Geiger counter. Next, Mike pointed Jason out, stating, "Do you see that man? He's with the ATF."

Rodney nervously responded, "Alcohol, Tobacco, and Firearms?!"

"Yes," Mike replied. "You're in *big* trouble, Mr. Millspaugh. Do you have your copy of the letter that was sent from the health department?" Mike then whipped out a copy and started to read. "You can see this section that mentions the chemicals that were banned by the Todd Keppenheimer Act? These chemicals were banned because they are used exclusively in the manufacturing of synthetic narcotics." Mike then glared at Rodney. "Do you know anything about the manufacturing of narcotics here, Mr. Millspaugh?"

Rodney responded a tremulous, "No!"

Mike continued, "Mr. Millspaugh, there are several State Bureau of Investigation agents en route from Asheville. My job is to take you into custody until their arrival." Mike then proceeded to "arrest" Rodney. He had Rodney place his hands on the hood of the vehicle and he cuffed him behind his back. (Rodney later mentioned to us that at this point he was completely freaking out and "almost lost all my bodily functions.")

Rodney's "arrest" was the signal for Jason, masquerading as the ATF agent, to move in. In the deepest voice he could muster, Jason leaned down, and nose to nose with a cuffed Rodney, murmured, "Why hello, *Jerome!*"

At this point, Rodney knew he had been had. With some pretty colorful language, he laughingly said this was the best practical joke that had *ever* been played, and he was honored to be a part of it.

One of the great things about this practical joke was that it was completely caught on Mike's highway patrol dash cam and body mic. And just like Mark Sandell's classic films, "Walk like Buck" and "Center Tragic," the video was played at many of NOC's Christmas in August parties. Another fun thing was that Mike Canata, Rodney's passenger, was so caught up in the ruse that when he recognized Jason's face under the ATF cap, he told us he muttered to himself, "Oh my God, Jason's a narc," which sent everyone into gales of laughter as well.

The late 1990s were a great time to be at the NOC. It was full of creative, talented people who loved to laugh, play, and paddle. Ray, as the person who hired most of us, was directly responsible for the quality of the NOC staff for over 40 years. That being said, don't mess with Ray McLeod.

 ## *About the Contributors*

Susan White Hester worked for the NOC from 1990 to 2000 as a waitress, raft guide, kayak instructor, adventure travel trip leader, and the manager of the Rafting Reservation Office. She met her husband, Bill Hester, working at the Chattooga after he threw her a rope when she flipped a raft in Jawbone. She currently teaches nursing at Western Carolina University.

Ray McLeod and his wife, Jackie, were spending the night at Bob Benner's waiting for a call from an executive recruiter; they were both determined to move from Memphis to the mountains and had scheduled several interviews to try and make that happen. Looking up from the *American Whitewater Journal*, Jackie said, "Well, if this interview doesn't work, I see that the NOC is looking for raft guides." They both exploded in laughter, but the germ of an idea had been inserted into their psyches. They decided to stop by the NOC on the way back to Memphis and talk to Payson. The idea was to spend the summer at the center and to use it as a base of operations to look for a new accounting job. After all, they were only planning to spend the summer there.

Now after more than 40 years of doing too many different jobs at the center to be listed, it ranks among the best decisions they have ever made. The McLeods found a community atmosphere here that has been like nothing else they have ever experienced. The NOC is family.

THE LODESTONE

By Heather McLeod Wall

I am from the blue-green mountains,
    Rain-soaked hills and wandering water,
    The Cherokee's "Land of the Noonday Sun" but for us,
    Land of the Hippies and Granola-heads,
    Where the rafting company I grew up at occasionally clashed with the local tobacco farmers and church-going families.

Smoke rising from cobbled-together shacks in the midst of tobacco fields hewn out of the sides of mountains, fog hanging low over creeks and bony horses pulling plows along mountainsides

Folds of mountains rising above, pushing skyward, a small strip of blue sky emerging as the river fog lifts and sun finally warms the floor of the river gorge.

The musk of decaying rhododendron, water—always running water, deliciously cold over frozen toes, wading for rock snails and launching homemade boats carrying acorn people over treacherous rapids.

When from upstream the river begins to speak a little louder, rising from a trickle to a gurgle to a dull roar, and suddenly the ice-cold dam release from the depths of the lake miles above has arrived.

Bringing with it rafters, and paddlers, and my daddy, always calm and sure, guiding visitors in rafts who love him now, at the end of their trip, almost as much as I love him.

But he's still *my* daddy.

And these are my mountains.

Mountains that taught me to be grateful for what you have.

Accept. Don't wish for more.

Be grateful for the hardscrabble life carved from the mountains,

Because what more could there be beyond this blessed place?

And now that I've left for the land of flatness and orange clay, the land of more,

My mountains serve as a lodestone,

Pulling, always pulling me

So that I can sense the mountains north of me wherever I am.

About the Contributor

Heather McLeod Wall worked a variety of jobs at the center as a teen and then entered the field of education and became a teacher and instructional coach of other teachers. She recently completed her PhD in education. She continues to mountain bike and hike with her husband, Andrew, who was hired years ago by Ray McLeod to help start the NOC Bike Shop. They live in Georgia at the foothills of the mountains and visit the mountains of North Carolina whenever they can.

SECTION IV
Adventure Travel

AN INTRODUCTION TO ADVENTURE TRAVEL AT THE NOC

By Payson Kennedy

Into the Unknown:
The First Trip on the Usumacinta River

On a Chattooga trip in the spring of 1975, I was guiding a raft in which Nell Jones and John Milton were guests. As we paddled down the lake, they asked what we did during the winter months. I told them I was trying to find a good location to run winter trips to utilize our equipment and personnel through the winter. John, who was an anthropologist interested in Mayan culture, said that the Usumacinta River, which flowed through the jungle area of Guatemala and Mexico that had been inhabited by the Maya, would be an excellent choice and said that he would be willing to accompany us on a first trip. Nell volunteered to help plan and market the trip, and we three agreed to organize an exploratory trip the following February.

In February of 1976 we led our first adventure travel trip on the Usumacinta River in Guatemala and Mexico. We had four paying guests on what we billed as an exploratory trip. John Milton and Nell Jones accompanied the NOC staff. After an earthquake the week before our scheduled departure forced us to fly into Belize City, Belize, instead of Guatemala, our rafts and some camping gear, which we'd shipped by airfreight, were impounded by customs authorities. Because the customs office was closed until Monday morning, we drove a couple hours to a small river emerging from a limestone cave and spent the weekend camping in the shelter of the cave mouth and exploring the area.

Sunday afternoon we drove back to Belize City so we would be ready first thing Monday morning to begin the process of getting our gear. While the guests explored Belize City, we hired a customs broker and began the nightmarish process. Rather than post a huge bond to ensure that we took all the equipment out of the country without selling any of it, we ended up paying a customs guard to ride with us to the Guatemalan border to make sure we didn't sell any gear along the way. We employed Jimmy and his truck Sugar Baby to drive us to Tikal for a couple days and then on to the Río La Pasión in Sayaxché, Guatemala.

Tikal was fascinating both because of the extensive Mayan ruins of this large ancient city and because the surrounding national park offered frequent sightings of a great variety of unfamiliar animals, such as coatimundis, peccary, and agouti, and exotic birds such as keel-billed toucans, white hawks, and many species of colorful macaws.

We decided to make Tikal a featured part of all future trips. We spent a night at Sayaxché and set off downriver on the Río La Pasión, a tributary of the Usumacinta, the next morning in four rafts and several kayaks. Because this upper section of the river was flat and slow-moving and we'd been delayed leaving Belize City, we were now several days behind schedule. We decided to make up for lost time by floating through the night on our rafts, which we tied together. The staff took shifts staying awake to keep watch and make sure the enlarged raft did not hang up against the shore.

At the confluence of the Pasión and the Salinas Rivers, we stopped to search for the ruins of the Mayan city of Altar de Sacrificios. We later learned that one of the small hills that we climbed to survey the surrounding jungle was actually the ruin of one of the pyramids that was now covered by jungle vegetation. As we searched for ruins, we had actually been walking among them, obscured by the jungle.

Finally after three days and a night on the river, we arrived at the restored ruins of Yaxchilan on the Mexican side of the river. On the second day after leaving Yaxchilan, we hiked to the partially excavated ruins of Piedras Negras. Two days after that we ran the best rapids of the trip through the Grand Canyon of San Jose as the huge volume of the Usumacinta River was constricted to a width of about 80 feet between sheer limestone walls, which rose vertically for several hundred feet above the river.

On our eighth day of river travel, we reached our takeout point near Tenosique, Mexico, and traveled on to Palenque. The next day we visited the beautiful restored ruins of Palenque before traveling on to Villahermosa for our return flight home. Tom Gonzalez's slightly differing memories of this first trip and Villa Brewer's memories of a 1980 Usumacinta trip are also included in this section of the book. It is interesting to compare the perceptions and memories of a young adventurer who was an experienced paddler with those of a teacher and student of Mayan culture who had not previously paddled real whitewater.

Why We Went:
The Appeal of Adventure Travel

The NOC continued offering this trip until sometime in the 1990s when the activities of guerrillas in Guatemala made travel on the Usumacinta unsafe. To avoid problems with airfreighting equipment and to facilitate land travel, we began having some staff members drive a van, and later a school bus, with our river equipment to meet us at the airport. On one occasion when the van drove onto the ferry to cross the Río La Pasión at Sayaxché, the ferry had apparently not been adequately

Vehicle ferry, Río La Pasión, Sayaxché, Guatemala. January 1980
(photographed by Villa Brewer)

secured to shore and the van pushed the ferry away from the bank. For a time our van was precariously perched with the front wheels on the ferry and the rear wheels on the bank, and we had visions of it disappearing into the river.

On a later occasion, we took our bus across the Río La Pasión on the same ferry. When the bus was leaving the ferry and began climbing the riverbank, the steepness of the climb caused the bus to tilt upward so much that the rear bumper caught on the ferry. All the locals gathered to watch the entertainment as Slim Ray, our 6-foot, 7-inch driver and mechanic, lay on his back in the shallow water now covering that end of the ferry to remove the bumper. Once he got the bumper free, the bus was able to proceed up the bank and on to our hotel in Sayaxché.

These stories illustrate what I loved most about adventure travel: We never knew what strange adventures and problems we would encounter, but we always found the ingenuity to deal with them.

Another thing that I most appreciated about our adventure travel trips were the opportunities we had to get to know local people outside the tourist industry. We didn't visit many museums and never stayed in five-star hotels. When we did stay in a hotel, it was usually the only one in town and we were happy if it provided hot water. More frequently we camped in the yards of families along the upper stretches of the river or in the jungle as we went farther downstream.

Gonzalez farm, Río La Pasión, Guatemala, January 1980
(photographed by Villa Brewer)

The Gonzalez family, whom we visited each year, began to share their food with us and we shared with them. Over the years the most daring in our party were able to try such local delicacies as barbecued armadillo and roasted iguana. Having sampled iguana, I thought that, because they were common along the river, I could supplement our diet with fresh meat. When I saw a 4-foot-long one sunning next to a large boulder, I sneaked around the boulder and brought my heavy Norse paddle down across his neck with as much force as I could muster. The iguana simply dove into the nearby river, apparently unhurt. The locals had greater success using their machetes.

Along the upper part of the river, there was one newly established cooperative village, La Flor de la Esperanza. We began stopping to visit each year; the locals seldom saw strangers and always welcomed us. When we visited their one-room open-sided school, we noticed that they had no blackboard and few books. On subsequent trips we took a small blackboard to them and began taking children's books in Spanish and other school supplies.

For many years, this remained our most popular adventure travel trip. In some years we filled as many as three successive trips, and staff often had great adventures between the trips. On one occasion we paddled a raft and several kayaks to the cayes off the coast of Belize and spent several days paddling, snorkeling, and camping along the reef. Our only problem occurred when a 30-mile-an-hour wind came up two nights before we were due to meet our next group of guests in Belize City. Paddling a raft in that kind of wind is quite a challenge, even with six very strong paddlers. We had some anxious moments before making it back to the mainland the next day. On another occasion, we attempted to climb Popocatépetl, a volcano south of Mexico City that reaches an elevation of more than 18,000 feet. We were disappointed when blowing snow and limited visibility prevented us from making the summit.

On our trips, we usually had a high staff-to-guest ratio. Extra staff members who were not chosen to work the trip often went along at cost in hopes that their familiarity with the area would give them a better chance of being selected the next year. I expect that over the years as many as 100 different staff members made the Usumacinta trip.

Most of the stories in this chapter illustrate these two benefits of our adventure travel trips: learning to deal with unanticipated difficulties through patience, hard work, ingenuity and trust in the local people; and getting to know local people who were not part of the tourist industry in their country.

Into Nepal

In 1979 Don Weeden worked at the NOC. Don was a recent graduate of The Evergreen State College, where he studied under Willi Unsoeld, who, together with Tom Hornbein, had made the first traverse of Mount Everest climbing by the West Ridge and descending by the traditional South Col route. Don had spent a year in

Typical scenery as we trekked through the Middle Hills
(photographed by Arlene Burns)

A view of Machapuchare as we trekked toward the Annapurna Sanctuary (photographed by Arlene Burns)

Nepal, where he learned to speak Nepali and explored many of the rivers by kayak. Don agreed to help us plan and to lead our first trip in Nepal that fall.

That first trip included four paying guests and Don, Aurelia, and me as leaders. Aurelia and I continued to lead trips there for the next 11 years. Our first two trips began with trekking in the Langtang area before descending the Sun Kosi River through the Middle Hills for 150 miles to the flat Tarai lowland region near the border with India.

On the second trip, we crossed the Ganja La (pass) at 17,000 feet to travel from the Langtang region into the Helambu region. The third year we began trekking to Kala Patthar, which at an elevation of about 18,500 feet overlooked Everest Base Camp, and from which the entire popular South Col route up Everest is visible. We continued doing annual treks to the Khumbu region near

Everest followed by descents of the Sun Kosi through 1986. I had fallen in love with Nepal and considered living there for about six months a year and returning to the NOC during the warmer months. In the fall of 1981, we sent Gordon and Susan Grant to Nepal to begin developing a Nepal Outpost, but when they decided to return to the United States because of health problems from living in Nepal, we decided to give up on the plan.

In 1987 Arlene Burns suggested that we change our Nepal trips from the Khumbu region and the Sun Kosi River to the Annapurna region followed by a descent of the Kali Gandaki and Trishuli Rivers to Chitwan National Park. By ending the trip in Chitwan, we would able to see the crocodiles, peacocks, rhinoceros, and other exotic jungle animals to be found there, including the possibility of encountering a wild tiger.

We did finally see a tiger on the last Nepal trip that Aurelia and I led, when a large male tiger charged the elephant on which we were riding, along with guests Connie Harvey and Scott Collins. That was our single most terrifying moment in all our years of adventure travel, as I imagined how I was going to explain that two of our guests had been eaten by a tiger.

Another advantage of the new trip itinerary was that at Annapurna we would be camping at lower altitudes than on our Everest treks, thereby avoiding most of

David Dauphine

the altitude problems that had kept many of our guests from fully enjoying the Everest trek.

In the late 1970s and early 1980s, the number of adventure travel trips that we offered increased rapidly. By 1982 we published our first adventure travel catalog; it listed 18 different trips. We encouraged staff members to plan trips to areas with which they were familiar or to explore new destinations on their own, to include activities that they were qualified to lead and then to help fill their trips. They could then remain as the primary leader for that trip for as long as they were able to recruit enough participants to make the trip at least break even financially. Aurelia and I led scuba diving and snorkeling trips to Cayman Brac. Horace planned and led trips to Scotland, which included a combination of cultural activities and backpacking. Brett Poirier and Sherry Spurlin led bicycling trips in southern England. Brett also led our Grand Canyon backpacking trip. David Dauphine began leading Caribbean sailing trips and Grand Canyon kayaking trips.

In 1981 Les Bechdel did an exploratory trip on the Bío-Bío River in Chile and then began offering regular trips there in 1982. Bunny Johns began leading trips in Costa Rica. Aurelia and I continued to lead trips in Nepal until 1990. Bob Beazley, Nick Williams, and Arlene Burns continued to run the trips there until David Ennis eliminated most of our adventure travel program in 2000.

I am sure the interesting stories from our many adventure travel trips number in the dozens. A few of these follow in this section of our book.

 ## About the Contributor

See page 81 for more information about Payson Kennedy.

A THANKSGIVING DAYYENU [1]

By Dan Adams

O Lord, our God, how excellent is Thy Name in all the earth. You gave us life: Dayyenu.

Had you given us life but not given us America as our home, Dayyenu.

Had you given us a country but not given us a vision of the world, Dayyenu.

Had you given us an understanding of the planet but never given us a desire to experience it, Dayyenu.

Had you given us the will to travel but not led us to Nepal, Dayyenu.

Had you brought us here but not sent Payson and Aurelia to welcome us to Kathmandu with leis, Dayyenu.

Had you boggled our minds with the Old Town but not thrilled us with dances, Dayyenu.

Had we seen the dancing but not heard a little boy play "Alouette" on a sarangi, Dayyenu.

Had we heard the music but not seen the Lakeside in Pokhara, Dayyenu.

Had we gotten to Pokhara but never had the exhilaration of setting out on the trail, Dayyenu.

Had we made the start but never had the fun of watching Polly on the road, Dayyenu.

Had we been on the road but never had the blessing of seeing how other people live, Dayyenu.

Had we had the chance to see them but never received their friendly greetings on the road, Dayyenu.

Had we had their namastes but never seen Delishar's smile, even in the cold, Dayyenu.

Had you given us his smile but never let us see the warmth of big brothers hugging Scotty, Dayyenu.

Had we had hugs but never the gustatory delights of Ram Bahadur's dinners, Dayyenu.

Had you given us good food but never yak cheese omelets and chapatis, Dayyenu.

Had we had special treats but never a birthday party, Dayyenu.

Had we had parties without the laughter of seeing a dog with a mouthful of peanut butter, Dayyenu.

---

[1] *Dayyenu* means "it would have been enough." It's also the name of a traditional Jewish song for Passover.

Had we had laughter without the beauty of hearing Ngawang sing "Rasan Perede," Dayyenu.

Had we had beauty without the peace of lying in the straw in the meadow, Dayyenu.

Had you given us rest without the solitude of walking through the bamboo forest, Dayyenu.

Had you created solitude but never given us the joy of seeing camp already set up for us when we arrived, Dayyenu.

Had you given us camp without the warmth of chocolate at 9,000 feet, Dayyenu.

Had we had tea but never had the excitement of spotting a Himalayan tar, Dayyenu.

Had we seen sights like that but never seen Ngawang and Scotty in the bedroll, Dayyenu.

Had we stayed in our own bedrolls and never had stars in our face when going out to pee, Dayyenu.

Had you given us the stars but not the brilliance of the sun coming up behind Machapuchare, Dayyenu.

Had you given us the sun but not lunch on a glacial moraine at the foot of Annapurna, Dayyenu.

Had you given us food but not the reminder of our mortality, Dayyenu.

Had we been impressed with the dangers of this trip without the happy sight of a Thanksgiving jack-o'-lantern, Dayyenu.

Had we had the great gourd and not Pat's recording of "Amazing Grace" and Myra's beautiful place cards and kind words about each of us, Dayyenu.

Had we had all these appetizers and never been presented with Ralph and Herman[2], a Thanksgiving pizza, and all the Nepalese trimmings, Dayyenu!

How much more gratitude we have, then, on this festive day than on any other Thanksgiving we have ever known: the Lord has given us America and the world; Payson and Aurelia; Ngawang, Pasang, Dorje, Dev, Sunli, Ram Bahadur, Maila, and our Kancha; dances, songs, the trail, and the porters (maybe we should give thanks for *them* first!); food and parties and laughter and rest; bamboo forests and high mountain peaks; sun and stars and snow and a new love for Nepal, the Nepalese people, and for each other:

O Lord, our God, how excellent is Thy name in all the earth!

---

[2] A few days before arriving at the Annapurna base camp, the cook purchased two chickens, Ralph and Herman, in the last village. The chickens were carried and fed until they were sacrificed for the Thanksgiving dinner.

About the Contributor

Dan Adams spent the first half of his 50-year career as a Presbyterian pastor in four different parts of the country, and the second half as the psychiatric chaplain in a veterans hospital. He and his wife of 60 years, Tucker, have 12 grandchildren and 13 great-grands—with more on the way. Though he earned three postgraduate degrees and has various other titles, he prefers to be called "just Dan." Dan and Tucker were guests on the 1990 NOC Nepal trip.

AMERICANS SNEAK INTO MEXICO ON RAFTS!

By Tom Gonzalez

In 1976 the NOC ran its first international adventure trip on the Usumacinta River, which runs along the Guatemala-Mexico border and finally into Mexico. The trip was scheduled for February 1976 and a small group of us volunteered to drive from North Carolina to Guatemala. There was not much for us to do at the center, so we loaded up our three vehicles and headed south in early December.

The motley crew included Bob Bouknight, Kathy Miller, Jerry Gillette, Allie Funk, Florrie Funk, and me, Gonzi, the only Spanish speaker. We three guys were either bearded, long-haired, or both, so we decided to clean up a bit and got our hair trimmed in an effort to blend in and avoid hassles at border crossings. Given that we were driving a Toyota Land Cruiser FJ6, a huge red Dodge van, and a small Ford pickup with a big green homemade camper on the back, all with kayaks and canoes on top, we were not very successful in blending in.

Crossing the border into Mexico at Brownsville, Texas, we certainly received a lot of attention and were pulled out of customs lines for special scrutiny. A customs agent asked whether we had a Christmas present for him. He was OK with being told we didn't, smiled, and recommended we go to the Yucatán Peninsula, where a place called Cancún was about to open up and where the beaches of Tulum were an uninhabited paradise.

In our first crossing into Guatemala, we were given the choice of either unloading all the gear in our vehicles for inspection or paying for an expedited process without inspection. We chose the expedited process. In our crossing into Belize, we were asked whether we had any marijuana. When we said no, the customs agent told us not to worry, that we would be able to pick some up down the road. OK, so maybe blending in was not that critical.

We drove down the spine of the Sierra Madre Mountains through Mexico City, hung out for a few days in Oaxaca, and reached the Pacific Ocean at Puerto Madero. Crossing into Guatemala, we headed for Lake Atitlán, a landlocked lake that is the deepest in Central America. There we settled for a few weeks into an indigenous village called Santa Catarina. Our accommodations were a mud hut with dirt floors and a beautiful view of Lake Atitlán and the volcanoes Atitlán and Tolimán. We were the only gringos in our village, where not only was English not spoken, but very few villagers even spoke Spanish. We spent our time exploring villages around the lake, paddling our boats, and doing an overnight climb of Volcano

Atitlán; on occasion we hung out in the village of Panajachel with other young expatriates from North and South America, Europe, and Australia.

From Santa Catarina we headed to Tikal, where we spent a few days exploring the temples. We had the site all to ourselves and were overwhelmed with the tranquility, antiquity, and spirituality of those six temples. Climbing a temple and sitting on an altar overlooking the tops of the other temples peeking out over the jungle was magical. The spell was broken at sunset, however, when we heard the terrifying roar of what sounded like a huge, fierce, and menacing creature. In actuality, the sound came from a howler monkey, which is about 2–3 feet tall, is an herbivore, and is not aggressive to humans. What great lungs, though!

While the rest of the group stayed in Tikal, Bob and I headed out to scout the put-in and to find a person we had heard of who reputedly knew the river. We did not have much to go on, other than that the individual lived on a dirt road leading from the put-in at Río La Pasión, which flows into Rio Salinas to form the Usumacinta.

When we got there, we found that the dirt road was being paved and we followed it past the construction crew. The road grew progressively worse and muddier as we drove on. We got to one mudhole that spanned the roadbed and was about 50 yards long but looked passable. Halfway through, we sank the Land Cruiser down to the axles. Our only option was to hike back to the construction crew camp to see if they would help us out. It was getting dark and those little howler monkeys started their spine-chilling roar. We walked fast, and along the way we met a man who walked out of what must have been a jungle path. He walked along with us, and although we could not communicate, we were glad to have the company of someone who obviously knew his way around. He left us before we got to the construction crew, disappearing into the jungle just as he had appeared. It was surreal.

When we finally reached the construction crew, it was pitch black and they were finishing their dinner. The crew had a huge timber jack that looked like it could easily pull us out. They told us that they would do it for $20, which seemed very reasonable to us, but they would not be able to do it until daylight because the timber jack had no lights. We were not too thrilled about staying the night because our camping gear was in the back of the truck and it would be no fun to have to hike back to it. "But wait," we told them. "We have a flashlight!" So one of the guys agreed to drive that huge machine, with Bob and me hanging off the sides pointing a tiny flashlight to guide us back to the Toyota. We got the Toyota out, drove back to the put-in, and—because it was late and we still had a long way to go to Tikal—we camped overnight on the side of the road. After all, it was an adventure trip.

The arrival of Payson and the guests was still a few weeks off, so we headed for Belize, a former British colony, where we found that most people spoke English. We were exposed to Creole culture, which was different from the indigenous culture we had been enjoying since we left the United States. We spent time in Belize

City and also camped out for a few days in Hopkins, a Garifuna fishing village south of the capital.

When we got to Belize City, a couple of young kids latched onto us and offered to show us around. They told us that we needed to be careful because "There is bad people. They'll thief the eyes outta yo head, man!" They proceeded to show us all the highlights—that is, the bars, restaurants, and an alley behind the police station where a man with long dreadlocks was cleaning and bagging mountains of ganja. OK, so that was what the customs guy was referring to.

The kids were right. The place was friendly enough, but there was danger as well. We were easy marks for the wrong people. No big issues, though, other than on one occasion having to chase a thief out of our campsite and another dealing with the usual scammers trying to sell black coral.

Hopkins was a totally different experience from the capital. The villagers made us feel welcome. We camped on the beach next to their small thatched dwellings and had visitors at all hours. When we went fishing, they would bait our hooks, clean our fish, and help us cook. They would come and play music for us and dance. They spoke Garifuna among themselves, but all spoke English with that British Caribbean lilt. One of the guys, around our age, wanted so much to come back to the United States with us. He proposed to Allie and said that once he got to the United States he would become a famous musician and take care of her for the rest of his life. Allie thanked him but said she was already in a committed relationship. It was such a bittersweet experience to meet people who, though living in poverty, were very welcoming and filled with joy. This was one of two very emotional experiences we had on this adventure.

After Hopkins, we went up to the Yucatán to visit what was then a huge construction site that would become Cancún. To us it looked like they were re-creating Miami, so we headed back south and camped out for a few days around Tulum. There we enjoyed the deserted beaches and the beautiful freshwater limestone lagoons known as cenotes. The customs agent who recommended this area to us was right; it was paradise.

After Tulum, we returned to Belize to meet Payson, along with Nell and John, who helped organize the trip, and four customers. The group arrived in Belize City on a Friday, but Belizean customs officials had impounded the rafts and other equipment.

Because we had some time on our hands, we suggested to the new arrivals that we spend the weekend camping at the mouth of a large cave on the Río Frío. The river flowed out of the cave, and inside there were pools you could swim in. On Monday we picked up the gear and loaded it on Sugar Baby, the truck that transported us to Tikal and the river.

Everyone was excited to get going on an eight-day float; we'd be in a pristine wilderness, totally inaccessible by road. We had four rafts and a kayak as a safety boat and were loaded with camping gear and provisions to last us for the duration of the trip. The weather was beautiful and there was a good flow on the Pasión, although we could tell that it was on the low side. The first day was an easy float with few rapids but a wonderful variety of tropical plants, flowers, and fauna. One night we camped out at a small farm belonging to Oscar Gonzalez and his family. We were the first foreigners who had ever visited them, and they were thrilled to have us there. The next morning they were disappointed that we would not stay longer, and they cried as we were leaving. Later that day, we reached the confluence of the Pasión and the Salinas. Finally we were on the Usumacinta (Mayan for "howler monkey") River!

Over the next few days, we had great weather and, except for the people we saw in several indigenous villages that were not accessible by road, we saw no other humans. It was a gentle float in a thick jungle where we saw macaws, spider monkeys, toucans, and beautiful flowers. At night we camped on sandy beaches and listened to the roar of our little howler monkey friends. The flow of the river was slower than we expected, and because we had been delayed in getting access to our gear in Belize City, we decided to make up time by floating in our rafts through one moonlit night.

On the third or fourth day, we explored the ruins at Yaxchilan, which are on the Mexican side of the river. Because it was very remote, archaeologists had barely touched it. A caretaker on site, Julian, lived there with his family and showed us around. The highlight for river running was when we finally reached San Jose Canyon on day seven or eight. There were a number of Class III rapids, but they were fun with nice drops, waves, and boiling eddies.

After running the canyon, we were nearly to our destination of Tenosique, Mexico. The current was slow and we had no idea how long it would take to get there. It had started to rain, we were getting low on supplies, and we were looking forward to reaching the takeout. Then, just like in a movie, the sun came out and we saw the bridge! We all breathed a sigh of relief.

We had left from Guatemala and were now in Mexico, so we knew that we had to go through immigration and customs and get our passports stamped. Of course there was no point of entry on the river, so we wandered into town looking to see if we could be officially registered as having entered Mexico. We divided into two groups, one to find the police station and the other to find a bank to exchange dollars for pesos. We were a very ragged-looking bunch still in our dirty river clothes, so it didn't take long for the police to find us. They got us all together and tried to figure out how we got into Mexico. Tenosique is not a border town, so we presented a problem. There was no immigration or customs anywhere nearby. We actually had the honor of meeting the police chief, a very pragmatic individual, who told us that customs could resolve the issue with our passports when we left the country. At that point we found a bank to exchange our money, found transportation to our respective destinations, and had an emotional goodbye. After a great trip, we went on our way—as illegal immigrants!

We never found out how it had gone for Payson and the guests when they got to the Mexico City International Airport. When the six of us got to the Yucatán-Belize border, a Belizean customs agent did not want to let us in. He was concerned about the irregularity of our immigration stamps. Fortunately our passports had stamps indicating that our vehicles were in the customs compound in Belize City, so he reluctantly gave us an entry stamp and waved us through. We were once again legal! From Belize City, we headed back to Yucatán, visiting Palenque, Chichen Itza, and Veracruz on our way back to North Carolina. It was an excellent adventure.

 About the Contributor

Tom Gonzalez worked at the NOC intermittently from the summer of 1973 through the spring of 1976 and was known as Gonzi. Tom did a little of everything, from guiding on the Nanty and Chattooga, to canoe instruction for North Carolina Outward Bound School, to maintenance, to cleaning rooms and washing dishes. He was a guide on the first NOC international trip to the Usumacinta River in Guatemala and Mexico. He met his future bride, Florrie Funk, at the NOC and married in the summer of 1976 in a ceremony on Lake Rabun that was well attended by friends from the NOC. Florrie and Tom spent the next 40 years traveling around the world, living in Spain, Puerto Rico, Canada, Chicago, LA, Miami, St. Louis, Boston, and Atlanta. They raised two wonderful children, Candler and Emma, who live in Boston and Brooklyn respectively. He recently retired from a career in manufacturing pharmaceuticals and medical devices and now lives in Asheville. They still paddle and enjoy their return to beautiful Western North Carolina.

WHEN TRAVEL WAS AN ADVENTURE

By Villa Brewer

I t was the years of *The Love Boat* on TV, and Margarita, my cousin by marriage, was a faithful follower. I was in my 10th year of teaching social studies at North Iredell High School outside of Statesville, North Carolina, and since Margarita's marriage had broken up, we were working together to raise her two sons. She and a couple of friends decided to go on a Caribbean cruise.

Good, I thought. She'll realize how silly all this *Love Boat* stuff is.

But no. Margarita is Panamanian. The captain of the ship was Spanish, and most of the crew was Italian. They spoke no English, so for them the cruise was lonely and largely silent. Margarita became a lively diversion. Every night at the captain's table, every night dancing until the early hours of the morning. For her, that cruise was *The Love Boat* come to life.

No sooner did she return home than she began pushing me to go on a cruise.

"No," I'd say. "I don't want to eat four times a day and change my clothes six times a day!"

About that time an article appeared in *The Charlotte Observer* about a rafting trip in Guatemala and Mexico that took tourists to ruins unreachable by road. *Now, that's what I want to do!* I thought. I had taught Latin American history in Nicaragua, had explored more accessible ruins in Guatemala and Mexico, and was intrigued by new explorations.

Payson and Aurelia Kennedy had led the trip. I wrote Payson, telling him that I was a 38-year-old schoolteacher who had never been rafting or camping, but I really wanted to go. Did he think I could do it? Payson said I should come up to the NOC, go rafting, and see if I liked that. Then I should try camping. If I liked doing both those things, I could go.

I brought my cousins to the NOC in June. We went rafting with Payson and we all loved it. Later that summer, in 1979, one of my students and her fiancé took me camping at the Grandfather Mountain Highland Games. To fall asleep to the skirl of bagpipes, how could I *not* like it?

So I signed up for the first trip of the year in January 1980.

I met Payson and Aurelia and the other guests in New Orleans, and together we flew to Belize, where we were met by a blue NOC bus and the other NOC staff members who had driven from North Carolina to Belize. (It was Payson and Aurelia's daughter Cathy and her husband, Jim Holcombe, along with Slim Ray, newlywed Susan Bechdel, and Melissa Andrews.)

Epic mudhole. El Naranjo, Guatemala, January 1980 (photographed by Villa Brewer)

Belize was dirt streets, puddles after a rain, and large clapboard hotels. As we settled into our hotel rooms, I reveled in the sounds of Central America—motorbikes, horns honking, babies crying, roosters crowing, and over it all the sound of bagpipes and drums as the British flag was lowered in front of the government buildings down the street. So far from *The Love Boat*. So wonderful!

Still, this was Central America, and crime was rampant. Payson had to spend the night in the blue bus to protect against theft. The next morning he reported seeing a hand probe an open window. As he stood up in the aisle, the hand quickly retreated and was never seen again!

In the morning we headed west. I remember the border crossing into Guatemala as rather routine, but the staff was slightly anxious. On an earlier crossing they had had to pull everything out from the bus for a thorough inspection. Our luck held as we crossed into Guatemala, but a few miles ahead we ran into a monumental traffic jam. There was a mud hole several football fields in length, providing entertainment and business for the locals, who gathered along the sides of the road ferrying cargo from overloaded trucks and offering soft drinks, snacks, fruit, trinkets, and textiles for those waiting to pass. Was that a Winnebago up ahead, sunk up to its hubs?

Slim, our driver who stood at 6 feet, 7 inches, stepped off the bus to check and the local kids recoiled as if the circus had just arrived. "El gigante! El gigante!" they yelled. Not too many folks are 6 foot 7 in the Mayan area! Eventually, a team of oxen extricated the Winnebago and we were back on our way.

In Tikal we checked into the Jungle Lodge while Jim Holcombe went for a jog along the defunct runway. (I had been in Tikal in 1968, when we flew in from Guatemala City in a DC-3 for a day's excursion. Since then, there had been a deadly

Temple II. Tikal, Guatemala, January 1980 (photographed by Villa Brewer)

crash of a group of American teachers and the decision had been made to route tour groups through the larger, safer airport in Flores).

Tikal is a major ruin, referred to as the New York of the Mayans. The University of Pennsylvania and the Guatemalan authorities had done much exploration and reconstruction in the 12 years since I had last visited. Payson was a former anthropology teacher and we could count on him to have the latest publications in his day pack. A whole area, El Mundo Perdido, or "the Lost World," had been completely covered by jungle when I last visited Tikal.

Not as interested in ruins? One could follow Jim Holcombe as he pointed out ocellated turkeys, oropendolas, coatis, and agoutis on the site. Was that a jaguar I heard cough as I was halfway up the moist, sweaty stones of Temple I this morning?

After Tikal, our first glimpse of the Usumacinta, also known as the River of Ruins, came at Sayaxché, 35 miles down a sketchy dirt road from Flores. The river was somewhat anticlimactic—wide, dark, and slow moving. Sayaxché, unfortunately, was on the other side of the river and there was no bridge, just a rickety ferry and assorted cayucos. All the gear had to be removed from the bus and ferried across the river.

Rivers were still superhighways in flat, roadless regions such as Guatemala's northern jungle, called the Petén. We were to spend the next two days of the trip on a "corn boat," a motorized launch the size of an 18-wheeler used to bring corn and other agricultural products upstream to the road at Sayaxché and mail and consumer goods downstream to farming communities along the river. Payson and Aurelia went off to hire a corn boat while the rest of the guests checked into a large clapboard hotel. We were given large, rubberized river bags for our tents, as well as clothing and personal gear. Packing for nine days on the river, the rest of the staff began putting the food and cooking gear into coolers and gathering army surplus rocket boxes and plastic pickle barrels, along with the rafts, paddles, life jackets, and kayaks for our days on the rapids below Yaxchilan.

Three enterprising sisters from Philadelphia were curious about what looked like small, furry dead jungle animals that were being deposited behind the hotel's reception desk. I asked the proprietor what they were and he replied that they were testicles! They had been castrating several calves in the village that day, and the testicles were to be a special treat for the proprietor and his family for dinner that evening! Our own menu was much more prosaic: chicken and vegetables over rice, a salad, and a sheet cake for dessert.

Dinner conversation provided a clue as to how the NOC was expanding in the adventure travel realm. Payson and Aurelia had spent several weeks that fall in Nepal, trekking and rafting on the Sun Kosi River. Susan's husband, Les Bechdel, was in Chile exploring a wild river called the Bío-Bío while other NOC staffers had led a trip snorkeling and scuba diving at Cayman Brac in the Caribbean.

In the morning we met our boatman, Adalaido; his nephew and grandson, who were the crew; and Henry, a professional photographer friend of Melissa's who would document our trip. The river was glorious, warm, and primitive. Henry and Melissa took seats in the prow, where he photographed birds, mostly herons, that

Melissa Andrews and Henry, the photographer. Río La Pasión, Guatemala, January 1980 (photographed by Villa Brewer)

we surprised. Pairs of scarlet macaws, who mate for life, flying high, fast, and free, were a special treat. We heard our first *zaraguatos* (howler monkeys).

Our boatman Adalaido's face fascinated me. He seemed ageless and wise. He saw everything, ripples that might indicate a submerged log that could endanger his boat, changes in the jungle that flowed unbroken down to the riverbank. When he donned his yellow slicker during a brief rain shower, he seemed to be mythical, the reincarnation of the boatman Charon, who ferried souls across the river Styx.

Adalaido spotted a small dock that led to a path up the bank and into the jungle. A short, bug-filled hike led us to a carved stone monument. This was Altar de Sacrificios, a Mayan site dating back well over a thousand years. Only a trained eye could spot buildings and paths being devoured by the inexorable jungle.

Aurelia Kennedy preparing lunch on the corn boat (photographed by Villa Brewer)

We slowly learned river protocols. At bathroom breaks, it was men downstream, women upstream. Tuck your pants into your socks. The no-see-ums along the river are vicious. Too many bites can cause a painful edema. It's impolite to "strip-mine" the gorp (that is, to take all the chocolate out of the trail mix). Don't drink untreated river water. Watch your hygiene. The nearest doctor is nine days away.

We spent the night at the Gonzalez farm, pitching our tents in the cleared area around their grass huts. Population pressure, depleted soils, and political unrest had caused some people from Guatemala's highlands to migrate into the Petén. The Gonzalez family were frontier people: intelligent, optimistic, generous, and open to new experiences. They enjoyed our company and we enjoyed them. When we left the next morning, they gave us a gift, a Rhode Island Red hen. We called her El Regalo—"the gift" in Spanish. She spent the day trussed up on the floor of the corn boat, but we knew that soon she would be our dinner on the river.

Our second day on the river would bring more stops. The first was a Guatemalan army outpost on river right, where we showed our passports to the soldiers who boarded the corn boat. The guests' body language betrayed Americans' unease with submachine guns in close proximity. It was something I had experienced with regularity in Nicaragua, so I just relaxed and let the army do its job.

Several miles ahead, we pulled into the dock at La Flor de la Esperanza, a community of refugees from the Guatemalan Highlands who were hoping to make new lives for themselves growing cardamom and other exotic spices for export. Aurelia had brought some books and materials for their fledgling school. We took measurements for a blackboard the staff would bring them on a future trip.

After we left La Flor, the river became narrower and the current stronger. Adalaido sent his nephew forward to watch for rocks and snags. Yaxchilan sat on a horseshoe on the river, its entrance marked by a great ceiba tree. Soon there was the mammoth tree and, look! There was a nest of scarlet macaws several stories up in a cavity in its trunk.

We camped on river right in Guatemala and set up our tents as the staff unloaded the corn boat and made dinner. The next morning, Adalaido gingerly swung his boat around and headed upstream. The waters downstream of Yaxchilan contained too many rocks and shoals for corn boat traffic. We were on our own.

We inflated the rafts and paddled across the river to the base of Yaxchilán's small runway. Soon I was to discover my favorite of all the Mayan ruins I have visited and its ancient legendary caretaker, Juan de la Cruz. We walked through the dark passages of a building called the labyrinth, which opened up into the Great Plaza. Pyramids, temples, palaces, and a ball court surrounded this sacred space, and the largest ceiba tree I have ever seen presided over it all. Gaily colored tropical birds flew about happily. At one point we could spot dark shapes moving through the tree branches. Howler monkeys feeding.

"Not a good idea to walk under the trees with your mouth open," Aurelia cautioned us.

Stelae, tombstone-like monuments carved to commemorate the accession of a ruler or a particular date in their reign, are common features of Mayan cities. The ones at Yaxchilan are truly remarkable, and one is two stories high. At the far end of the plaza, Aurelia led us to a stela that lay on its back under a thatched building. Payson told us how robbers had tried to remove the stela but were interrupted by the wife of a well-known archaeologist and fled into the jungle. Trafficking in pre-Columbian artifacts is a problem, particularly at remote sites like Yaxchilan. Payson and Aurelia had warned us not to buy anything that looked like an artifact, no matter how sweet the child offering it for sale was. This may sound harsh, but the trip would continue without you, and you would be alone to extricate yourself from any legal difficulties that arose from such a purchase.

We climbed a long stairway to Temple 33, high above the Great Plaza, to view the stone lintels above their three doorways. Extraordinary. The Michelangelo of the Mayans lived and worked at Yaxchilan. In all the Mayan ruins I had visited, I had never seen such stone carving.

Another climb brought us to the highest temples on the site, where we could look out over the river and the jungle. Descending, I noticed that the back of Temple 33 had been planted entirely in aloe. The mixture of ancient and natural was intoxicating. Back at the Great Plaza, Juan de la Cruz plucked a grapefruit from the fruit trees he had planted and gave it to me. Returning to the caretaker's hut, I photographed Henry with the empty, dried shell of an armadillo. They say armadillo meat is sweet and tasty. The jungle was providing for Yaxchilán's caretaker, just as it had for its townspeople a millennium ago.

When we crossed the river to our camp, we found that Jim Holcombe had humanely dispatched El Regalo, plucked it, and gutted it. She was on the menu for dinner. It was a good reminder that there were no supermarkets on the Usumacinta and that meat did not come neatly butchered and wrapped in plastic. We silently thanked El Regalo for her life as we ate her.

The next morning we packed up and headed downstream. We had three rafts, a couple of C-1s, and a couple of kayaks. At one point the river narrowed, the current quickened, and we splashed through a series of waves, but no significant rapids. Toward the end of the afternoon, we spied a beach straight ahead. Could it be? Had we abandoned the jungle for a Caribbean beach? It was our first campsite, which the NOC staff had named Paradise Beach. In actual fact, it was an S-turn in the river, where floods had piled up sand. To our right, in Guatemala, were some low hills covered with vegetation. They were unexplored Mayan pyramids in a ruin named El Cayo. To our left, in Mexico, was a single grass hut.

Payson emptying a raft while Cathy Kennedy bathes. Paradise Beach, Usumacinta River, Guatemala, January 1980 (photographed by Villa Brewer)

We went about our chores, setting up our tents, flipping over one of the rafts to use as the kitchen/dining room. The inhabitant of the grass hut on the Mexican side of the river paddled over in his cayuco and hovered several yards offshore looking at us. I later found out that he approached the scruffiest-looking member of the group, Henry the photographer, and asked if he wanted to buy any pot.

Paradise Beach was so lovely that we were reluctant to leave, but Payson told us that our next camp would be at the Mayan ruins of Piedras Negras, on the Guatemalan side of the river. Piedras was a major Mayan city, the subject of a three-year excavation by the University of Pennsylvania just before World War II. Some remarkable stone stelae had been brought out and were on display at the University of Pennsylvania Museum of Archaeology and Anthropology in Philadelphia, but after that excavation, the ruins had reverted to jungle. We learned of Tatiana Proskouriakoff, a young, beautiful Russian émigré who lived there for three years making elegant drawings of what the city might have looked like in its heyday.

Piedras had a romantic aura about it. Many declared it to be their favorite of the cities we saw on the trip. It was utterly deserted—no airstrip, no caretaker, no planted fruit trees, no one selling pot. It was easy to imagine that you were the first person to visit this abandoned metropolis. We camped in a small alcove on river right about 0.5 mile upstream of the city. As the sun set and the moon rose, I felt a mental kinship to the Mayan astronomers who contemplated the universe and their place in it.

I found myself growing apprehensive, particularly as one of the guests prattled on about the Dead River in Maine and about the people she'd known who had died on whitewater rivers. There's a river called the Dead? People die on adventures like this?

Fortunately, there were distractions. A large waterfall appeared on river left, at least 60 feet in height. It was a tributary of the Usumacinta, draining a large portion of the Lacandon Jungle. We slid past the base of the falls and anchored just below it. It was a travertine waterfall, an amazing bright blue-white, and it was not slippery, so the most adventurous of us could climb all over it.

Back in the current, we scanned river right for our last campsite in Guatemala, which Payson and Aurelia had nicknamed the condominium. It came with entertainment. Across the river there was a tree with a large oropendola rookery. These are the largest birds of the oriole family, measuring about 18 inches in length. They look like a large, nondescript blackbird but when they fly they reveal brilliant yellow wedges on either side of their tail. Their cry is loud and burbling, kind of like water coming to a boil in a pot. Their nests are long and baglike, with the opening at the top near where the nest attaches to the branch, but the young are safely cradled in the soft, round bottom until they are ready to fledge. We took our binoculars to the condominium's penthouse to observe our neighbors across the river. As the sun set across the river and the oropendolas roosted, we were a little more subdued than usual, wondering what the canyon would bring.

We were up early, ate a basic but hearty breakfast, and began rigging the rafts. Everything had to be packed away and tied down. Life jackets now became mandatory.

A couple of the guests, who paddled kayaks but did not have the river skills to paddle the canyon, joined us in the rafts; their boats were tied on top of the gear.

We eased out into the current. The river narrowed, the walls on either side rose, and what had at first been a murmur became louder. Payson took the lead. He stood on the tube, staring ahead. It had been a year since he had seen this rapid. Aurelia and I were in the second raft, which Cathy Kennedy was guiding. Jimmy was in the third raft, running sweep. Payson told us to stay back at least a hundred yards so we could help in the event of a flip. The sound increased to a roar, and we could glimpse the waves ahead. I guessed 12–18 feet high. We saw Payson's raft top a wave and then disappear. It reappeared at the top of the next wave. We kept up a slow, determined cadence with our paddling. Speed would give us control and maneuverability, Cathy had told us. Waves broke over us and we were soaked to the skin, but we kept moving forward. The river took a slow bend to the left and then it was over. Jimmy's raft emerged in the run-out. The kayakers had all made it too!

I began to breathe again as we slowly spun around and marveled at the new world we had entered. The enormous river draining a large portion of Guatemala and Mexico was now no more than 30 yards wide. The walls of the cliffs rose at least 500 feet on either side. Swallows screamed above us, furious that aliens had invaded their secret nesting spot. I had never seen anything like it.

The roar of the entrance rapid died away, but soon we became aware of another murmur. The second rapid lay ahead. Payson stood up in the raft. I learned later that just about every river had a rapid named Maytag, since it tossed you around like a washing machine. But this was *Maytag!* It was a tricky, fine line to tread between two recirculating eddies, each with eddy walls 5 or 6 feet in height. Payson's raft rode that fine line with precision and we followed dutifully. Once again, all of us made it through safely. We high-fived each other with our paddles and slapped the water with joy.

The water widened, the cliffs receded, and we found ourselves in a Shangri-la. Children fished from cayucos. There were grass huts. There was even a crude woven footbridge across the river. Who were these people? How did they get here? I wanted to hear if they were speaking Mayan, perhaps a dialect not heard since the pyramids were built. But they were too far away.

Slowly the river narrowed again and the walls became steeper. Then a murmur, a cackle, and finally a roar. The third rapid passed in a slow, steady paddling rhythm. I did not see it so much as I felt it. I felt the muscles in my torso and arms. I felt the sun drying my back.

One more rapid to go. These waves had to be the largest yet, and this, the longest wave train. This was nothing like the Nantahala. Big water has a character all its own. It's as if the molecules unite. Sheets are formed. Tectonic plates. You do not control your movement on the water; it controls you. If it is merciful, it spits you out. If it is not, it keeps you. Even the run-out of this fourth rapid seemed deadly.

Whirlpools, but movable ones. You successfully pass one, but then it moves, grabs you, and spins you about. It's impersonal, inexorable, but indifferent. This time it doesn't want you. It wants to keep moving to its promised reunion with the sea and you are no more important than a water spider.

We moved along, exhausted.

The sun was lowering in the sky. We looked for a campsite but nothing appropriate appeared. A small tributary flowed in on river right. It was muddy and buggy but there appeared to be enough spaces to set up tents. We called it the Arroyo. It would have to do.

As we had since the beginning of the trip, guests helped untie gear, remove bags, clean the rafts, purify water, and set up tents. I helped Aurelia with the kitchen chores. It had been nine days since we'd left the vegetable markets of Flores and Sayaxché. All of the ice in the coolers had melted. What remained were a few battered potatoes and some carrots trailing green fungus.

"Oh, dear, what will we eat?" I wondered.

Aurelia handed me a vegetable scraper and a paring knife. She had held back one large can of bully beef. Jimmy found a can of corn and a can of string beans in his raft. Soon, with the help of garlic, flour, and Aurelia's ammo box of assorted spices, a beef stew was heating on the stove. We finished off the last of the gorp and crawled, exhausted, into our tents.

The next morning, the river widened and became placid. The jungles gave way to cattle pastures. We paddled for about 3 hours and finally saw a concrete bridge across the river, the first we had seen since we put in. Something was wrong. There was no blue bus on the bridge. But there was a white school bus and Slim and Susan were smiling and yelling.

The story spread like wildfire. Five miles after leaving Sayaxché, the brakes went out on the blue bus. Slim Ray drove the bus across Guatemala, Belize, and the Yucatán Peninsula to the nearest Ford dealership in Villahermosa, with Susan Bechdel hanging out the door and frantically yelling, "No frenos!" to everyone she saw! The bus was still at the Ford dealership undergoing massive repairs. Susan had mustered all the Spanish she knew to rent another bus to meet us at the takeout.

We rode into the small city of Tenosique and stopped at the best hotel in town for lunch. Inexplicably, the college professor, who had pondered all those she had known who had died on whitewater, was the last to be served. She broke down and sobbed. She might have had low blood sugar or an overabundance of nerves.

The next morning, we took public transportation to the ruins of Palenque, a few kilometers outside of town, while Slim and Susan returned the white bus to Villahermosa and reclaimed our blue bus from the Ford agency. Europeans had known of Palenque, a major Mayan ruin, since the mid-18th century. German Count Waldeck lived at the ruins for several years starting in 1829. Later, American John Lloyd Stephens and Englishman Frederick Catherwood visited Palenque and published a travel book with gorgeous illustrations. In grade school, I had been taught that the pyramids in Egypt were tombs but that the pyramids in the New World were temples. A gross oversimplification. Mexican archaeologist Alberto Ruz Lhuillier opened the tomb of Palenque's principal ruler Pakal under the base of the Temple of the Inscriptions in 1953. And now here I was working my way several stories down steep Mayan steps to view the final resting place of this legendary Mayan ruler. The thrill was incomprehensible.

I knew that efforts were being made to read the words the Mayans had left us, carved in stone, but I was not aware until later of Palenque's role in this search. First deciphered were emblem-glyphs that seemed to identify specific cities. Then my old heroine from Piedras Negras, Tatiana Proskouriakoff, chain-smoking in the basement of Harvard's library, speculated that many of the glyphs were names and lineages of kings. Flash forward to the Palenque Round Table of 1972, in which Linda Schele; Merle Greene Robertson, who lived in a small house in La Canada; and Moises Morales of Palenque deciphered hundreds of inscriptions.

We crawled all over the splendid buildings of Palenque and later assembled at Palenque's railroad station, where we boarded a sleeping car that Aurelia had rented for us from the Mexican National Railroad. The car was attached to a train headed to Mérida in the Yucatán, and we slept on sheets (*sheets!*) in berths as we rattled across some 300 miles in the Mexican night. In the morning, we left the train at a small station in the Yucatán and what should we see but the blue bus! Slim had driven all night to meet us and take us to the ruins of Uxmal.

Temple of the Dwarf. Uxmal, Yucatán, Mexico, January 1980
(photographed by Villa Brewer)

I had been to Uxmal before. Now a massive tourist site, Uxmal was constructed after the heyday of Tikal, Yaxchilan, and Palenque. The Temple of the Dwarf is the world's only oval-shaped pyramid.

John Lloyd Stephens, an American explorer and writer, called the Governor's Palace "the most beautiful pre-Columbian building in the Americas." Unlike the carvings of the Usumacinta cities, intricate stones fitted together form the intricate roof combs of the Nunnery Quadrangle. Vegetation is different. The Yucatán is arid. There are no rivers. Rainwater seeps through the porous limestone and is trapped in underground wells. Still the soil produced enough food to support the huge population of the area.

As the day wound down, we boarded the blue bus and headed east to Mérida, Yucatán's capital. Aurelia had arranged for us to have a farewell dinner at a well-known restaurant there, El Faisan y El Venado ("The Pheasant and the Deer"). It featured wild game, along with other classic Yucatecan dishes, very different from the usual Mexican fare. I even remember what I ate—carne *desmenuzada*—a cold dish of shredded venison and green onions and spices. *¡Que rico!*

At the close of the dinner, Payson distributed our T-shirts. He was a firm believer in T-shirts that could not be bought, only earned during a race, a clinic, or an adventure. Our T-shirts had been designed by a guest on a previous year's trip, taken from a Mayan design called "the paddlers" incised on a bone found beneath Temple I at Tikal. The guest, an art teacher, worried about the copyright of the ancient Mayan artist, so she reversed the position of one of the paddlers in the canoe. The color of the T-shirt was bone and the design on it and the words "River of Ruins Expedition—Nantahala Outdoor Center" were printed in cinnabar ink, similar to the ink used on the bone fragment. I still have my T-shirt, although it's pretty well worn.

An interesting feature of NOC Adventure Travel in those years was a reunion of trip guests at the NOC the following summer. We gathered at the NOC one Saturday in June and had a dinner and slide show, all wedged together on the living room floor of the Stone House, where Payson and Aurelia were living at that time. Aurelia remarked that my slides were as good as Henry's, the professional photographer who'd been on the trip too. I became a frequent visitor to the NOC, even taking a kayak clinic taught by Payson and Bunny Johns. Aurelia mentioned that the NOC was thinking of hiring another photographer for its Nantahala Photo Service and asked if I might be interested. Of course, I was! After a couple of summers working at the NOC, a year-round position opened up, and as they say, the rest is history!

About the Contributor

Villa **Brewer** wandered very happily in the groves of academe until she was 38 years old. School never was a paper chase to her. It was an opportunity to read interesting stuff and to discuss important ideas with students, colleagues, and friends. College and graduate school led to teaching—in New Jersey, in Nicaragua, and in the Piedmont of North Carolina. But she was always looking out the window. If a dog, a cat, a horse, or an eagle wandered into the schoolyard, she was always the first to notice. In Nicaragua she had the most beautiful classroom in the world—a third-story aerie with glass on both sides, overlooking a lake and volcanoes. But when she was relegated to a classroom in rural North Carolina with 2-foot-wide slits for windows, something snapped. It started with the trip to the Usumacinta detailed in this book and morphed into a summer job. Later she permanently stepped out of the classroom and into the outdoors, working primarily in taking photos for the NOC but also in serving as staff on adventure travel trips, answering phones in the reservations office, and caretaking NOC's permits with government organizations. The NOC community is her family. She retired after 31 years with the NOC and still lives in the area.

ADVENTURES WITH CHRISTINE

By Bill Hester

Working and living at the NOC for 10 years (1982–92) had allowed me to see and hear about the travels and adventuring of other staff. In those years, my life had intertwined with some fantastic people whose talents and adventures inspired many, including me. I had been on a staff Bío-Bío trip in 1985 with some of the NOC's best. That trip left an indelible mark on my brain and heart that I couldn't shake. I would often have dreams of Chile that would leave an ache in my soul. I knew that at some point, I would be going back.

By 1991 I had become pretty much entrenched at the NOC while guiding at the Chattooga during the summers, and had a teaching and coaching gig in nearby Salem, South Carolina, during the winter. In my mind, though, all I wanted to do was go back to Chile, so in the fall of 1991, I decided to resign from my teaching and coaching position on Christmas. I remember asking my assistant principal what he thought. His answer sealed it. He said I had to go. If I didn't, I would regret it for the rest of my life. He was right. I would have regretted it. Now, looking back, it was one of the best decisions I ever made.

Shane Benedict, Bob Beazley (Beaz), and I agreed to go to Chile. We didn't have a plan really. We just thought we'd find some transportation, talk to other boaters, including some Chileans who had come to the NOC, and figure things out along the way. Serendipity helped us in the form of Jib Ellison, a friend of many at NOC, who had Lars Holbeck's handwritten notes on the rivers of Chile. These were like gold. It was like the Bible's first print edition had been given to us.

That's how things seemed to go on this adventure. While everything we did seemed difficult, there was nothing that wouldn't get figured out with some hard work, patience, and trusting the people around you a little.

The legendary Christine

With notes on the rivers, we now had a plan. All we needed was transportation. Rent or buy? We decided to buy. Not a brilliant idea, but one that we thought would save us some money, extend our trip, and make things easier. Shane and Beaz had originally found the car and thought it was a great idea too. A day later, we met a Kiwi named Peter. He liked the idea too, so he joined us for the adventure.

So we bought a very sharp-looking, deep-red, black-vinyl-top 1967 Chevy Impala for $1,500.

We were to be in Chile for three months to kayak and explore as many different rivers as possible. Two nights prior we'd bought the car, but the hitch in the deal was that if we could get it back to Santiago at the end of the three months, the owner would buy it back from us for $1,000. Seemed like a good deal.

We needed to head south on a checkout run for the car. We needed to make sure the car could handle the more rigorous roads of Chile's Lake District and possibly Patagonia beyond. We had driven up to the hotel, and the kids oohed and aahed at the classic, graceful lines and shiny paint of the Impala. We thought the car looked good too. The shiny black vinyl top and the rich deep-red body paint made the car stand out. At least we thought that's what they were oohing and aahing about. When I finally translated what they actually were saying, it turns out they were saying it looked like a big fat tomato: "Tomato grande." Put four kayaks on top and four people inside, and yeah, I guess it did look like a big fat tomato.

We headed south on the Pan-American Highway. Along the way, the car's name changed from the Big Fat Tomato to Christine because she started acting like the possessed car in Stephen King's novel of the same name. Christine did what she wanted, when she wanted, and was only going to go, or stop, when ready. We'd turn the key off and nothing would turn off, or everything would go off at the most inopportune times. We'd give her a little time to cool and off she'd go, good as new. Later on during the trip, we started talking to her, coaxing her, apologizing to her, and yes, even begging her to make it. We ended up just accepting this as part of Christine's personality.

Our second stop was the Río Tinguiririca, what we nicknamed the Ting, one valley south of the Río Maipo. This was a wonderful valley with stark volcanic rock and a beautifully contrasting green river valley. We were heading high up into the mountains and the roads were getting worse. As we got toward the top, the road narrowed to one lane right next to the river. Our tires were literally 1 foot away from the water on one side and 1 foot away from a rock wall on the other. As we rode along with our eyes glued to the water and the rock wall, we encountered a bus coming the opposite way. Yes, a bus! There was hardly any room for our car. Luckily, we found/made a nook for us to slide our car into. The bus lumbered past us with millimeters to spare. As it did so, it honked loudly and everyone in the bus started shouting and waving at us. We thought it was because we looked so strange with all the kayaks and gear so we just waved back.

Balancing our four kayaks on top and two gringos on the hood, we did look strange, and we happily waved back. A little while later we encountered another one and the scene repeated. We ended up passing at least four more buses along the way. Thankfully we were nearing the top of the river and our put-in point. We had a tremendously great day paddling back downstream. The river's bright green waters were full of bouncy, fun waves and narrow, challenging rapids.

We ended the day of paddling at a small store beside the river. While we waited for Beaz to hitch a ride back upstream to get the car, Shane and I settled under a shady grape arbor and ordered a beer. We joked about the traffic on the way up to the top. As we sipped, we saw that the traffic pattern had switched. Now the traffic appeared to be going up the road. The same way we had gone that morning. However, much like that morning, when we set off toward the top, Beaz, driving Christine, was making his way against the traffic on a very narrow road. We were sure we could hear horns honking in the distance and knew that somewhere up that road Beaz was still smiling and waving back.

Curious, I asked our hosts and proprietors, in my broken but happy Spanglish, about the road: "Why is it we see traffic going that way this morning, and then the other way this afternoon?"

After picking up a few words and several gestures I realized that this road is actually a one-way road . . . and we were going the wrong way. The honks and waves weren't to four gringos in a strange-looking car in an effort to make us feel welcome. They were telling the four gringo idiots to get off the road! Evidently, the one-way changes. In the morning it is one way down the road, back toward the highway. All the guests from the night before needed to leave. In the afternoon, more guests come in and the road changes to one way going the other direction. Leave it to us to get it backward.

Our stay in the Ting ended with one of my more memorable moments. We were tired after our long day of playing and driving, so we ended up staying. After drinking a few beers and eating loaves of fresh bread and home-raised honey for dinner, I pitched my tent on a sandy island in the middle of the river valley about 100 yards from the store. I fell asleep quickly and happily. In the middle of the night, I was wakened by the brightness of the moon and looked out my tent flap. Just above the horizon was the most glorious full moon I had ever seen. I sat and watched the summer moon filled to the brim and washing the entire river valley with its brightness and warmth. That moon, framed by the mountains that surrounded the valley on each side, made me feel like this was the place I was meant to be. Nowhere else on earth could've been better.

The next morning I awoke to the smell of fresh bread baking in a fire-stoked, earthen oven. The only thing that could've made this better would've been coffee. I sleepily went up the hill to our impromptu hosts, who were making the bread, and greeted them: "Buenos días." They smiled and returned the greeting with a warm, steaming piece of bread and a jar of honey to dip it in. Coffee could wait. Life was good.

Did we make it? Even more important, did the car make it? The answer is yes, but barely. We ended up logging about 6,000 kilometers over some of the roughest road imaginable. Christine's stories could fill a book, but remember, at times it's not the goal that counts; it's the journey and with it, the experiences along the way.

After three months we were finally headed home. We had just left Pichilemu and three days of some of the biggest ocean surf I had ever experienced, and we were tired but pretty happy. Spirits were up as we drove in the late afternoon sun toward Santiago. About 300 kilometers south of Santiago, we started hearing a noise coming from underneath Christine. We had been hearing noises like this, but that was in second gear and Christine still seemed to run OK. We didn't use second gear much, so we didn't think it was a big problem. However, third gear was important. We needed third gear, but the sound was getting worse. We decided to give third gear a break and slowed down and shifted into second gear. She wasn't as loud, so we kept moving up the road, slowly. Not the best, but we would make it if . . . if . . . if . . . Christine would be kind enough to cooperate.

To ward off the insanity and worry, we all donned our Walkman headphones and cranked the music up. Anything to drown out the noise and the stress it caused. All we needed to do was get to Santiago. We were hoping, praying, and begging her to make it. The stress of it was killing me, but hope still lived.

Until second gear died. It died near a truck stop/restaurant on the side of the Pan-American Highway, where we spent the next few hours wrestling with the gears and ignoring the truckers who kept shouting offers to buy Christine. Still, we got her going again and arrived in Santiago just before the morning rush hour and fell exhausted into our beds at the Hotel Caribe.

The next morning we called the car dealer and arranged for him to come over and check out the car. We washed and cleaned her and made her look like new again. When our friend the car dealer arrived, we told him about the trip and how great the car was. We told him most of the details but left out the transmission issues of the night before. We wanted to see his face when he started her then put her into gear. He climbed in and started her. The engine roared to life and the muffler backfired. He laughed. We told him to go ahead, drive around the block. As he put her into gear and released the clutch, he just about died laughing. We ended up eating a late lunch and recounting all the stories we had experienced along the way. In the end, he agreed to pay us $600 to buy her back. Wow, this was a steal, considering what we had put the car through, but she still looked good and labor was cheap. We were to drop her off the next day at his bar and restaurant.

Our experiences with Christine were a prelude to many years of fun and exciting trips with incredible people. For me, she was the spark that ignited the flame that travel and adventure travel holds. Many people ask if I would buy an old car again and do the same type of trip. I tell them no way, but I wouldn't trade those experiences for anything. She's out there somewhere. I'm sure of it. Christine is plowing down some road somewhere in search of adventure.

About the Contributor

Bill Hester grew up the son of a career Air Force pilot, moving every few years. Luckily he ended up in New Iberia, Louisiana, where he began racing marathon canoes around the country. He came to the NOC in 1982 and continued to push his paddling abilities through teaching, guiding, and leading trips; he counts his time working, and paddling in unique and beautiful places such as Chile, Costa Rica, Mexico, and Vietnam, as the highlights of his 20 years with the NOC. His last trip guiding for the NOC was a Section IV Chattooga trip in 2013, where five of the guides were the kids—now adult guides—of the talented people that he'd spent his NOC career working with. That trip marked 31 years since he first guided for the NOC. Still living in Bryson City, he now spends his time teaching physical education, while also finding new places to explore and travel with his wife, Susan, and kids, Rye and Callie.

MISTAKEN IDENTITY

By Susan Bechdel

In Lonquimay, Chile, NOC staff members were shopping for provisions for a nine-day river trip on the Río Bío-Bío. It was 1982. Six of us were filling the coolers and dry boxes in this frontier town on the banks of the Bío-Bío. Meanwhile, two other guides were escorting our guests south from the capital, Santiago. We planned to be fully provisioned and launch-ready when they arrived.

The six of us finalized our menu and divided up shopping lists. Kathy Bolyn (KB) and Dick Eustis went to the produce market. Les Bechdel and Mike Hipsher went to the fish market. And Chris Spelius and I were assigned the grocery store for canned goods. We would meet up later at our hotel to pack.

This was a little town with more horses than cars, and it was certainly not a tourist destination. At that time, the Bío-Bío had yet to register on the list of international classics. We were some of the first gringos to descend on Lonquimay. Our crew stood out like rafters out of water in a town of caballeros. KB and I were the only girls on our crew, both with short hair, jeans, and Patagonia vests, clearly nothing like the local women wearing dresses, with babies on their hips. We strolled down the unpaved streets, empty rubber river bags in tow, our flip-flops leaving tracks among the cowboy boot prints in the dust.

The grocery store was the size of an American convenience store and staffed by several uniformed clerks. Chris is 6 feet, 6 inches tall, much taller than anyone who worked in the store. He pulled full cases off the top shelves as I read from our list. The clerks scrambled to find all we needed. They clearly hadn't had a day like this in the history of their little market. After over an hour, we pushed our carts to the counter, rechecking our lists.

One clerk tallied the cost and gave us the total. I quickly translated pesos into dollars to make sure we were within our budget. Sure enough, it was a huge sum for the little store, but a bargain for nearly 20 people's food for nine days. I handed over several bills, including one very large one. There was much fussing behind the counter, and it was determined that one clerk would run to the bank for some change and be back momentarily. When she returned, she carefully counted out the change. I looked at it and was initially confused, but then realized she had given me not only our change but also the large bill I had initially given her. In pesos, it was the equivalent of several hundred US dollars.

Essentially, we'd have had free groceries and change to boot! Of course I told her of the error and passed back the big bill. Tears welled up in her eyes as she realized she just about bankrupted the little store. She and her coworkers spoke rapidly in Spanish, gesturing madly with their hands. We understood nothing, but knew

162

this would have been a catastrophic mistake for them. The employees ran around from behind the counter and hugged and kissed us; they started pulling candy bars and trinkets off the shelves and stuffing our bags. Tears poured down their cheeks and they couldn't thank us enough.

Chris and I walked out feeling pretty good about the impression we as Americans had given them. When we met our fellow guides at the hotel, we couldn't wait to tell our story. But KB said, "No, no, I have a fabulous story to tell," and ours would have to wait. We argued with her, knowing ours would be hard to beat, but she won.

KB began, "We found just about everything on our list at the produce market, but a few types of fruit were missing." So off they went to the grocery store for canned fruit. KB continued, "I had barely entered the store when four short little clerks looked at me with instant recognition. I, of course, had never seen them before, but they seemed to know me. They rushed me, hugged me, and kissed me and filled our cart with candy and gifts. They wouldn't even let us pay for the four cans of fruit. They babbled and babbled, far too rapidly for us to understand anything except thank you." KB and Dick left, canned fruit and gifts in hand, but baffled by their reception.

Even though the Bío-Bío has since been dammed and few river runners now shop the markets of Lonquimay, I'd like to think we left a positive and lasting impression on the dusty little town.

 ## *About the Contributor*

See page 121 for more information about Susan Bechdel.

KIND OF LIKE THE NANTAHALA

By Villa Brewer

The tale isn't told very often. It needs to be fueled by alcohol and the smell of a campfire. It starts out simply beside a river "kind of like the Nantahala" and ends up being "the day Villa saw God twice in one day on the Filobobos in Mexico."

At this time, NOC adventure travel was transitioning away from the Usumacinta. There had been incidents other companies had had with the Guatemalan guerrillas, and our clients tended to be kayakers rather than rafters. We had run several kayaking trips to Veracruz since 1988 and had found an enthusiastic supporter in Ed Culp, the US consul in Veracruz, a C-1 paddler. Ed had encouraged us to add the Filobobos to our itinerary, as it was farther north in the state of Veracruz, closer to the ruins of El Tajín, a tourist attraction, and the beach at Tecolutla, where we would conclude our trip.

Villa Brewer with ball court artifact, unknown ruins. Río Filobobos, Veracruz, Mexico, 1993 (photographed by Tom DeCuir)

Sue Magness leading paddlers down the Río Filobobos in Mexico
(photographed by Villa Brewer)

Sue Magness and Phil Watford, who had done previous Veracruz trips in the 1990s, had gone to work for another outfitter. New leaders for the trip would be Tom DeCuir, who had led the trip in 1988, and Wayne Dickert, a member of the USA Wildwater Team, which had spent a winter training on the Río Antigua in Veracruz. Tom's wife, Ellen Babers, who spoke good Spanish, would take over for me as "road warrior" and backup instructor in case one of the instructors fell ill.

This was just a Saturday sojourn to introduce our instructors to a new river. Ed Culp brought a couple of Mexican teenagers from the local kayaking club and an English teacher from the American School of Veracruz who knew nothing about paddling but was up for adventure. Ed brought a ducky for him, one for me, and another for Ellen.

We camped in an idyllic pasture beside the Filo, where the trip had camped the previous year. I secured the camp while Tom, Ellen, and Ed drove cars to the takeout for the return shuttle. The river had been described as "kind of like the Nantahala," a river with Class I–III rapids with waves and eddies for good play but not pushy, not big water. By this time, I had spent 10 years taking photos on the Nantahala, interspersed with stints as a shuttle driver and camp cook for instruction clinics along other rivers and creeks in the Southeast. I knew, theoretically, that whitewater could be dangerous, that people had died on wild rivers, and I even had a friend who had died on a river in West Virginia. But this was a supposedly easy river in Mexico, and I was with friends who were experienced paddlers. It never even occurred to me that I might die on this river. All I felt was a vague impatience, waiting for the shuttle drivers to return, anxious to get on the river and to see these two new ruins.

In previous years I had walked to the lower pasture to take photos of our paddlers negotiating the first rapid. It was a good fun wave, constricted a little by protruding rocks on either side, but no pour-overs, no holes.

The drivers returned. We outfitted and put on, Ed and Tommy in the lead, followed by the Mexican teens who did not speak English, the three duckies, and Wayne running sweep.

We punched the first rapid. "Whoa!" A lot more water than I had anticipated from the shore. But then I remembered that Nantahala Falls looks huge when you're in it but not so scary when you're sitting beside it taking pictures. "Kind of like the Ocoee!" I laughed. Then the river turned sharply to the right and we entered the unknown.

At that point it started to rain, gently at first but then a little harder. I smiled ruefully, remembering a conversation with my aunt in Mexico City more than 10 years earlier. "Why doesn't Mexican TV news have weather reports, like the States?" I asked.

"We don't need them," my aunt had replied. "If it's the rainy season, it's going to rain. If it's the dry season, it's not. Why have weather reports?"

It's November, the end of the rainy season, I thought. We could have used a forecast today. Soon the rain was coming down in sheets, the water turning brown. The river rounded a bend to the left and we saw that the face of a whole cliff, maybe 30 or 40 feet high, had come off some weeks earlier and had fallen into the river. It was a rock garden, no huge boulders, but it slowed us down as we picked our way through.

We paddled another couple of miles. The rain slacked off a bit, but because I was wearing glasses, it was still hard to see. The river made a sharp bend to the left among towering boulders, but maybe there was a sneak route to the right. I eased over to take a look and then started a hefty back-paddle. The route was too constricted for a ducky, and if I was not mistaken, those rocks were undercut! I knew enough about whitewater to know I did not want to be there! There was not even time to say, "Oh, shit!" The current grabbed me and I flipped over and went underwater. All I could think was, *I hope I come up!* Had the crack been stuffed with branches or debris, I wouldn't have. But fortunately, I surfaced and there was Tommy DeCuir in his kayak. He gave me his grab loop and pulled me into an eddy on the riverbank. Someone grabbed and beached my ducky.

The others gathered and began getting out of their boats. We had reached the first ruin. My camera was in a dry bag carabinered into the duck. I walked around shooting a few pictures, hoping no one noticed how much my legs were shaking.

Wayne slipped a PowerBar into my hand. I always thought they tasted like cardboard, but this afternoon it was delicious.

There were pyramids and platforms covered with green grass. Hard to tell who had built them. Northern Veracruz was a border area between pre-Columbian groups. The Huastecs were given credit for building El Tajín and the Totonacs inhabited Zempoala, closer to the city of Veracruz, when Hernán Cortés invaded. But this city had a distinctive stone ball court piece like none I had ever seen before. It resembled pieces I had seen in the Maya-Toltec ruins of Uxmal and Chichen Itza in the Yucatán, some 700 miles to the south, except that the opening was much smaller than the stones in those cities.

But as the sky began to darken again and my legs continued to shake, I realized that someone else would have to figure out the story and even the name of this city. Intellectual pursuits would have to wait. Our journey was about survival on the river. We got back in our boats. It began to rain again. There was thunder, lightning, sheets of rain, and brown water growing in speed and intensity. Tributaries came bubbling in from the right and the left. Ed couldn't seem to find the second ruin. The Mexican boys were antsy; they knew we were running out of daylight. We could hear the roar of a big rapid up ahead.

Ed, Tom, and Wayne boat-scouted the rapid and took strategic positions in eddies to guide the duckies through. Tom motioned to me how to work my way through the rapid, and I was following his directions when I got swept up onto a rocky shelf. I was just working myself back into the current when the out-of-control English teacher in his ducky hit my ducky. I was over in a second, but Tom was there offering his rear grab loop. I couldn't see much but I could see his eyes widen. "Villa, you have to kick," he yelled. "Kick *hard*!" I did and then we seemed to be in the run-out of the rapid, and there was Wayne with my ducky and its paddle. He grabbed my personal flotation device (PFD) and pulled me in. "Kind of like the Gauley," he said, referring to the famous river in West Virginia.

We paddled on for a couple of miles and the rapids smoothed out. Through the rain and the growing darkness, I thought I saw the footbridge that would mark our takeout about 0.5 mile ahead.

"I know where I am," I said, easing over to river right. "I'm going to walk from here!"

"Me too," Ellen chimed in. "I've had enough!"

Ed and the teacher and the Mexican boys had gone ahead. Tom and Wayne carabinered our duckies to their kayaks and headed downstream. Ellen and I began walking. Cane field. Then cornfield. It was full dark now. We came to the bridge. But it was not a bridge! It was a 3-inch irrigation pipe or a sewer pipe across the river! I had no idea where we were. We yelled for Tom and Wayne, but the roar of the water drowned our voices out. We had no flashlights. We knew that there was a bridge downstream, but we weren't sure how far downstream. Every time the lightning flashed, we fixed our sights on a tree or fence post about a hundred yards ahead and made for that and then waited for the next flash of lightning. We didn't even think about snakes. After about 15 minutes, we heard voices speaking English. Tom and Wayne had found Ed, taken out, crossed the bridge, and were coming upstream to look for us. They had flashlights. We were safe!

In retrospect, what do I say about this misadventure? People do die on rivers. When things go bad, they can go bad very quickly. They go bad in ways one might never have anticipated. In this case, I escaped. I survived. I'm grateful that no one in my family has heard this tale. But, to this day, I'm still involved with rivers, with whitewater, and with people who run rivers. It's the stories, like this one, and the people who had my back and who know I have their backs that keep me hanging around. And to me, it's the adventure travel stories, where we have put ourselves out there to encounter new countries, cultures, and people that are the most vivid, the most worthy of telling when you're drinking beer around a campfire.

 About the Contributor

See page 156 for more information about Villa Brewer.

RÍO UPANO STAFF TRIP:

ADVENTURE OF THE MILLENNIUM!

By Leigh Boike

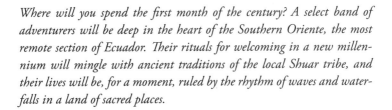

Where will you spend the first month of the century? A select band of adventurers will be deep in the heart of the Southern Oriente, the most remote section of Ecuador. Their rituals for welcoming in a new millennium will mingle with ancient traditions of the local Shuar tribe, and their lives will be, for a moment, ruled by the rhythm of waves and waterfalls in a land of sacred places.

After reading this pamphlet about the Ecuador trip, who wouldn't want to go, right? Celebrating the turn of a new century in a foreign country paddling Class II–IV+ whitewater with a bunch of your friends? Sign me up!

This was my first time traveling outside of the United States, along with many others on the trip. Remember, way back in 2000 the Internet wasn't really a thing (at least in the land of the NOC), but if it had been, we might have known a little more about the economic and political situation that the country was in at the time. Ignorance was bliss, so we (me, Nathan Boike, Erika V'Soske Brock, and Adam Breidenbach) hopped on the plane.

After some time in Quito, we met up with more NOC staff in Tena, which felt like a jungle paradise. Several of us paddled the Río Jatunyacu to get warmed up before the big week on the Río Upano. Nate ended up losing his paddle, but some local kids playing in the river offered him one with a makeshift wooden blade that they'd found. We still have this priceless keepsake, and it only cost Nate $2.

The government unrest caused many speed bumps just getting to the river, and it all started in Tena. The word on the street was that a transportation strike was going to be happening a day or two before we planned to leave Tena for Macas. What this meant was that the buses we were planning to take to Macas were not going to be running and that the already sketchy roads to get there would contain roadblocks by locals who chopped down trees with their ever-so-handy machetes.

We ended up hiring several taxis to take our group of 10–12 people along with all of our gear. As we came across the first downed trees in the road with a crowd of locals standing "guard," we realized that this was going to be a long ride. We probably encountered three to four of these between Tena and Macas. Dan Dixon was among our group and led the negotiations at each of the roadblocks. For at least two of them, we had to pool our money together and pay them to let us through.

Dan Dixon in a waterfall in Honduras (photographed by Villa Brewer)

We finally reached Macas way after midnight, and we hiked and played soccer with local kids to pass the waiting days. *Muerto* and *peligro* were just some of the words that the locals used to describe how crazy they thought we were to go on the Upano. The morning of the trip, we loaded up our gear and ourselves into two cattle trucks and started out for the put-in. If memory serves, it was supposed to be about an hour away. Not far out of town, we ran into yet another roadblock, but this time, no matter how hard Dan tried to negotiate, there was no deal to let us through. Our only option was to head back to Macas and put on the river there, a full day upstream from where we were planning on starting.

It seemed like forever before we got everything unloaded, blown up (hand pumps on two oar rigs = not fun), and packed for the river. We were all a little deflated by the difficulties of our travel so far but excited to get on the water, where roadblocks wouldn't be an impediment. With boats ready, we hit the water. Our new local friend Pedro was going to accompany us in case anyone questioned why we were on the river.

The pamphlet described the next part of the adventure:

> *As our journey on the Upano begins, we will meander through the valley which separates the Cordillera de Cutucú (Mountains of Moss) from the*

Andes. This area is the center of the Shuar tribe, once famous for their custom of shrinking the heads of their enemies. Although many Shuar have adopted contemporary lifestyles, there are still a number of traditional villages deep in the rain forest.

The first night on the river was nerve-racking. The only place that we were able to find to camp was an island that had little elevation from the riverbanks. We knew that rain was on the way, so once we got camp set up and the poop/fire/water crews were assigned, Dan put a stick in the ground about 8 feet from the edge of the water. This was our flood warning of sorts, so if the river got up to the stick, we were all going to have to scramble into the jungle.

The trip down the river was breathtaking, magnificent, and so very secluded, like nothing I had ever experienced before. This was also the biggest water I had ever paddled, which took some getting used to. You could just feel the power beneath you at every ripple. One of the most memorable camps was in a bend in the river at Tsunki Falls, which is named after the Shuar word for "river god." It was here that we camped on the opposite side of the river to the falls, and we took a trip over to get water and bathe in the rain forest pool.

The next night we arrived at the camp by a traditional Shuar village that consisted of two families and four generations. They'd invited us up to their village for a celebration that evening, and we were to bring alcohol to share with the tribe as they would be sharing their chicha with us. The hike to their village was nothing short of Class V and in complete darkness. When we arrived at the building, there was music, dancing, and immersion into their culture. The men had to ask the women to dance, so that was a lot of fun. One of the best parts of the night was a man approaching Nate, asking him if he would dance with the man's wife . . . who was breastfeeding their child! I about died. Nate danced with her, even as she breastfed! I think the song lasted 5 minutes and was pure torture to him.

After some dancing, we all sat around and shared our drink. I liked to call this the passing of the bowl of hepatitis. The chicha was in a small orange Tupperware bowl. Whether they used the traditional method of making it (where the women chew the maize or yucca root and spit the juice in a bucket to then ferment for the drink) or not, I was not a fan of this part of the celebration. There had to be at least 50 people passing this bowl around and it would have been rude to not accept. I think it went around the circle at least three times. I actually tried it the first time and managed not to gag in front of everyone. After that, I pretended to sip and finally we shared our liquor with them. Tequila!

The next morning, one of the villagers, Bosco, showed us around before we headed out. He would be joining us as our interpreter the rest of the way. The next morning, many from the tribe came to see us off, but several who would have joined us were missing due to the liquor from the previous night.

We decided to add a day onto the end of the trip, which would take us farther downstream than we had originally planned. One of my biggest regrets of this adventure was not going up to the next village that we came to where we would have been able to visit a school. Sand fleas were seriously attacking us all, to the point that it was almost unbearable, and I simply didn't want to let those little buggers get to my legs anymore. So, I missed a once-in-a-lifetime opportunity and stayed in my boat by the river with a few others. The group that did go not only met many school children but also got to use handmade blow darts.

The end of our trip and getting back from Santiago, Ecuador, to Macas proved to be as much of an adventure as the trip from Tena to Macas. We arrived in this small town in the middle of the afternoon. We had a truck there to load all of our boats and gear onto while we would be taking a bus. Because we were so close to the border with Peru, we had to stop and have our passports checked at a military base. After a while, we all started to get pretty nervous about what was taking so long. Dan came back to inform us that they were concerned that we were Peruvian spies and that they weren't going to let us leave until things checked out. We couldn't have looked more gringo, but OK, we just sat there and hoped we'd get to leave. I think we were there for more than 2 hours before finally being cleared to continue on our way.

We boarded our "bus," which was just a truck transformed into a passenger vehicle with bench seats and a little deck on the roof. The trip back was very, very long and it was helpful to be able to climb out of the windows, up to the rooftop deck for a change of scenery along the way. The tune that played for the entire trip was "The roof, the roof, the roof is on fire . . ." It is a drive that I will never in a million years forget—or want to make again.

Once the river trip had come to an end, Adam, Erika, Nate, and I traveled together for the next week and a half. Some highlights of our following adventures would certainly include the visit to Baños, which was supposed to be under a man-datory evacuation because of the active volcano. Additionally, the visit to the surf town, Montañita, was a major highlight and it included the best piña colada con banana on the face of the planet. Finally, a trip to Ecuador would not have been complete without a visit to the equator and the surrounding shopping villages.

The more I write about this trip, the more memories keep flooding back. When I was in high school, I remember drooling over the NOC Adventure Travel catalogs that were mailed to our house. I never in a million years thought that I would have the privilege to work for this amazing company for 18 years, much less experience a trip like this. I am forever grateful.

About the Contributor

Leigh Boike applied for a job too late in 1997 and got her rejection letter from Ray McLeod, so she started in May 1998 in the Rafting Reservations Office under Susan Hester as an intern for her outdoor recreation degree from Murray State University. Leigh agreed to a two-season commitment, never imagining that she would work her way up through the ranks of the reservations department and lead the charge there for more than 10 years (doing taxi squad in several different departments along the way). Now, 19 seasons later, she is the executive vice president of the NOC.

ORIGINS OF CLINIC NEPAL

By Payson Kennedy

O ne year when we arrived in Chitwan, Nepal, we heard that in two days the elephant polo world championship match was to be played on the airstrip at Meghauli, across the park from our campsite. We decided that this was too good an opportunity to be missed and that we would hike across the park to be at Meghauli in time for the match. Our bus would drive with our rafts and gear around the park to meet us at Meghauli. We had an interesting hike across the park, seeing lots of wildlife along the way, and arrived at Meghauli in midafternoon.

As we waited in the shade for the bus with our tents and gear to arrive, a boy of about 15 joined us and began conversing to practice his English. As it began to get dark and we were getting hungrier, we became increasingly worried about the whereabouts of the bus and our gear. This young boy then offered the hospitality of his village for the night. The villagers would feed and assign us to several different homes for the night. By the time we were ready to eat, the bus had arrived with our gear, but by this time we now felt it would be more diplomatic and more interesting to stay in the homes to which we had been assigned.

It was a very festive evening, with a village elder and then me giving short speeches, which had to be interpreted as we spoke. The gist of the elder's speech was that the people of the village watched as wealthy individuals landed on the airstrip at Meghauli and were picked up and driven to their fancy accommodations at Tiger Tops Jungle Lodge. The villagers seldom had any interaction with them, and the village did not benefit much from the proximity of the airstrip and Tiger Tops. They were happy to finally be meeting some of the park visitors. While the guests were less comfortable spending the night in village homes than they would have been in their tents, the entire experience is one that I am sure none of the guests will ever forget.

Half of why we took adventure travel trips was the draw of strange adventures and our always finding a way to deal with problems that arose; the other half of that equation was the people we met. Years after this meeting, in 1997, I was contacted by Hari Bhandary, who explained that he was the young boy who had befriended us years earlier at Meghauli. He had since obtained a university degree, worked for several years in health field jobs, and now was working to establish a clinic at Meghauli to provide medical care for the people of the surrounding area. Up until then, to obtain medical care villagers had to walk or be transported by ox cart several miles to a highway and then go by bus to the nearest city, where medical care was available. The whole trip took several hours.

Growing up in the village, Hari had kept a notebook in which he recorded the names and contact information for the foreign visitors he struck up friendships with. He was now contacting them and asking for support in his project for the benefit of the village. Soon Hari was making fundraising trips to Germany, Spain, Gibraltar, the United Kingdom, and the United States. He now heads a thriving social service organization that not only supports a clinic for the people of the Meghauli region but has also established a kindergarten and a scout troop and has built sanitary latrines. The organization is now building an extensive community water system using a deep well after it was determined that the shallow wells in the area not only were often polluted by sewage but also contained an unhealthy level of arsenic in the water.

Hari now makes an annual fundraising trip to the countries named above and usually visits the NOC on his visit to the United States. Two individuals from the NOC community have spent time at Meghauli as volunteer workers in the clinic programs, and the NOC community regularly supports the clinic financially. As I look at the annual report of Clinic Nepal each year, I am astonished and inspired to realize the impact that this one man has had in bettering the lives of everyone in his community.

For anyone interested in learning more about Clinic Nepal, there is a Facebook page and several websites: a somewhat limited website for the Nepal organization (clinicnepal.com) and a website for the United Kingdom organization that supports the clinic (friendshipclinicnepal.org). The story there of how cofounders Peter and Beryl Shore got involved is remarkably similar to my own story. The US organization founded to support the clinic does not have a website, but it has a 501(c)(3) designation, and its address is Clinic Nepal, Inc., 1837 Chasewood Park Dr., Marietta, GA 30066.

 *** About the Contributor***

See page 81 for more information about Payson Kennedy.

SECTION V
Life Changes
at the NOC

NEVER, NEVER GIVE UP

By Tommy Yon

When I was a kid, from around the age of 8 until about 15 years old, I was considered an overweight child. I weighed a maximum of 220 pounds by age 15.

At 8 years old, I discovered kayaking, and by the age of 10, I had finally learned how to roll my kayak in the frigid Nantahala River, where I grew up. After I got my roll down, I started doing more things in my kayak than I had ever imagined I could. I was learning tricks like stern squirts and cartwheels, playing around Nantahala Falls, and eventually wandering out to the Ocoee and other rivers around the Southeast.

As an overweight kid, I found it hard at first: hiking my boat, putting on gear, getting in a boat, and pushing myself when I faced a challenging new river. Kayaking was truly the most intense workout I had ever experienced, but back then I didn't think of kayaking as a workout. It was addictive and out-of-this-world fun to me! Every kayaking trip was an adventure, a chance to make friends, and another chance to push myself in my boat and to practice that old-school pirouette I didn't quite nail the previous week.

With the drive to become a better athlete, I decided that it was time to change my diet and truly get fit. I spent every free moment (aside from kayaking and school) hitting the gym and trail running. With no guidance from others but headstrong determination, I lost 90 pounds.

Needless to say, 21 years later and I'm still at it. It's a curse, but a good one. I couldn't have asked for a better life. Kayaking changed mine! It's kept me fit and young at heart, and it never lets me forget how to have fun.

I hope it can do the same for you.

 ## *About the Contributor*

Tommy "TR" Yon's father operated a boiled peanut shack near the Nantahala River. As a youth, TR spent countless hours entertaining himself by playing on the river in an inflatable kayak. When he was 8 years old, several NOC staff members took an interest in TR. The people who influenced him included, but weren't limited to, Horace Holden, Wayne Dickert, Craig Parks, Andrew Holcombe, Adam Clawson, and Forrest King. Nathan Maddox taught TR how to roll. TR worked at the NOC intermittently 2003–2015, first as a cook at River's End and Relia's Garden restaurants and eventually as a full-time raft guide and occasional kayak instructor. He is now a top-level competitor in freestyle kayaking.

FROM THE MOUTHS
OF THE CONVERTED:
LETTERS FROM NOC GUESTS AND STAFF

Editor's Note: The following letters were received by NOC staff over the years and exemplify the type of life-changing experience that people have rafting, learning to kayak, and working at the NOC. Payson has a folder full of such letters, but these three really tell the tale.

From Barbara Holliday-Evans

October 3, 1995

Dear Payson,

I have suffered from multiple sclerosis most of my life. Sports were not something I could do, ever—or so I thought. Extreme sports, only in my dreams.

I have been paralyzed, blind, incontinent, lost my short-term memory, had no energy whatsoever. . . . In short, I had something of a life but there was no reason to live it. Until June 3.

I wanted a whitewater trip for my birthday. At that time I didn't know why. The French Broad is close, so my husband made reservations there. When we arrived there was a high river. Eight times the normal volume, Bruce Tarbox, the trip leader, said.

Bruce was also our raft guide. I didn't tell anyone about the MS because I wanted to see how far I could go with this, just like a real person, and it was the ride of my life. I had no left side for two days after, but it didn't matter. I had seen the face of the river.

The whitewater experience was repeated two weeks later. And then again on the Nolichucky on July 9. I was very full of myself at that point and decided to do a ducky. This with a semi-paralyzed left side. And of course the Nolichucky took a major bite out of my ass that day. I got thrown over the first rapid and slammed into a rock. It ruptured a disc at the base of my spine. You fished me out of the water and I spent the last day of the Nolichucky season in your raft.

I was bruised, battered, and semibroken . . . I knew that if I didn't get back on the water immediately I would never go near it again. So we did it again twice more that week. Fear conquered.

SECTION IV (of the Chattooga) has always been in capital letters in my mind, an incredibly scary place where only the "well above average in shape" could go. Some place where I'd never be able to go.

Of course we went. I got tossed out right after Seven-Foot Falls. And again when we just brushed into a rock. I laughed the second time while the Chattooga bounced me around and tattooed my hands and knees with little bloody marks. Dan offered dry clothes and first aid, both of which I refused because, damn it, I was having the *Section IV experience* and this was part of it.

Dan helped me up the path to see Long Creek Falls and held my hand tightly because I am unsteady on my feet. His secure grip allowed me to see one of the most holy places on the Chattooga. . . . Everyone I have met has been wonderful.

Today I have been kicked once again by the hobnailed black boot of multiple sclerosis. About three quarters of my eyesight began going the way of all flesh yesterday, and I'm scrambling to finish this before everything gets blotted out. But guess what? We have reservations this weekend on the French Broad. I have become a strong paddler. Even though my left side is badly weakened, I can paddle like hell when I sit on the left side of a raft. I've not done the river mostly blind yet, but this will be just another experience in the most wonderful summer and fall of my life. Please don't let this feeling end.

I dream of the river nearly every night. Always powerful dreams, beckoning whitewater. Always calling me back. I dream of a pitch-black night where rafts bobble against each other in the water and the only light that can be seen is the tip end of cigarettes. We are going to follow the river as soon as we figure a way to light it.

From Dick Graham

April 23, 1994

Dear Brooks [Ryan]:

I am blessed with a good full life with most everything anyone could want. But two days before I came to the NOC my dearest friend and companion of 13 years, my old springer spaniel, died in my arms. I saw lots of death in Vietnam but I have never hurt so much as with the loss of that old dog. So I came to you with a very heavy heart and my mind not so much on the trip. I bet it showed some—sorry for that.

You and my friends who tolerated me made that go away. I learned everything I ever hoped to learn and have memories I will treasure forever. I marveled at your talent and gentle enthusiasm. . . . You are never intimidating and never lose patience when we old guys get a little tired or disgusted with ourselves.

So I just wanted to thank you for what I truly believe was the best week of my life and to let you know that what you do is far more than teaching people to paddle a boat.

From Gordon Grant

August 4, 1988

Even on the worst days—on crowded August weekends with the traffic jams on both road and river, and the waves of humanity that wash through the Nantahala Gorge, displaying nearly every unpleasant trait that characterizes the species—there would be for me a second or two of a nearly transcendent delight. It might be caused by the witnessing of a certain arrangement of light and cloud above the river, or the inhalation of one of those cleansing gusts of cold air blowing up from the rapids, or the rowdy hilarity of a group of guides—all those nameless, unremembered moments sort of coalesce into an overwhelming evidence that for 12 years the center gave me daily opportunities to apprehend a moment of living fully. No small gift. And that is really what I perceive the business of the center to be: the dispensation of moments of joy, both for guests and staff. Everything seems subordinate to that.

Now realize, I make the distinction between fun and joy. Fun is a moment or so of pleasure and satisfaction—generally sensual. . . . But joy is more than that; it is an elevated state that consumes a person's entire being and brings them up to a much,

Payson Kennedy guiding a crew through Corkscrew on the Chattooga

much larger place than they would normally occupy—brings them out of themselves, out of egocentricity and pettiness. I have seen it so many times—the incredulous delight of a kayak student after her first roll, or the exultant whoop of a rafter below Corkscrew, a person so terrified initially that he almost backed out of the trip—these are transformative experiences, and they are going to last the individuals who undergo them for longer than the few seconds of the direct experiences themselves.

By small degrees, I believe we change the world by providing such experiences. But you can't *tell* people that: "I'm trying to save the world, and myself, by being a raft guide." Yet that is what I've been trying to do all these years at the center. I've always thought the most important distinction between the center and other businesses is that it has been based on ethics and philosophy, rather than business and profit.

 ## About the Contributor

See page 12 for more information about Gordon Grant.

MORE THAN PADDLING INSTRUCTION

By John Lane

Years ago, on a busy Labor Day weekend, Thayer and Allen Grumbine decided they needed a good teacher. The Grumbines, from Greenville, South Carolina, had come to the Nantahala River in Western North Carolina to canoe. Their only prior whitewater experience had been a quick Saturday trip down the ripples of the Green River near Columbus, North Carolina. Looking back, I remember they called themselves typical goonies in an aluminum canoe.

The Grumbines were a little afraid when they put on at the top of the most popular whitewater river in the Southeast. The river had fast, cold water. And rocks.

"We were so bad we didn't even make it down the whole river," they said now with a laugh.

Since the early 1970s, whitewater sports have turned into a multimillion-dollar business at the Nantahala. Most come to raft the river, but many—like the Grumbines—choose to study boating skills.

In the 1980s, much of what drew people to the NOC was the clear sense of community. Clinic participants ate family style with their instructors, slept in modern cabins built by NOC employees during the off-season, and were offered a discount in the Outfitter's Store. Learning to paddle at the NOC was the equivalent of learning dance at the American Ballet Theater. The core staff members were expert paddlers, certified by the American Canoe Association, and they had years of experience competing, running rivers, guiding rafts, and teaching clinics.

The experience and certification make for a good staff, but what made the NOC special at that time was the high level of personal achievement. Wendy Gordon (a wildwater national team member in 1986) spent weekends and summers at the center, but he also taught full-time in the psychology department at Warren Wilson College. Kathy Bolyn had taken part in first descents and expedition paddling all over the world. Angus Morrison, who taught canoeing, had been a world outrigger champion, national wildwater champion, and was a member of two Olympic flatwater canoe teams. Mark Hamilton, a member of the 1986 flatwater, wildwater, and slalom teams, taught regularly when not training. Mike Hipsher and Bunny Johns won the world tandem canoe championship in 1981. Arlo Kleinrath won the Colorado freestyle contest, and Eric Nies was a master of a newer form of whitewater playing called squirting.

With such teachers, a student could progress from beginner to advanced level in as few as three clinics and many weekends on rivers practicing the skills acquired at the center. Many guests took a clinic and then returned to the gorge year after year. "Repeat business, we thrive on that," Kent Ford said. "People feel like they are part of a club here. The exhilaration of the river brings out the best in people. They are very focused when they are here. They are taken care of, and they feel good."

While rivers were always at the heart of the NOC's business as a recreational opportunity, mountains have always been healing places, and there is much evidence, in the mythology of the Cherokee, that the Nantahala Gorge has always been a very special, powerful place. Among the waters and landscape of Swain County, the center began to see the potential for other possibilities. It was while teaching kayak clinics that NOC staffer Nancy Pettit discovered that the beauty of the gorge could serve an additional purpose: to help urban people manage stress.

The NOC's stress clinics of that era drew from a different group than the typical paddling clinics. Most who came to the stress clinics had no prior whitewater paddling experience. While watching beginning paddlers, Pettit observed that while learning a new skill, which for many was a stressful situation, these beginning kayakers discovered their own ways of managing stress. Pettit said, "We use the stress that students feel to take a look at how the body responds. When someone is stiff, he or she is much less likely to complete a full paddle stroke. You can hear the stress in their voice, see it in their balance."

So Pettit used this situation to teach people how to manage stress: Put the person in the boat, teach them to take the right stroke, and help them learn to deal with the stress created whenever they face change (learning a new skill) in life.

Managing stress? The Grumbines can relate. They began spending nearly every weekend, April through October, in the North Carolina mountains, running rivers and exhibiting more than a little paddling skill. You could say they were obsessed. In their Toyota Land Cruiser with the kayaks on top, they seemed indistinguishable from the men and women who drove all night from New Orleans for a monthly whitewater fix.

One warm fall afternoon, the Grumbines were eating peanuts and raisins in front of the Outfitter's Store. Thayer Grumbine said, "In Greenville, there aren't many people who are interested in taking risks. Up here in the gorge, it's just a different outlook on life: more living for the present."

Much of the enjoyment they'd found in paddling can be attributed to their discovery of the NOC clinic program. In three years, Thayer and Allen took seven clinics, and their sons, John and Peter, attended one clinic and weekends of personal instruction. Under the eyes of their instructors, they worked their way from canoe goonies to advanced kayakers with good strokes and an unbounded sense of play.

Why did they continue to drive 3 hours every Friday afternoon? They had a good life in Greenville. Thayer Grumbine had many friends, even if they didn't understand her river running. Allen Grumbine was a lawyer with a firm where "several folks love the outdoors. One senior partner even went trekking in Nepal, so I'm not that unusual."

It wasn't the risk of danger, Mrs. Grumbine explained, that drew them back each weekend. "It's something that takes you beyond your controlled environment."

"On a river you have a real fear of something," Mr. Grumbine added. "You go ahead and make a decision that you'll run a rapid. You've gotten outside yourself and made a decision. That's difficult to do in life. It's the closest thing I know to trying a case."

Allen Grumbine ate a few more peanuts, looked toward the river, and shook his head. "I've done things in the clinics I didn't think I'd ever do."

 ## *About the Contributor*

See page 114 for more information about John Lane.

THE LIFT

By Joe Jacobi

"And the winner of the gold medal, from the United States of America . . ."
Thirteen words that would change my life. A moment later, Scott Strausbaugh and I would step onto the top step of the awards podium at the 1992 Olympic Games in La Seu d'Urgell, Spain.

The thing is, it wasn't really a step. It was more of a lift.

Lifted up by so many others who had established a culture of excellence. A path
for doing the hard work. A spiritual connection to something bigger.

As proud as I was to represent the United States of America, the connection
I truly felt was to the people who did the heavy lifting—my Nantahala Outdoor
Center (NOC) community.

Lifting is what NOCers do best. For others. For themselves. A concentration of
energy, ideas, and action that helps us all find flow. Anywhere. Anytime.

How does this happen?

When I think about what it is that makes NOC so different, it's not so much
the place where we come together so much as the places and experiences we bring
from elsewhere. In other words, it's about the deep contrast that the NOC provides
as the backdrop to our performance and contribution: the lifting.

It's the collaboration of these contrasts that creates something special.

My own contrast starts with being raised in the Washington, D.C., area, close
to the Potomac River and one of the highest-performing whitewater slalom groups
in the history of this sport. The group consisted of the canoe/kayak's top athletes
and legendary coach Bill Endicott, who together dominated whitewater slalom for
over a decade. World-class competition fueled the twice-daily training sessions on
the Potomac River.

While we fought each other for excellence on the water, we also fought off the
grind of the conventional D.C. work-intensive culture that lived 100 yards from
our training venue. They were thousands of car commuters on the parkway going
to and from their in-town jobs.

In 1989, when whitewater slalom was added to the 1992 Olympic program,
the sport saw new Olympic resources come into play. With those resources, my
NOC contrast began.

Scott and I moved to the NOC full-time at the start of 1990 to begin a three-
year push toward the Olympic Games.

My memories of this period focus on three elements of performance: time,
community, and innovation.

Time

The context of time radically changed for me in the move from the D.C. area to the NOC. The NOC became my place to put all of the proverbial eggs in one basket. Time became an ally, not an enemy.

We had time to prepare. Time to settle into a workflow on the water. Time to analyze. Time to question. Time to reflect.

What I always looked forward to at the gate workouts was that little bit of time to gather beforehand. In the chase for Olympic excellence, the time to greet and check in with each other and set the context for the work that was about to happen was invaluable.

Away from the water, we had time to build friendships and learn about others and their journey to NOC. For me, this frequently happened over staff meals at Relia's Garden. I had long lunch conversations with the best kayak instructors in the world, digging into concepts, strategies, and techniques that make paddle sports better.

Community

In his speeches, Al Oerter revealed a progression that unfolded through his athletic participation in four different Olympic Games. The American discus athlete became the first Olympian to win a gold medal in the same event at four consecutive Olympic Games.

At his first Olympiad in Melbourne, the big motivation for Al was being a part of Team USA. He won a gold medal.

At his second Olympic Games in Rome, Al wanted to beat the very best, his rivals, the Russians and East Germans. Checked that box. Another gold medal.

At his third and fourth Olympic Games, Tokyo and Mexico City, Al wanted to throw farther than he ever had before. Mission accomplished. Two more gold medals.

Al's Olympic journey marks an evolution of excellence to which anyone can relate:

Level 1: Belong. Value the shared experience.

Level 2: Win. Nothing less than the top step of the podium.

Level 3: Do your best. No boundaries.

Not long after researching the life of Al Oerter, I was a part of a video production team who interviewed some of the NOC's world champion and Olympic canoeing legends: John Burton, Wayne Dickert, Bunny Johns, Gordon Grant, and Lecky Haller, to name a few. The conversations focused on a lineage of excellence that threads together our generations of high performers at the NOC.

Throughout the NOC interviews, Al's story was on my mind.

No matter how the questions about performance were framed, the answers from our NOC legends aligned with Al's third level of excellence—just do your best.

This third level anchors exactly what I've experienced throughout my years at the NOC. The concept of "just do your best" can be replicated and applied anywhere, any time. That's the system.

But, of more significance to me is the art—the element that can't be replicated by someone else or something else. So I dig a little more.

Where does "do your best" come from?

Why does it matter so much?

Slowly and thoughtfully, these NOC legends—all of whom were interviewed separately and never crossed paths during the interviews—shifted to a deeper place of commonality. In their own personal and profound ways, they outwardly pondered community and shared purpose.

Though decades have passed, the clarity with which they articulated their experiences would have you believe they had just finished a morning workout on the river in the prime of their athletic careers. Their eyes light up. And tear up.

The collective spirit of these legends inspires a thought—perhaps Al Oerter's first level of excellence—to belong—isn't a step to the second and third levels. Perhaps "to belong" encompasses all the steps:

Belong to Good: Whether you choose or are chosen, if it doesn't feel aligned, purposeful, and enriched, why belong at all? Think teams, jobs, friends, and partnerships.

Belong to "Bigger than You": The core belief in a collective action offers greater purpose and intention.

Belong through Contribution: There's no need for a scorecard to measure what you give. Investment should feel effortless and know no limits.

Belong to Moments: Results such as money and medals don't facilitate deep belonging. Meaning and memorable moments, which inspire reinvention and reinvestment, do.

These are neither strategy nor system. They are art. The art to belong. This was the community I experienced at the NOC.

Innovation

If you believe in the basic premise of Malcolm Gladwell's book *Outliers,* the idea that we are products of our own fortuitous circumstance, you would be hard-pressed to find a paddling situation more fortuitous than mine.

Mine looked like this:

 Live less than 5 miles from the Team USA training site on the Potomac River.

≋   Take an increasing interest in the sport about the same time the legendary coach of the group who trains at that training site starts to worry about the lack of up-and-coming athletes.

≋   Show up every day.

≋   Become the youngest training partner and teammate to the best whitewater slalom athletes in the world.

I was 13 and paddling with the all-time greats. At every workout, I was getting my butt kicked by one world champion except when the other world champion would step up and kick my butt even more. Slowly, I was distilled into one of the greatest whitewater slalom legacies the sport has ever known.

What the NOC offered, though, was not the chance to uphold a legacy but to reinvent one. Every day.

The NOC challenged me to grow my sense of innovation. From workouts and training plans to building a club scene to equipment design, innovation wasn't a nice-to-have. It was the foundation of our athletic existence at the NOC.

There was not one element of our training that was held safe as the status quo—everything was on the table. But, my favorite innovation was the design of the Patriot C-2, the boat that Scott, Horace Holden, Wayne Dickert, and I designed for the 1992 Olympic season.

Throughout the first five years of our racing career, Scott and I were always on the lookout for C-2 designs that favored smaller, lighter-weight pairs. However, the 1992 Olympic whitewater channel in La Seu d'Urgell changed that approach.

The Olympic course in Spain was a continuous section of whitewater defined by lots of hydraulics that would constantly reduce boat speed. So we wanted a boat a little bigger, especially in the bow, which would stay on top of the water and above the hydraulics.

The idea of a larger bow on the C-2 that Scott and I were already paddling was of interest to Horace and Wayne, our C-2 training partners at the NOC. Together, the two C-2 teams worked together to create the new C-2 design.

In the design phase, instead of working on the shape as a foursome or by C-2 pairing, Scott and Horace, the bowmen of the two teams, would take a work shift together. Then Wayne and I, the sternmen of the two teams, would take a shift together. Our pairings created different questions and conversations, which ultimately led to greater refinement of the design.

Both teams paddled the Patriot boat at the Olympic Trials that spring on the Savage River in western Maryland, and then Scott and I went on to paddle the boat at the Olympic Games in Spain.

Today, our 1992 Olympic boat hangs in the NOC's River's End Restaurant. I sometimes overhear restaurant staff tell their particular take on our Olympic story

Scott Strausbaugh and Joe Jacobi racing on the Ocoee River
(photographed by Villa Brewer)

to diners who ask about the boat. There are no right or wrong versions—the boat
is art, which means everyone can decide what it means to them.

For me, every time I walk into the restaurant, the same three thoughts come
to mind:

Scott had a powerful vision for what the Patriot could be and how it could work.

The spirit of innovation and experimentation never ends.

The spirit of partnership among friends creates great innovation.

All of these years later, the NOC remains an important part of my life. I met
my wife at the NOC, our daughter has grown up around the NOC, and my professional pursuits align with NOC core values. The right steps with the right people
at the right time create the lift.

Never stop lifting.

About the Contributor

Joe Jacobi and Scott Strausbaugh teamed up in the doubles canoe to
win America's first-ever Olympic gold medal in whitewater canoe slalom at the 1992 Olympic Games in Spain. Today, Joe shares 40 years
of whitewater concepts and strategies as an athlete, coach, and CEO
to help leaders and executives perform better at work and in life. His
platforms include performance coaching, professional speaking, and
writing, including his weekly newsletter, *Sunday Morning Joe.*

TRANSITIONS

By Michael Inman

For about 10 years (1984–1994), I worked as a guide for Southeastern Expeditions and Wildwater Ltd. and continued my river career on the Chattooga and Ocoee Rivers, guiding for the NOC. I first visited the NOC shortly after finishing up a three-year stint in the 82nd Airborne to attend Slim and Kent's river rescue course in the early to mid-1980s. As an Army infantryman, I enjoyed being out in the woods in all types of weather, so after I left the military, becoming a raft guide was a great transition for me back into civilian life. As a guide, making that final commitment to "go for it" by peeling out of an eddy and entering a challenging rapid was akin to parachuting out of an aircraft at night. You are committed all the way. The feeling of euphoria after getting through the experience is fun to share, and as a river guide, I loved introducing folks to something they may not have ever done before.

During the time I was working for Dave Perrin on the Chattooga River as a guide, we had a former Green Beret, a Navy SEAL, and a paratrooper on staff. Cold rainy day on the river? No worries. These guys had the natural ability to get everyone's morale sky high. We were all embarking on a wonderful adventure, and heck, we were planning on getting very wet anyhow! The guys I am referring to were not macho ducks. They had a charisma and chemistry with our rafting guests that made everyone feel like a coconspirator in this great adventure that those poor souls stuck in offices down in the cities could never imagine!

For me, one of the things that distinguished being a guide at the NOC was that Payson Kennedy would do all the grunt work that would be expected of myself or any other guides, things like washing dinner dishes for staff members and scrubbing guest toilets and showers. In my professional guiding career, I've worked for a number of outfitters on the Chattooga, Ocoee, and Gauley Rivers, but I've never once observed the other outfitter honchos doing this type of menial labor down in the trenches on a regular basis like Payson did. That selfless work ethic made Payson one of us, and to me and the other staff members, that was one of the big differences between working as a guide for the NOC rather than any of the other top companies in that era.

Working for various outfitters, you get a good sense of when you are with a solid group that runs trips that are as safe as possible. While there are definitely a number of reputable companies, you'd have been hard-pressed in the late 1980s and early 1990s to find a better-prepared trip per capita than a Section IV NOC commercial rafting trip. The Nanty and Ocoee were usually very crowded, so I favored the Chattooga because it afforded more of a wilderness experience. As a whole, the staff I worked with at the NOC on the Chattooga River under the leadership of Dave

Perrin was the most competent, professional, and safest group that I ever had the honor to work with on any river. I had worked at other regional outfitters, and while they were solid, the NOC was operating on another plane.

The guides I worked with at NOC Chattooga were very informative and understood how to communicate effectively with their guests. We always kept it light and set the tone with the guests, but just underneath that happy vibe there was always a well-oiled and serious machine operating. When there was a mishap on the river, I always knew I could count on my colleagues to be the most highly trained and prepared people around.

At that time, I also had already been a guide for Class-VI River Runners on the Gauley and discovered that we NOC Chattooga guides were highly regarded by many of the West Virginia outfitters because of our ability to read water and improvise, as well as our high safety standards. Not to take away from some of the great river pros at other companies (I enjoyed working for Southeastern Expeditions, Wildwater Ltd., and the NOC, what some of our colleagues would refer to as the triple crown), I still believe that the average NOC guide during that era was the gold standard for safe, competent professionalism on commercial river trips. I'm proud to have played a teeny-tiny little role in the history of the NOC. Mostly I treasure the loyal friendships forged out on the water every day.

 ## *About the Contributor*

Michael Inman served for three years as a paratrooper in the US Army's elite 82nd Airborne Division. From 1984 to 1994 he worked as a guide for several different river outfitters, including the NOC. While he was guiding, he attended Ringling College of Art & Design as an illustration major, finishing in 1991. These days he works as a background painter and concept artist for the major animation studios. With a taste for adventure, he spends his weekends as a whitewater river guide. He is also an adjunct professor at Kennesaw State University.

UPPER NANTAHALA, 1974

By Florrie Funk

Friends together late at night
lean into one another in that space
between college and the world.
Conversation spirals down like petals after a storm.
Someone draws forth
from the communal spring of random ideas
this one: to crowd into a car and drive
the narrow winding road up the gorge.
Wheels crunch on the gravel of the turnout.
Doors thump shut.
Sound is absorbed by a forest
that rises invisibly up the steep slopes on either side of us
toward a swath of beneficent summer sky.
Laughing, touching,
skidding on bare calloused feet
down the bank toward the sound of tumbling water,
T-shirts and torn jeans piled on a smooth rock,
stripped down to immortal youth, we slide
into the icy black pools,
into the deep places between cascades and boulders.
We breathe sharply, treading water among
imagined speckled fishes.
Then, back out on the smooth rock,
we lie against its memory of the afternoon sun.
We look up at the stars and read in them
a hundred glorious tales of a future that
waits for us with open arms,
that will welcome us just as we are:
unadorned and smelling of fern and spring water,
draped around by purple raspberry flowers
that glow faintly
from the star-shadows
on the riverbank.

In this one summer night we each
store in the coffers of our memories
enough dizzying freedom to last,
if managed wisely,
at least a modest lifetime.

 ## *About the Contributor*

See page 102 for more information about Florrie Funk.

LEARNING TO LEAP

By Arlene Burns

M y roots with the NOC began in the early 1980s at the Chattooga Outpost. I was part of the migration from Wildwater Ltd., which included Dave Perrin and Scott Kolb. Considering that beginning, it is a miracle that I ever escaped the Chattooga's lure.

I thought I knew how to kayak, but I quickly learned from the great boaters of our time that there was much yet to learn, techniques more precise and efficient to move through fluid time and liquid space. The NOC was the ultimate adult summer camp, an ever-evolving tribe of inspired, passionate, athletic beings. Always game to immerse in nature while aspiring to the highest level of safety and skill. We lived together in an infectious community in a form so rare in this modern world. We collectively shared our passions with the clients and honed all life skills, perhaps with the exception of saving money—neither abundant nor prioritized as our basic needs for food and shelter were provided as part of the package. Payson's experiment in community was well under way.

Those seasons on the Chattooga are my roots, lucky me. As a kayaker, I most loved to safety boat or photo boat or otherwise guide the black rubber barges down the very bedrock of Appalachia. Folds of folded folds in solid rock, made precious by heat and pressure and eons of flow sculpting holes through folds. The Five Falls, with its mysterious underbelly and different character at various levels, kept us alert as we navigated it. Learning the dance of ropes and knowing that people's lives might depend on nailing that throw. Bonds between guides were woven with threads from our life lived on the river in her many moods. The fabric was rock solid.

Some stayed year-round and hunkered down for the cold and quiet winter in Wesser or Long Creek. Others followed the seasons like migratory birds, to our wintering grounds in ski resorts and along the earth's liquid arteries in the wilds of the world: Chile, Ecuador, Costa Rica, Panama, New Zealand, Nepal. Stories trickled back into our summertime conversations, a fresh waft of heroic tales, of perspective and experience that made our lives richer, our world smaller, and me excruciatingly curious.

After my first season, a quiver of Chattooga guides was aiming for New Zealand. Intrigued, I applied and got a work permit as a river guide! I arrived to be told that no way I was working. They had mistaken Arlene for Arlen and assumed I was a guy. "Women have never guided rafts here, never will!" they said. I was devastated. The irony was that I was actually holding NOC-honed skills and experience that had not yet arrived in the Kiwi Wild West train wreck rafting industry.

As a concession for not hiring me, they invited me to join a rafting trip. I was not even given a paddle but instructed to scream and bail like a good Sheila. I was doing my best at bailing, anyway, and at some point we pulled out to portage Tree Trunk Gorge, aptly named for the logs sticking out from a very narrow chute through the volcanic rock. Definitely a portage! I was perched on a buttress overlooking the scene when the owner of the company hit a rock and was ejected. He swam to shore. A raft with eight people and no guide was heading for the falls, with no clue of what was ahead of them. Instinct honed in the Chattooga's Five Falls compelled my leap into the river. I swam to the raft, got on board, and took the helm. At this point we were on the bubble line of the eddy between certain death and safety.

Obviously we made it to shore. Just.

The owner approached, dripping wet. "Do you want to work tomorrow?"

As fate would have it, on the same trip I met a group of kayakers including David Allardice. A few of us loaded into his van and headed to the Bay of Plenty to hang glide. Eventually, I did return, and David and I guided in the North and South Islands until curiosity propelled us to leave the English-speaking world and meander through Southeast Asia. Our compass pointed to Nepal with hopes to hook up with the NOC clan.

At last we had arrived in the enchanted Kingdom of Nepal. The NOC had a scheduled trip that I hoped I could tag along on, but upon arrival I got a letter from Payson, explaining that the trip did not fill and that they could not send any guides over from the States for only two people. Would I like to lead these two on a 30-day trek to Everest Base Camp and down the Sun Kosi River, leaving in three weeks? I felt a surge of adrenaline and loyalty as I read his words. Payson believed in me and trusted me far more than I trusted myself.

The NOC had standing contacts in Kathmandu that would help organize the trek, and somewhere in the maze of Kathmandu was the NOC's rafting equipment. We met up with the local trekking agency, which assured us that everything we needed would be waiting for us upon arrival at the airstrip in Lukla. In the meantime, I found the raft and had

Arlene chatting with local children

Sometimes getting to the river is as challenging as going down the river.

time to do a scout trip on the Sun Kosi. The raft had been stored in very humid conditions, and the glue that formed the chambers had failed. When we inflated it, large tumors erupted all over the raft. We soon discovered that the very special glue was not available in Nepal, so we had to get some delivered disguised as luggage from someone heading to Nepal, just a few days before the trip started.

The two clients finally arrived. They had been a couple until the night before in Bangkok, and they arrived with no intention whatsoever to even speak to each other, much less share a meal!

We arrived in the Everest region to find no Sherpas waiting for us, no guides, no gear. We got a message that in a few days they would meet us with the gear, when another trip returned. So off we went. . . No porters, no cook, no tents, and with a couple who were no longer a couple.

Fortunately, the nature of the region is such that we could stay and eat in lodges along the way, so we did until our staff caught up with us. The trip was a success, and one of the clients even became a doctor in Kathmandu, where we shared a house for several years.

This was just the first of what became a decade of trips in my new home of Nepal, with great characters from the NOC family becoming part of the tapestry of the experience. Payson and Aurelia, Bob Beazley (Beaz), and Nick Williams usually arrived at the tail end of the monsoon. Every year, the monsoon rains transformed the rivers, while also cleansing the beaches of human excrement and depositing much-needed firewood. Where landslides scarred the mountainsides, the river was predictably choked with debris, keeping us alert to the dynamic character of Himalayan rivers. I remember so fondly the many long trips, moving via our own means from the high peaks of the Himalayas down the drainages, on rivers small and growing larger, camping on sandy beaches, interacting with the flow of humanity that emerged from dense jungle shortly after arriving at camp.

The locals we interacted with became like family over the years, adding a rich element to our experience. Down, down to the plains with crocodiles lurking in quiet eddies, tall grass holding tigers and rhinos and elephants.

The fortunate folks who joined us could not help but be transformed by the place, the gentle people, the stunning beauty, and by our time together. On these long trips, we shared stories and read books aloud, huddled around a fire or in a big tent. Night after night we took turns reading Maurice Herzog's *Annapurna* while snuggled on the flanks of the ridge. Drinking chai, of course.

Whenever we put in on a confluence, especially on the Kali Gandaki, we had to prepare our clients for seeing a cremation or even dead bodies in the river, as all of Nepal's rivers are tributaries to the Ganges, the mother of all rivers. Confluences are particularly sacred. Every river runner knows that too.

A yearly flow of NOC guides would join us on great adventures into the mountains then down one of a variety of

Wherever she went, Arlene always made lots of local friends.

fine rivers: the Sun Kosi, the Marsyangdi, the Seti, the Trisuli, the Kali Gandaki, the Arun, or the Karnali.

These gave fodder for further exploration, like when Greystoke (Dan Dixon) and I hitchhiked to Tibet in 1986 with our kayaks, or when Beaz and the gang headed to Bodh Gaya in the deluxe (nonexistent) bus. We immersed in what became decades of perpetual once-in-a-lifetime trips. Then we added Project RAFT and the rallies in Siberia, Nantahala, and Costa Rica. The NOC held the standard as true professionals.

I think back to that leap into the river in New Zealand. That leap has been a bit of a theme of my path. Leap before fully assessing the situation and hope it forms in midair. There is that poignant moment when leaping is just the right move. That is what the NOC and my fellow guides sculpted in me. That discernment of circumstance, to be tuned in body and mind while surfing the edge. That fine line of focus and fluid freedom when you tune into energy and become the river itself. And now we have a template for life itself. When obstacles arise that limit direction, there are other ways to flow. Water only needs gravity to find flow.

Over the years, the family has grown, morphed, reproduced, and transplanted itself to other areas of the country and the world. The tribe itself ripples through time and space and generations.

We were weaned on Payson's vision of community, of sharing nature and adventure with our friends and clients. Whatever has become of each of us was

Aurelia Kennedy, Payson Kennedy, and Slim Ray carrying their gear to the put-in for an exploratory run of the Arun River in Nepal

formed and forged at the NOC. How is it otherwise that a river guide like me became a film festival director and now a mayor?

Like salmon, after years away, we all make our way back to the place we were hatched. That is the NOC.

About the Contributor

Arlene Burns became part of the NOC tribe in the early 1980s, working mostly on the Chattooga River and teaching kayaking clinics. Her lust for travel landed her in Kathmandu in 1984, where for the next several years she led the NOC's Nepal trips. Also involved with the Baylor School's Walkabout, she has returned to the Chattooga Outpost most years since the mid-1980s to accompany the graduating class down Section IV. In more recent decades, Arlene has worked in the film industry, including one Hollywood gig on *The River Wild,* and a decade of TV work on outdoor adventure series and specials. She has directed two film festivals (Telluride Mountainfilm and BLUE Ocean Film Fest) and now produces and directs documentary film projects. She is now mayor of Mosier, Oregon, where she incorporates all the skills she developed while river guiding to manage her little town and is currently fighting oil trains.

A SON'S TRIBUTE TO HORACE HOLDEN

By Howard Holden[1]

M y earliest memory of whitewater is 50 years old and not to be trusted. It is colored with sights and sounds accumulated decades later as an NOC guide and embellished by countless retellings of the first trip my parents, Horace and Jody Holden, took down the Chattooga River with friends Aurelia and Payson Kennedy.

It was in late September 1965. I was 4 years old, so words like *US 76 bridge* or *the border of Georgia and South Carolina* meant nothing to me. All I remember is the late summer sunshine slanting through the steel skeleton of the old bridge, dragging an air mattress across the sand, imagining the fun of riding the Chattooga's current. And the Kennedy family. No doubt it was John Kennedy—then 6 years old and therefore worthy of my admiration and trust—who filled my head with fantasies of floating. It was John; his older sisters, Cathy and Frances; and my big brother, Charlie, whom I longingly watched splashing and playing in the river, for I hardly ventured past being knee deep, having just learned the first and most cruel lesson of river-running: water is cold. I suppose I was satisfied, if not exactly content, to play on the beach with 3-year-old Stewart Kennedy, under Aurelia's watchful eye.

On that late Sunday afternoon, as the sun dropped below the mountains and the sky grew red on the Georgia side, Aurelia piled the six kids into the van and readied for the 120-mile drive back to camp. Yet, as we kids lay about the van drifting in and out of sleep, our driver had ample reason to be frightened and alarmed. Her husband and two of her best friends were stranded somewhere upstream of Bull Sluice, in an unfamiliar wilderness with little to keep them warm.

Good river information was hard to come by in the early 1960s. Probably fewer than 100 people had canoed what we now call Sections II and III of the Chattooga in any craft more modern than a dugout, and they were scattered and unfamiliar to each other. Dad had obtained some notes from a camp director in North Carolina, but he lost them before putting in.

Names and landmarks became confused. They unwittingly added a significant part of Section II to the beginning of the trip, then spent a few hours at Earl's Ford helping some folks unstick their Jeep from the riverbed. They had no idea there remained 13 miles of Section III at low water to paddle in just a few hours.

---

[1] This essay was adapted from an article in *NOC Newsletter*, "The Visionary Who Likes to Start Things," edited by Gene Smith.

This story appeared in John Lane's book, *Chattooga: Descending into the Myth of Deliverance River* (Athens, GA: University of Georgia Press, 2005):

By 3 p.m. Payson and Horace figured they weren't far from the Highway 76 bridge. It was only in retrospect that they realized how wrong they were.

"We weren't strong paddlers and we all found some of the rapids hard to scout," Payson explained. . . . They portaged some rapids. Some they stood and studied a long time before running. Payson remembers that one they studied was what would later be known as Second Ledge, which back then looked a lot worse than it is now.

By the time it was dark, they were only through what is now Eye-of-the-Needle, still 6 miles above US 76. They ran some of that stretch of the river—including a rapid called Roller Coaster—in the dark. They decided to stop for the night, not knowing what was below. Payson had matches in a bamboo match case and some extra clothes. They lay by the fire all night. First light, they went downstream and found they were above Painted Rock, the Class IV known in the early days as Keyhole. When they reached Bull Sluice, they portaged that Class V and made contact with a search party headed upstream.

Later they learned that Aurelia had waited at the highway crossing until dark and then walked upstream and seen Bull Sluice. "I knew all the paddlers had good sense and would hear the rapids," she said. "I was calm and I had a lot of faith in their ability." Still, she went to the sheriff's office and told them they were missing on the river when they did not show up. The search party assumed they were hurt, and Aurelia took the kids back to Atlanta that night. She actually went to school and taught the next day, not knowing the fate of the Chattooga adventurers.

Not everyone shared Aurelia's calmness. My grandfather, a federal magistrate in Atlanta, called out the National Guard. They were about to launch a helicopter search when they received word that the paddlers were safe. My big brother's clearest memory is of being called to the principal's office on Monday to be told his parents were alive and unhurt. He shrugged his shoulders, never having known they were in any danger.

Yet, if the Kennedys and my parents were undaunted, they were changed by their experience. They learned from it and others. In 1966, on a different North Georgia river, bad information resulted in a boy's death by exposure.

My father was quite disturbed by that death, and soon after called a group of his paddling friends to our house at Camp Chattahoochee. "How can we participate more safely in whitewater?" he wanted to know. "How can we promote and enjoy our sport and prevent needless deaths and injury? What ways are there to spread information and develop skills and awareness?" His concerned reaction was the seed that grew into the Georgia Canoe Association (GCA).

By the time the GCA was well established, the Kennedys had moved away from camp. Our family stayed active with the GCA, hosting meetings at the camp and taking occasional river trips, but keeping the camp and school going took lots of time, and Dad's ideas took up more. He started a tennis club on the property, and even built a 100-foot AstroTurf ski hill, complete with a rope tow—the first of its kind. The Kennedys spent many more weekends paddling and, together with Doug Woodward and Claude Terry, ran a very active Explorer Scout post and a Boy Scout troop. Some of the Explorers—John Kennedy and Michael Terry, to name them—became world-class paddlers in their teens.

The GCA soon promoted paddling through instruction, a newsletter with information about rivers, weekend and day trips for specific skill levels, and a white-water resource library. Over the weekend of July 4, 1969, Dad chaired the first whitewater races held on the Nantahala River. That annual event grew to become GCA's Southeastern Championship Canoe and Kayak Races.

For the first year or two, most of the racing took place on the upper half of the 8-mile run. The first slalom course was at Delabar's Rock. As racers improved, the slalom moved to Patton's Run, and in subsequent years, the focus was on Nantahala Falls, and the GCA rented room number one of The Tote 'N' Tarry Motel, just downstream of the falls, for its race headquarters.

"After the third season of races, I went up to the Tote 'N' Tarry Motel one fall Friday in 1971 with the intention of talking to Mr. Vincent Gassaway, who owned the motel complex, café, service station, and combination gift shop/general store," Horace Holden said. He took along a blank Camp Chattahoochee check, a typewriter, and carbons and checked into room number one.

The next morning, he ran into Mr. Gassaway. "You've never thought about selling this place, have you?" Horace asked. Mr. Gassaway allowed that circum-stances had led him to consider just that, and asked if Horace might also want the 90-acre farm off Wesser Creek Road.

"After looking around, I sequestered myself in room number one and drew up a contract to purchase the complex on the river and the farm from the Gas-saways." Horace presented Mr. Gassaway with the agreement, both parties signed, and Horace made the blank check out for $1,000 in earnest money. They agreed to close the deal in May of 1972 with the first of 15 equal yearly payments coming from funds made at Camp Chattahoochee.

That summer, Horace hired Payson and Aurelia to run the motel, restaurant, and store on the Nantahala. Most of the employees—including the Kennedy kids and my 14-year-old brother, Charlie—were members of an Atlanta-based Explorer Scout post that the Kennedys led with paddling friends from Atlanta.

When summer ended, The Tote 'N' Tarry Motel, the restaurant—basically the entire operation—closed for the cold season, as did most mountain tourist attractions in those days. Payson and Aurelia brought their family back to Atlanta, but over that winter they decided to make their home at the Nantahala. Naturally their influence over the organization began to increase as they became permanent residents.

As the Nantahala Outdoor Center took shape over the years, Payson feels Horace Holden's continuing contributions were expressed in two ways. "First, Horace's role is primarily as a visionary, as a person who can have all kinds of new ideas and dreams."

And second "was his willingness to share the ownership of NOC," Payson said. "I think it's important to realize that initially he had sole ownership. We were just working for him as managers the first year. It was when we moved up here the second year that we became partners, and it was March of 1974 when we became incorporated and several people who were working here at the time acquired stock."

My father, Horace Holden, has always been restless. He always liked starting things more than running things, and often my brothers and I had to rein his youthful heart in. We have talked him out of an awful lot of projects and purchases, and he still wears us out with his endless ideas.

Looking back now, if we had known what he was up to, I wonder if we might have tried to talk him out of buying the Tote 'N' Tarry and starting the NOC. Thankfully we did not. We were young then, and the NOC helped make us who we are now.

 ## *About the Contributor*

Howard Holden is the second son of Jody Holden and NOC founder Horace Holden Sr. Howard grew up at Camp Chattahoochee in Roswell, Georgia. He first worked at NOC as a 14-year-old dishwasher and stable boy and returned in 1984 two days after graduating with a BA in English from Guilford College. Between 1984 and 1989, he was a raft guide on five rivers; a canoe and kayak instructor; and head guide, assistant manager, and manager at the NOC Ocoee Outpost. In 1989 an automobile accident left most of Howard's body paralyzed, but by summer 1990, he was at work for NOC in the reservations office, where he stayed until 1994. Since leaving Wesser, Howard has worked as a freelance reporter, computer consultant, and web designer. He lives in Decatur, Georgia.

ON THE EDDY LINE

By Greg Hlavaty

"Let's go." I clapped my hands, stepped back beside the bus, and checked the rafts stacked on top. While I tightened the ropes, a group of camp kids filed past me, their faces rife with acne, their sweating arms extending from orange personal flotation devices (PFDs) that smelled from a busy season of river use. We'd wrapped the kids tightly, and though they had yet to set foot in a raft, they were too afraid to loosen the straps. Some already had their paddles in a death grip, and I couldn't help but smile while remembering the first time I'd been on the Nantahala and how new the world had looked after dipping in that cold water. I'd come out wide-eyed and determined to return to this place, and nearly 10 years after my first whitewater trip, here I stood in the middle of my third season as NOC staff. Though I had tried to return to the city after my first two seasons, I had quit my throwaway job to return for another season by the river. The place that had healed me kept calling me when I left; it was a voice that would never quiet, much like the feedback of my teenage bands, but far less discordant. Appalachia had become a thing I thought I would never again find: home.

Stephan Hart, a veteran raft guide who'd encouraged me to stay at the NOC, leaned against the bus's front fender and watched the river. A trained botanist who had fled 60-hour workweeks in Florida, Stephan loved southern Appalachia and spent much of his time studying local flora, gaining a knowledge attained by a seeming stillness, a staying in one place that, to a modern culture bent on movement and change, may at first seem like failure. For 12 years, he had run various river trips around the Southeast, as well as the Grand Canyon, and his river experience and local knowledge set him apart from transient seasonal workers who passed through, partied for the summer, but never really connected to this place. His knowledge of place and his laid-back yet confident demeanor made him a hero of mine. He was different from people who had not given into the riparian lifestyle—happier, or so I thought.

When the last camper stepped on the bus, I nodded to Stephan. "That's all of them."

Ignoring his group, Stephan half-smiled at me then turned back toward the river. "Look who's back."

The camp kids banged paddles on the floor, a noise so loud and jarring that nearby squirrels, accustomed to human presence, darted up the adjacent black walnut tree. Even when the bus started rocking, Stephan said nothing and just watched this stranger cross the bridge over the river.

"Who's that?" I said. "He work here?"

"Not anymore."

"Old school?"

"Could say that." Stephan watched this stranger descend the bridge's far steps, turn a corner, and disappear into the Outfitter's Store. "Guess he couldn't leave the eddy."

"Leave the eddy?"

"Yeah." Stephan stared into the space the stranger fled and slowly turned to me. His eyes seemed to focus and then he smiled. "It's what we say when someone tries to leave this place to join the real world then gets sucked back in."

"That a bad thing?" The thought of spending my life in the mountains as opposed to idling in city traffic seemed more pleasant than threatening. I pictured an eddy, a calm spot behind an obstruction where paddlers can relax, and found it an apt description of why I'd sought an outdoor lifestyle, but I didn't see eddying out as defeat, more like taking control of a life badly lived. By personal choice I'd eddied out of city life, I guess, and usually I felt no shame.

Stephan glanced through the bus's open windows. Camp kids packed the vinyl seats and clamored for him to start their trip.

"Seems like a good place," I said.

"Yeah, but you spend a long time here and it's too scary for some people to get back out into the current and go back to the real world, you know? So we call it being stuck in the eddy."

Stephan had always seemed happy and at peace with his chosen work, but I began to wonder if his sense of calm, rather than being a hard-won gift from the wilderness, was actually resignation. Labeling Stephan, whom I admired, as a victim did not seem accurate, but I wondered how I would feel if I ever tired of seasonal work and one day edged closer to the current I'd supposedly fled. Though I had moments of self-doubt, I mostly saw this conflicting desire mirrored in people who expressed jealousy at my way of life and at times lashed out at my irresponsibility for not moving into a white-collar career—or as we called it, the real world.

Turning from me, Stephan boarded the bus, quieted the camp kids, and began a routine trip talk that I already knew by heart. I guessed it hadn't changed for many years. As the bus pulled away, I could hear his booming voice through the lowered windows: "What's the most important thing to do when going over Nantahala Falls?"

As they'd been trained, the kids yelled, "Smile!"

My morning's euphoria, bought by physical work and mist slow to burn off the river, had fled, and though I tried to fight the image, I imagined Stephan's weakly lifted mouth and how he likely spun the trip talk while his mind wandered into more intellectually challenging directions, places he often spoke of but would not, by his own admission, try to enter. The current there was too fast, I guess, its underwater obstructions unmapped.

The bus turned onto the far bridge and crossed the river. As I walked back to the rentals building, I hoped the morning's work would bring sweat, but instead it brought time, so I thought about the eddy, and why I kept angling into it, and why someone like Stephan had never left.

Inhabitants of the eddy move more slowly than those in the main current, it's true, and it is this slower pace of life that outdoor industry lifers often seek. In their more hurried moments, some of our coworkers would get frustrated with Stephan when he moved slowly and accuse him of working only on "Stephan time." As a manager at rentals, I first wondered at his slow movements, but even in his slowness, he always appeared just downstream of a runaway raft or on shore with throw rope in hand when a swimmer floated by. He was there when someone needed him, which is all any person can ask of another.

I used to think the eddy was where the current simply stops, so it sounded like a good place to rest without worry, but eddies are a bit more complex to the trained eye, and those who sit and look closely will notice that eddies actually move, and rather than being still, the water in them can form a slight upstream current. It's very subtle. To feel that current, you have to really stay awhile, to sit still, and for the modern person on a 3-hour river trip, stillness is an elusive quality eclipsed by the promise of thrills. Tourists come for the rapids, but those who remain often stay for the calm.

When I slowed down and looked closely, I saw that those in the eddy moved slightly upstream, slowly, in opposition to those riding the main current and seeking big waves. Lovers of the eddy have a more refined taste that requires stillness and a certain element of awareness that is not visible to neophytes. Jon Young, the famous naturalist and mentor, once said, "the quality of your awareness is directly related to your ability to sit still," and the eddy can provide the haven for such stillness. It's also the only place river-lifers can relax awhile and talk with those like them, as the current is full of people who miss out on such camaraderie, for camaraderie implies friendship, and real friendship takes time.

The truly dangerous part of the eddy is the eddy line, that liminal area where the swift downstream current and the slower upstream eddy meet. Any boat that lingers too long at this line will almost certainly destabilize and flip. People like Stephan sit firmly in the eddy, and many of the guests firmly in the current, and my foolishness and indecision about remaining at the NOC left me squarely on the eddy line. I was always trying to balance myself between two worlds, the urban and the riparian, and I was scared to commit to either place, the end result of such indecision being that I could not fully connect to my new home in Appalachia, could not fully slow down, could not fully become a riparian inhabitant.

≈≈≈

One morning I was on a bus headed for the French Broad River with other members of NOC's raft guide school. Because I worked in raft rentals, I'd never really had formal guide training, so I was looking to fill gaps in my knowledge. The guide school students were asking the instructors how they had turned a fun job into a career. Most of the students were college kids; they knew the river was just a vacation and a blip on a résumé, something to enliven conversation at future corporate mixers: "Ever tell you guys about my summer as a raft guide?" "Ooh, I'd love to do that. If only . . ."

"If only" was the source of our bus ride conversation. An older and hesitant student named Eric, probably in his early 30s, really wanted to quit his office job, and he had been excited at the prospect of guiding professionally until he heard how much it paid. I think I told him—hell, I had to tell him. Guide school glosses over economic reality, and as a recruitment strategy, it tries to sell students on promises of fun, but Eric had real problems and no safety net.

When I laid out best- and worst-case scenarios for pay, the bus quieted and Eric blinked. "Seriously?"

"Yeah."

"You really make that little?"

"I make a little more cause I'm a manager. But not much."

He looked from me to the instructors. "How do y'all do it?"

For a moment, there was silence. Maybe the students were embarrassed. From a monetary aspect, we seemed such obvious failures. Outdoor sports instructors are often idolized, but this idolatry conflicts with a cultural prejudice that places a value judgment on how much money someone earns. We make nice and act like it's not there, but if you had lived on the wrong side of that stare for as long as I had, you'd see it quite clearly. In our low-income line of work, we got that quiet stare a lot. Sometimes it's subtle; other times it's obvious, like when I asked to see a guest's waterproof iPod and he simply said, without humor, that I couldn't afford one anyway. He pocketed the device and left without another word. He was right, of course, I could not have afforded the iPod, but he missed this key detail: I had *chosen* to not be able to afford it.

When the silence on the bus grew too awkward, Cathy Kennedy, the lead instructor who'd been at the NOC since she was 15, sat forward and gripped the back of my seat. A severe introvert, she watched always and spoke little, so when she did speak, we all listened. This is what she said: "You have to learn to like being poor."

She looked at each of us, nodded, then sat back and stared out the window at passing mountains. She had seen those mountains many times before, but each time she looked upon them her eyes seemed wide like she was taking in such scenery for the first time. You might think her childlike if you hadn't seen her reset a dislocated shoulder or take charge when someone was in danger of drowning. She was no fool. Her words mattered and all of us knew it. For some of us, a conversation had ended; for me, it had just begun.

≈≈≈

When I first vacationed in the mountains, I breathed the fresh air and stood by rushing water and thought, *Yes, place fixes everything.* If I could simply live in this area, then I'd be happy. Even at 18, I'd already succumbed to the real estate sales pitch for any area that seems idyllic and connected to nature. According to this logic, habitat determines attitude and experience.

Biology textbooks distinguish between an organism's habitat and its niche. An organism's habitat is its preferred type of neighborhood, to use a human metaphor. For river people, proximity to water seems the obvious habitat, which is why so many of them have settled in Western North Carolina. Until I started thinking about such things, I assumed that place was the defining factor in this equation. If an organism has found its preferred habitat, then should not all happiness follow?

This is where niche comes into play. The same textbooks define niche, again using a human metaphor, as an organism's occupation, which is dependent on place but not solely defined by it. Take, for example, the horseshoe crab. Its niche is walking on the bottom of shallow coastal waters while feeding on a range of food items. If we were to go down the list and specify all of the things that make up the horseshoe crab's niche, probably no other organism would fit the description. A niche, then, is a function of place and action; in human terms, it's where you do your best work. This is what self-help gurus are always proclaiming: find what you love to do and then go do it.

True riparians like Cathy and Stephan have found their niche, and the very specificity of its requirements, the coming together of place and action, pretty much dictates their life path. To thrive, they have to stay near water and work; they could do something else, but they probably would not be as happy, and they would likely not be as accomplished. They knew themselves well enough to stay by the river and do not seem to trifle with endless "What if I did this?" questions.

If you take the horseshoe crab from its underwater shallows and throw it on the beach, it doesn't lose its identity. It's still a horseshoe crab, although it may be a dead one. Beaches are often littered with shells of this prehistoric creature. They are still recognizable as horseshoe crabs, but their sand-encrusted legs are drawn in over the body, a posture not too different from the depressed person who has wandered away from his most meaningful work and is doing what he can to pass the days. It's a kind of death that breathes.

To a human observer, the most valuable part of the horseshoe crab is its shell, a remnant from a time we vaguely intuit as being mysterious and possibly less complicated, but the force that imbued that shell with life is gone, and with it whatever magic attended its actions. Most people put the shell down and go back to a hurried life; there are so many things to do that inhibit reflection. Still I stood awhile, too long perhaps, with that shell in hand wondering what the creature within it had been like, what it could have been had it stayed in its niche, and if it could yet be. And more: Who chooses the niche? The will of the self or the will of God? Still I hold that shell and wonder.

There are few people I can think of who, if given the choice to create their life around a feeling of happiness, would say no. But that choice does exact a price. Most river-lifers, excepting the few bitter ones who stayed purely out of fear and a lack of direction, had taken Cathy's advice and learned to like being poor, or to paraphrase Henry David Thoreau, they had decided to be content with less rather than always wanting more. And as someone who daily took upward of $35 per person for a 2-hour raft trip, I can honestly say that our monetarily poor lives, grounded primarily in a desire for happiness and community, were for all appearances more vital than those of the comparatively wealthy, who visited the mountains for a brief salvation from their city routine. It's a value judgment on my part, I'll admit, but I think it's more than just a defensive reaction, as I have lived in both worlds. If you're going to live at all, then you have to draw a line and decide which side to live on. All of us, perhaps unconsciously, have drawn that line; the difference for most river-lifers is that they've *consciously* drawn that line and feel no shame in choosing their side. A painting where no forms dominate is static; such art lacks movement, and art that lacks movement is nothing if not dead on the canvas.

Perhaps Cathy *can* become a paradigm. She is no failure because she is where she wants to be. Though in appearance she lives the life that success-minded people flee, her life is far richer than their vacation, for hers is not a reaction to a life poorly lived. She says yes daily and the river hears. With legs like roots extending deeply into forest loam and arms outstretched to encircle friends, she must see eddies everywhere. Maybe when she shuts her eyes she feels the water and whatever is within her shift. On her best days, I hope she finds no space for regret, as the river rises each morning and carries all that evening's accumulated debris downstream.

In spite of all romantic philosophy, the truth is that being a lifelong river guide will stress the body to its limits and sometimes breaking. Cathy, like the others, has her scars. But what's better? Those who, like Cathy, live and have bodies with scars to start the story? Or those who prefer protected soft skin, unburned, but also untested? Protection from exposure lengthens life only in the biological sense; I suppose that's one type of success. My heart still beats? But what good is that beat without purpose? And why pump that blood to eyes that see no new sunrise but days, just like yesterday and tomorrow, with no new adventure?

Death too is a rock that breaks the surface, and we're all rushing toward it. Is it the fool who eddies out?

 ## *About the Contributor*

See page 45 for more information about Greg Hlavaty.

RELOCATION

By Maggie Parkes

O n a warm, clear day in June 1981, I loaded up my '69 Volkswagen van with a summer's worth of essential items; my three sons Matthew, Adam, and Jonathon; and some travel cassettes. I then headed out of Salt Lake City for the Nantahala Outdoor Center, which I'd heard of from a friend who went for the summer and never came back.

Back in those days, GPS and cell phones didn't exist. I had an atlas and a general idea of where I was headed. On our second day on the road, my van started to lose power climbing a hill in Colorado. I pulled over to let the van rest and told my boys we were just taking a break to explore the area. We limped along like this for another three days before we reached Andrews, North Carolina. I stopped to ask for directions from a very friendly older gentleman who appeared to go to great lengths to explain to me how to get to the NOC. I thanked him, bid him farewell, and rolled up my window. When my son Matthew asked what the old man said, I replied: "I have no idea." The Southern Appalachian dialect was as foreign to me as Arabic. It took me at least two years of living in the area before I developed an ear for it.

We eventually made it to the NOC in time for staff lunch at the River's End Restaurant. I had given my sons my usual spiel about how children should behave

Mike Hipsher

when in grown-up environments, and they'd promised to be good. During the course of our lunch, there was much merriment from a large group of people, and to my astonishment, a very tall gentleman picked up a very short gentleman by his ankles and shook him vigorously, apparently to extract coins from his pockets. Matt observed that it wasn't the children who needed to behave but the grown-ups. I subsequently learned that the players involved were John Worstell and Eric Reagan.

I worked at River's End that summer as a cold prep, hot prep, and occasional line cook. Some of my fellow River's Enders were Mervyn Readman, Frances Glass, Gail Shoemaker, Sue Magness, Ramelle Smith, Judy Boone, and of course Aurelia Kennedy. My sons had the run of the NOC and kept themselves occupied in ways they had never experienced living in the city. It was for them a playground with unlimited opportunities for fun. They were thriving. By the end of the summer, I had decided that the NOC and country living was the perfect environment in which to raise children.

Adam especially adapted to country life and water sports by acquiring an old inner tube from Mike Hipsher, who worked in the vehicle shop.

Adam cinched the tube together with a piece of rope, donned a life jacket and helmet, and on his knees paddled the tube down the Nantahala River from the raft room takeout to the pavilion. He became obsessed with this pastime to the point that someone took pity on him and put him in a C-1 and worked with him at the slalom gates. The rest is history.

Our summer adventure turned into 17 summers. During that time I raised my three sons; watched the building of the cabins, Kleinrath Hall, Relia's Garden, Slow Joe's, and Basecamp; and watched the demolition and rebuilding of River's End and the Outfitter's Store. Work and play really did merge for us at the NOC. I was proud and honored to have been a part of Payson's vision. It was a magical time in a magical place.

Editor's Note: Adam Clawson became a top C-1 paddler and made the US team for the Barcelona Olympics and the Atlanta Olympics.

 ### *About the Contributor*

Maggie Parkes started working at River's End Restaurant in 1981. Until 1997, she worked in the reservations office, custom programs, and finally, ran the instruction reservations office. She spent a few months working in Leeds and London, England, before moving to Austin, Texas, where she worked as an HR trainer for the Lower Colorado River Authority. She moved back to Western North Carolina with her husband in May 2016 to become a farmer.

MY ACCIDENTAL COMMUNITY

By Janet Smith

A fter a couple years of teaching overseas in dry desert locations, I was ready for a green wet landing. During my first year of teaching in the 1970s, I'd gone to North Carolina from Michigan to raft and hike on the Appalachian Trail (AT) with my brother, Paul. Remembering this trip, in the early 1980s I wrote Paul from Saudi Arabia and asked where that place was where we ended our raft trip; I found out it was the NOC. So NOC became my goal for a job the summer of 1981; I never dreamed it would become my home.

That first summer drew me into a new world: bicycling the Blue Ridge Parkway, kayaking on Lake Fontana and then the Nantahala, rafting all the rivers that the NOC rafted, and running on the AT during lunches with new friends. I read a lot while living in a room tucked away in Horace Holden's barn above the NOC's trail horses' stalls. Nights were quieter and the skies more full of stars than what I had seen while living in the Middle East. And more profound than the fun was the camaraderie.

That season led me toward a winter job at NOC and the promise of another summer of taking reservations since Allyson Gernandt took a maternity leave in the fall of 1981 when she gave birth to Eric. So, I decided I'd take just one more year off from teaching and stick around, and I worked another year for Jackie McLeod in reservations. Toward the end of that year, I proposed establishing a new position, becoming an executive assistant to Payson Kennedy and Bunny Johns. It was accepted and I loved the independence and challenge of the new position.

After being an executive assistant for a time, the Adventure Travel Department head position opened up and was given to me to pursue. Already understanding many of the intricacies of traveling abroad, I found the quest to find ways to fill the trips and make the program profitable intriguing. I jumped in with both feet. I knew I was leaving the world of education behind, at least for a while. I became a more proficient boater, found I loved camping along rivers, and many multiday water adventure opportunities came my way. For the next five years, I planned my seasons around the next adventure: sea kayaking with California gray whales off the Baja Peninsula; paddling the Usumacinta and Nahanni Rivers; traveling to Pakistan, India, Malaysia, and Sri Lanka with Bunny and the Rio Grande with Sandy Melton and Villa Brewer of Texas Water Safaris; as well as Grand Canyon trips, two of which we took in a tandem open canoe with Bunny; and Alaska's Noatak River. So much traveling and so many adventures and always with wonderful people, many of whom still live in this community I call home.

Janet Smith and Bunny Johns in an open canoe atop the big wave at Hermit in the Grand Canyon

After Payson and Aurelia returned from a Nepal Adventure Travel trip one year, Payson spoke with great excitement about the concept of the NOC becoming employee owned and those who were committed to the NOC being given the opportunity to actually own part of the company. He and I spoke about what forms commitment could take; my desire to always completely throw myself into my work and his desire to say, "I am committed to the Nantahala Outdoor Center." We agreed the love of what we do and where we loved doing it trumped all.

During a restless period, I went to Western Carolina University's graduate school and immediately put my master's in education degree to use, teaching middle school English for a year in Barranquilla, Colombia. Then I returned to the NOC and received another administrative job—and the years continued to fly by. During that time my sense of community deepened further. More marriages happened, more children were born, and inevitably tragedies struck. We were there for each other in person and spirit, and I realized the allure of living elsewhere continued to lessen.

In 1992 I married John Mordhorst. We became parents twice, and many trips involved diaper bags and car seats until we reached a destination for more water adventures. Car seats were left in the car and off we went with some very short paddles on some craft that floated. The four of us and friends with their own kids and friends who were kid-tolerant had amazing watery trips together in the Boundary Waters, the Everglades, Colorado, Wyoming, and down different parts of Idaho's Salmon River.

Life continues on here in Wesser. I did not intend to stay this long, but I would not have it any other way. It feels great to ask myself if I have any regrets and find myself responding, thinking that life is too short to live with regrets. That I love what I have chosen, my community—and not by accident, yet not with intentional foresight. What good fortune. My good fortune.

 ## *About the Contributor*

Janet Smith was born and raised in Kalamazoo, Michigan. She graduated from Grand Valley University in Allendale, Michigan, and later earned a master's degree from Western Carolina University in Sylva, North Carolina.

Before coming to the Nantahala Outdoor Center, she taught middle school in a rural Michigan community for two years and then taught abroad in Pakistan and Saudi Arabia. After traveling extensively throughout the Mideast and Europe, she came to the NOC for a summer job and stayed about 20 years. Janet first worked in reservations, then as an assistant to Payson Kennedy and Bunny Johns in the Instruction Department before becoming the department head for the Adventure Travel Department. During her years at the NOC, she enjoyed numerous water-related travel opportunities, including Alaska, Mexico, Canada, the Grand Canyon, Siberia, and Malaysia. During her last five years at the NOC, she worked as the vice president over the Programs Department. Janet then decided to return to teaching in public schools, which she continues to do today.

LUCK

By Florrie Funk

It was simple
when I was twenty-one.
I decided to fall
in love. It was time.
It was summer.
The future was opening like dawn across the ridge tops.
Your shoulders were brown in blue denim overalls,
nothing else.
I decided to love you
as if the decision were mine
alone,
as though you
were a beautiful stone that I chose
from among others
on the bank of the river
where the water rushed clear
from the heart of the mountain.
I held you in my hand. I
took you home.
Later I learned
that where the sun didn't touch,
your skin was as white as milk,
that you had deep wells of kindness,
glittering veins of anger,
that we had arrived at that meeting place
from very different sources.
What does rushing water care about its sources?
It was luck, then, those thirty years ago
when you decided to love me,
to hold me in your hand, to
take me home.

About the Contributor

See page 102 for more information about Florrie Funk.

MEMORIES

By John and Margie Zubizarreta

W illiam Faulkner's famous line, "The past is never dead. It's not even past," comes to mind as Margie and I reflect on our years in the gorge. Such are our memories: never dead, never past. As I slip toward slumber, I think about the wonderful years at the NOC and flirt with the notion of giving up the pace of professional life and homebound obligations to return to the river.

"One could do worse than be a swinger of birches," said Robert Frost, and I would add, "than be an NOCer!" From 1976 to 1982 and off and on a few years after that, Margie and I spent summers at the NOC. Margie worked grounds; worked maintenance; guided occasional rafts; and drove the truck with the trailer, stacking rafts vertically between outer slats, like dominoes ready to tip one after the other, which is exactly what happened on one occasion. But the gasps on that day were not as loud as the ones when she tried to make a U-turn with the top-heavy trailer just before the narrow curve beyond the old bridge below the original NOC store. The trailer tipped over, spilling bouncing rafts all across US 19. All of us preparing for that morning's raft trip stopped pumping rafts to clear the highway and reload rafts—even John Barbour and James Jackson came dashing out of the store; Jackie McLeod gazed wide-eyed at the scene from the main office across the pavement, and Ray McLeod dropped everything to come to Margie's rescue. No problem: a routine day at NOC.

I remember stacking rafts in the back of the flatbed truck we used to transport boats to the put-in. Two guides would pick up a raft, balance it overhead, take a running start, and sling it onto the truck, one on top of the other. I should have known better, but I took the back end of a raft one day with John Worstell at the front. Being twice as tall as I am, John tossed the raft up, the raft hit the crossbar at the end of the truck, and all I remember is regaining consciousness with John Burton kneeling beside me, asking me if I was OK after the raft bounced back, knocked me in the face, and laid me horizontal. The blow gave me a serious headache all day (but I still guided faithfully—the NOC inspired such loyalty) and prevented me from turning my head, which was a near catastrophe because the National Whitewater Canoe Championships were a week away, and Margie and I were racing to defend our previous national title in OC-2 slalom. Negotiating slalom gates without the ability to turn one's head quickly left and right was a challenge, but we managed to earn a medal anyway, mostly due to Margie's work in the stern. I also teamed up with Robert Harkness to win gold in men's double, but I confess that my stiff neck probably made me more of an albatross around his, and we won probably on the strength of his awesome skill. A forgiving and loving wife and friend: all part of my lasting NOC memories.

John and Margie Zubizarreta racing C-2 at Nantahala Falls

But like Faulkner said, the past and its memories are sometimes more than just recollections. Sometimes the past lives in the present. For example, I honestly can credit the NOC for playing a key role in cementing my relationship with Margie, my cherished wife of more than 35 years. We lived together in the block house, the white house, the brick house; we shared living quarters with John Barbour, Dennis Counts, Homer King, and others. One night of torrential rain at the Ocoee River, we even shared a tent with Alan Mandrell, wedging him between the two us so he would fit in the longest part of the tent, but he jumped out in the night and slept under a leaky picnic table because we teased him that we would probably cuddle with him while sleeping.

Today, Margie is still the love of my life, a devotion that grew unshakable as we shared countless unforgettable experiences and relationships at NOC. In fact, we married in Bryson City in the summer because we wanted all our NOC friends to be with us. The wedding party at the Fryemont Inn was an incredible gala: John

Barbour in his tailored suit; Bunny Johns and Sherry Spurlin in their finery; Robert Harkness handsome as ever; Steve Holmes doing acrobatic gymnastics while dancing; Drew and Judy Hammond eyeing each other, unaware that they would one day be sailing their boat *Maria* throughout Europe "at wine-tasting speed" (Maria, by the way, is our youngest daughter's name—is that "Center Magic" at work?); John Burton twirling girl after girl in disco patterns; Les and Susan Bechdel on the verge of a relationship that would result in marriage and their own whitewater company on the Salmon River in Idaho; the McLeods making sure their children, Michael and Heather, behaved in the ruckus; Payson and Aurelia taking in the foot-stomping glorious scene as testimony to the special community they built from the old Tote 'N' Tarry—so many fit, competitive athletes and adventurous, fun-loving people all together in celebration, all bonded in love!

Margie and I remember the late-night caving trips, returning black as coal; moonlight paddles on the river, the blue light dancing on the white foam guiding us around invisible rocks in the darkness; paddling in the snow, the river quiet and serene, a treasure all to ourselves; John Barbour's wrestle with a huge rattlesnake that took up residence under the white house front steps; my hooking a giant snapping turtle while wade-fishing with Bob Gernandt in the pond beside the railroad tracks on river left. We remember Margie, Stewart Kennedy, Bob Beazley, Nancy Pettit, and others led by Judy Hammond, practicing massage therapy by candlelight in Payson and Aurelia's newly constructed house; when I barged in, clueless after a hard rowdy day on the river, the mood was shattered, and disheartened sighs filled the room as I tiptoed out. We remember Robert Harkness's ballet lessons after long days of instruction and guiding on the river. Just imagine a bunch of sun-browned, buff NOC guides doing plies and pirouettes. We remember a bunch of NOCers piling into a van for an excursion to John C. Campbell Folk School, and also how Aurelia would lead hunts in the woods for edible mushrooms and other delights.

Always driving the NOC crowd was competition: slalom and downriver racing; outdoor triathlons; mountain bike contests; fast treks up steep mountains; ender, pop-up, and surfing duels. And when competition through sports wasn't enough, we would invent other challenges: "crotch rock," pull-up or push-up showdowns, ice cream eating rivalries, and other shenanigans to keep the evenings lively after a day on the river.

Memories. The spectacular beauty of the gorge. The ubiquitous morning mist over the river, like a mysterious blanket just over the peaks of waves. Swims in chilly Queen's Lake. Literary and other intellectually stimulating chats with Gordon Grant, now a distinguished educational leader in Asheville who even met with the Dalai Lama; Kim Fadiman, whose father, Clifton Fadiman, is a legend in academic circles; Angus Morrison, a mountain of a man who has a cultured mind to match his formidable Olympic brawn; and Billy Richards, a lawyer-turned-raft-guide with a giant heart, quick wit, and considerable learning. Just a few examples of the intellectual and professional caliber of NOC folk. They represent the accomplished lawyers, physicians, professors, bankers, real estate professionals, veterinarians, horticulturists, architects, nurses, accountants, teachers, therapists, carpenters, and other professionals who gave up their busy careers to settle in the gorge, at least for a while.

No matter what challenges the NOC may face as outdoor adventure becomes a luxury (some of us would say a necessity!) in a hectic world of instant gratification, Facebook and Twitter communication, virtual relationships, and tightening economies, I am confident that the NOC will prevail because of the magic of the place: a spirit of joy, generosity, and humane goodness that has always characterized every person and initiative that I have come to associate with the NOC for four decades. This spirit, this magic, has been at the core of the NOC's integrity and reputation. It is what drew me and Margie to Wesser in the 1970s, kept us there throughout the 1980s, and continues to sweeten our dreams and memories.

My life has become so disproportionately dominated by professional details that I'm continually haunted by Thoreau's quip in *Walden*: "We live meanly, like ants. . . . Our life is frittered away by details." One lesson I treasure from the NOC is how much simpler and more fun life was for me and Margie during our years there. I slip frequently into such reveries and fantasize about ditching academia and returning. The NOC made an indelible mark on us, and we will forever be grateful for the memories, flowing and flowing like the river in the land of the noonday sun.

About the Contributors

John Zubizarreta and his wife, Margie (Carlisle) Zubizarreta, worked summers at NOC from 1976 to 1982 and periodically after that until 1988, when they finally settled down in Columbia, South Carolina, after journeying throughout the Pacific Northwest, Canada, and Alaska. John is a professor of English at Columbia College (a distinguished Carnegie Foundation/CASE US professor of the year), and Margie is a physical therapist specializing in neonatal intensive care at Palmetto Richland Hospital. They have two daughters, Anna Ruth and Maria, who to some degree have inherited their parents' embrace of challenge and adventure. They deliberately married in Bryson City to include all their cherished NOC friends. They were multiple national champions in open canoe slalom. John was an instructor and guide, while Margie was the center's versatile handywoman, driving shuttles, working in the store, tending the grounds, guiding on the river. For them, the NOC will always be deep in the heart's core.

FAMILY MATTERS

By Heather McLeod Wall and Michael McLeod

In 1975 our father, Ray McLeod, decided to take a two-month sabbatical from his profitable job at a large corporation in Memphis, Tennessee, to live at the NOC, then a fledgling whitewater rafting company. The experience proved so successful that, in the true adventurous spirit of the 1970s, he managed to convince our mother, Jackie, to leave her life of relative comfort and move to Wesser with us, their 4- and 6-year-old children, in tow. We eventually moved into a house at Hellard's Motor Court, a 1950s-era property apparently built long before building codes had been invented. The *motor court* portion of the name was scrapped, but *Hellard's* remained, and this became our home for many years.

Payson and Aurelia's children were older than we were by a fair margin, and thus we became the youngest children at the NOC. What a childhood! We were free range before free range was cool! Summers meant playing in the creek or exploring the woods, using rafts as trampolines, and constantly preventing employees from completing their work by asking endless questions.

Our experiences at the NOC were limited only by our imagination and US 19, which we were forbidden to cross without adult supervision. Utilizing a trusted staff member, or occasionally an unsuspecting guest, we easily circumvented this hindrance. Once across this parentally enforced barrier, we made liberal use of our parents' charge account at the store or forayed into the restaurant kitchen, where a friendly kitchen staffer often facilitated our assault on the fountain drink machine. We scrounged for money that had been dropped through the slats in the floor of the changing room to repay our parents when our excessive charging habits were discovered, and to save for trinkets at the store.

Most summer mornings we'd arrive early at the center with our parents as the mist drifted off the shrunken riverbed awaiting the arrival of the dam release. If it wasn't too cold, we'd sit in the swing set, wet with dew, and watch the workings of the world as the center awoke. As 8 o'clock turned into 9 o'clock, guides began running back for last-minute forgotten items, dressed in their racing life jackets, the safety boaters decked out in spray skirts and souring paddling jackets. The ubiquitous through-hikers brought their packs with dirty laundry to the washer/dryer porch beside the swing set, reading their Kerouac as the machines churned behind them. Car doors slammed as the final guests arrived, late and panicky after spending precious minutes searching for a parking space. And if we were lucky and there was room, our dad would call us to gather our miniature guide life jackets and join him on a trip. After countless trips down the river, we knew every rock and rapid and had each of our dad's jokes and stories about the Nantahala Gorge committed to memory. Come fall, we had plenty of fodder for the required summer essays at school.

Once the season ended and the guests left, NOC staff seemed to scatter across the country and the globe, leaving only a core group to pass the winter making repairs and paddling the gates below the NOC until ice formed on their mustaches. But we knew that once people returned each spring from Telluride or Chile or Nepal, they often brought us gifts from these faraway lands. We still have a beaded necklace that supposedly came from a sacred cow in India, a pottery flute from Guatemala, and dozens of stamps and coins from around the world.

Perhaps the most generous gift we received came from Aurelia Kennedy. Part of being an NOC kid was the privilege of tagging along to practically every corner and outpost of the organization, and one of our favorite outings involved joining the horseback riding trips whenever we could. Our favorite horse was Old Rabbit, Aurelia Kennedy's personal horse, who was a bit smaller than the others and as trustworthy as they came. We would spend hours brushing him and making clover flower crowns for his head as the guests arrived to experience trail riding in the mountains. One Christmas, Aurelia took us to check on Old Rabbit in the cold weather. A note was pinned to Rabbit's stall that read: "I think that if you live at the center—sooner or later you will get everything you want. You want a horse at just the perfect time—because I am ready to give one away. I know that you will love him and take good care of him. So Rabbit is yours. Merry Christmas, Aurelia."

Aurelia's amazing gift of Rabbit meant that we had the resources to be a regular part of trail rides and work our first unofficial NOC job by playing "sweep" at the back of the group. It also meant that we began to learn responsibility by saving the money we gathered from the changing rooms for Rabbit's grain and tack supplies, which were needed even when the summer season was over.

Fall and winter was a double-edged sword; it meant that we were able to spend more time with our father, and participate in Hellard's dinner parties and large-scale snowball fights. However, it also meant that we returned to school, where local children and teachers judged the NOC community very suspiciously. We learned early in our school career that keeping home and school as separate worlds was a wise practice. Being teased for "wearing a life jacket to school" when wearing a new down vest, or seeing suspicious, scornful looks when we'd get off the bus at the NOC, was not unusual. We gradually understood that the other kids couldn't relate to stories of going camping or joining raft trips on the weekends or mountain biking on the horse trails. Eventually, as the center grew and became a source of employment, the community warmed to the hippies in their midst, and tensions began to wane.

Around the time that we both turned 12, we began working in various departments (generally repair and maintenance and the restaurant) at the center, in clear violation of whatever child labor laws existed at the time. Fortunately, this employment proved uneventful, and we benefited from being exposed to the tremendous work ethic exhibited by NOC staff. Eventually we began guiding and leading trips down the river alongside other staff.

Exposure to the many cultures and personalities that composed the center proved to be invaluable. In many ways, growing up at the center was like having 75 slightly older siblings or surrogate parents who modeled and nurtured in us an appreciation of the natural world and a sense of joy about working in a tight-knit community with a common purpose. When we remember the center, our memories always come back to the constant laughter and stories of the remarkable people who made up the essence of the NOC at Wesser.

About the Contributors

See page 126 for more information about Heather McLeod Wall.

Mike McLeod worked on river staff through college before moving, oddly enough, into a career in law enforcement. Mike continues to live in the area and involve his wife, Whitney, and daughters, Abby and Adison, in adventure sports. Despite cutting his hair short and shaving every day, Mike still refers to the NOC using the pronoun *we*.

By Betsey Lewis Upchurch

I had recently divorced and didn't have much of a social life, so when I went on an NOC raft trip with a youth group and one of the guides asked me out on a date, I was flattered and also ready to move my life forward. Soon after, I garnered a job as a guide and moved my three small children to Wesser. They were not wild about moving away from their friends, family, and neighborhood. There weren't any kids their age among the staff children, and there were no local kids who lived anywhere near us. They were used to being in a neighborhood with kids their age and having ready playmates. I regularly got a scowl, and my youngest asked every day, "Why did you have to move us to the stinky old mountains?" They were often lonely, and while they loved the freedom of wandering the woods and streams, it was a very hard adjustment.

One of the biggest concerns I had was moving my kids to an area where there was little opportunity to be exposed to the larger world we live in. My job barely paid enough to feed them; travel was out of the question. Even though the staff regularly

The Russian team (photographed by Villa Brewer)

traveled in the off-season and brought back slide shows and tall tales, little kids were not often included in the reminiscing. For this reason, growing up at the NOC was both wonderful and hard; you could be surrounded by interesting and caring people yet still be lonely. There were limited resources in some ways, and there were limitless opportunities in others.

When the NOC hosted Project RAFT's Nantahala '90, the festival started with a parade and gathering in a park in Bryson City. My kids fanned out, and while I was attending the first aid tent, they managed to make friends with various international groups, some of whom spoke no English. Having come from a big city, where you had to keep an eye on your kids every moment, I was always a bit nervous when I couldn't see them. When they showed back up at the tent to introduce me to those they had met, I was astounded. They had managed to meet various competitors who seemed very glad to know them. Little English, lots of smiles!

A couple of days later, my 9-year-old, Chip, walked out of the house with his chess set. I asked him where he was going and he said, "I'm going to play with my Russian friends."

Every day after that, I found him playing chess on a stump in the parking area with the Russian team members. Chip was only 9, but they treated him like an equal. They taught him chess moves and listened to him talk away in English, which they understood very little of. I watched his skills grow, but more important he seemed to belong in a way that had been missing for him. He found a place for himself that week and understood for the first time that he had the power to engage with others, whether they were like him or not.

That weekend, my doorbell rang. When I answered it, there were four members of the Nepali team. They asked, with big smiles on their faces, if Will, my 10-year-old, could come with them to play. He'd met them at the parade and with little language in common formed the bond of boys who love to play in water. He walked out to go raft the raging Nantahala that huge rains had formed that week. He was competent in whitewater, but was he as competent to manage with a bunch of young men who were likely to take risks beyond his physical ability? I tried not to worry. When he arrived home wet, tired, with a huge smile, and four hungry partners in adventure, this relieved mother fed the whole gang.

Twelve-year-old Brooke was more problematic for me because she had befriended the French team and had a mad crush on those sexy athletes! I was a bit worried, so I hung out near them to see how it was going. Without being inappropriate, they were kind to her and made her feel like a queen, when she had been feeling a bit awkward and uncomfortable with the new braces on her teeth. I don't know what they talked about or how she understood much of what was said, but she and another young girl got their first taste of attractive male attention that week. She took on a new self-confidence after that. It was good to see her begin to smile again.

That event changed my kids. It was the beginning of their understanding that there was a great big world out there and it was populated with some very interesting people. They were so happy that week to have new people to learn about

Another family raised at the NOC. From left: Ben, David, Anne, Abby, and Dave Perrin. All have worked at the NOC.

and to relate to. That exposure to different cultures would never have happened anywhere else in Western North Carolina. Project RAFT was created to expand people's understanding across borders and to help bring peace to the world. For my kids, it was all that and more magical than I had ever dreamed it would be.

After that, they began to reach out to the other kids at school more. They were more interested in hearing the staff's stories from the off-season. They began to see themselves as having a place in a world beyond their neighborhood, and I heard far less about "the stinky old mountains."

That experience carried over into their adulthood. They now have jobs that serve others: one in law enforcement, two in the medical field. They see differences in race, nationality, beliefs, and religion as a basis for learning about something new. They are confident and meet others with curiosity and acceptance. I believe the seeds of their acceptance and curiosity about all people were sown that week.

About the Contributor

See page 119 for more information about Betsey Lewis Upchurch.

By Jennifer Holcombe

I was born into a whitewater family. My father, Jim Holcombe, had multiple first descents on many rivers up and down the East Coast, which are now known as premiere whitewater runs. My mother, Cathy Kennedy, is part of the founding family of the Nantahala Outdoor Center. From my grandparents on both sides to my parents, being outdoors and on whitewater was part of who we were and our heritage. So it's no surprise I grew up in and around the NOC.

I was born at home in room 5 at Hellard's, which was one of the Brown Houses in staff housing. I remember my first personal flotation device (PFD) was yellow. My mother used to hike with my brother and me into the Five Falls on the Chattooga. When we reached the river, the rule was we had to put on our PFDs, so if we fell in we would float. Some of the other rules I remember include the following:

1. There were specific people at every outpost we could go on the river with if we were not on our parents' trip.

2. We had to listen and follow the directions of every guide or employee we were with. If they said it was too busy and we needed to go somewhere else, we had to.

3. I was not allowed to spit on anyone but Eric Nies and that was because he would spit on me first.

4. We could not spray any guide with the hose above the knees.

5. In middle and high school, when we needed rides home from town after practices in the summer, we were supposed to walk to Joe and Kate's Laundromat to see who was doing laundry and catch a ride to the gorge with them, or we could catch a ride on the Smoky Mountains Railroad. The ticket agents knew both my brother and me. Sometimes we got to ride the engine. They would stop at the NOC on the way up the gorge and drop us off.

6. We were not supposed to curse, and if we did repeat one of the words we heard, my mother would tell us the real meaning of the word and ask if that was what we actually meant to say.

When the NOC had Raft Room parties, my brother and I would hang out with other kids. We'd play on the rafts, run around until we got tired, and then we'd head to Dad's van or Mom's truck and go to sleep in the beds they'd set up for us in the vehicles. My mother has a picture of me at one of these parties: I'm in a sleeping bag with my head in her lap, sound asleep. I was about 4 or 5, I think. I don't know how old I was when someone first streaked through the party, or changed into nothing but

Three generations of raft guides. From left: Cathy Kennedy, Payson Kennedy, Aurelia Kennedy, Andrew Holcombe, and Jennifer Holcombe (photographed by Villa Brewer)

Cathy Kennedy takes her children, Andrew and Jennifer Holcombe, through Nantahala Falls—June 26, 1984 (photographed by Villa Brewer)

a spray skirt and danced. I just remember not being surprised or thinking such things were odd. Mom just told me not to stare, as that would've been rude.

I never thought we were poor or even low income. The experiences and happiness I grew up with in this community made me rich beyond measure. Growing up, I never lacked for things to do, or when at outposts, adults to play with me. They would help me climb trees, set up rafts as slides, take me on hikes. The cooks at the Chattooga and French Broad would let me help in the kitchen. Ellie Feinroth used to take my brother and me with her to take pictures at Bull Sluice or to hike into the Five Falls for Section IV trips. When we went on vacation with my dad, it was to North Georgia or the Florida Panhandle to paddle. He'd put in for a Grand Canyon permit when I was still in the single digits of age, and we got the permit the year I turned 16. I had my birthday five days into that trip. This was also when I learned how to rig a boat and to row.

There was never a lack of being loved or taken care of, whether it was by my parents or the community that helped raise me, but as I grew older and started working at the NOC, from about 18 until 30, I did not see my family heritage at the NOC as a blessing. Many times it was a weight holding me back, or I was seen as a member of "the family," but not as my own person. Many people told me that I was only getting to the rivers that I was guiding on because of who I was and not because of my skill set. I felt I had to work twice as hard as most other first-year guides on every river just to prove myself and my skill set. Many times I was hazed, challenged, or not given the same kind of help or understanding as other guides. Some people seemed to think that I had influence I did not have or that I would tattle about things to the management at Wesser. This got especially bad once my mother became director of rafting. Because of this I learned to keep quiet, work twice as hard as everyone else, and not ask for help, as that would be seen as weak. Most of all I learned to take care of myself.

As one of the early generation of what has been described as the NOC kids, on some level, I always knew I was raised differently from other kids in my elementary school. It was definitely sinking in as I went through middle school and graduated high school. By the time I got ready for college, I joined the community that raised me as a raft guide myself.

Jennifer Holcombe throwing rope at Nantahala Falls, August 2001 (photographed by Villa Brewer)

At that time I thought that this was something I would do as a summer job through college. I was still planning on being a history major and becoming a teacher. Little did I know then that what I had grown up thinking was normal had had such an influence on who I was, what my goals in life were, and what I wanted to do.

From my childhood I had learned to take care of those around me, to work endlessly hard, to value being able to support myself on only a shoestring budget. So when I started guiding at NOC, I was willing to work any job, from cleaning bathrooms, mowing lawns, doing dishes—anything to get hours and make a paycheck.

As I moved from guiding to management, I tried to support and take care of those who worked for me, just the way I'd seen others do at NOC as I was growing up. I tried to constantly put myself between the staff members who worked for me and the politics that sometimes interfered. I worked to help the staff succeed and to foster a protective, open environment. This was the behavior I had seen from the managers as I grew up at the NOC, and although the NOC culture was shifting as leadership changed hands, I still tried to live by "old NOC" values. The departments had been like a family, and the families took care of each other and supported the other departments. Even after I left the NOC, I took this philosophy with me into the world of outdoor programming at a university.

Now at 32, I know I want to live in a community like the one I was raised in. Where members are like a family. When someone loses everything, people step up to help; if you need help or support, it's right there. A village raises the kids, knowing that no matter what happens, they will be taken care of and loved. Because of the NOC, I know that family is both genetic and something more than that. I am now proud of who I am and my family heritage. I am a proud part owner of the company I grew up in. It is my heritage and it helped make me who I am. I am able to chase my dreams and will work ceaselessly to reach them because of the people who raised me.

 ## *About the Contributor*

Jennifer Holcombe worked at the NOC 1998–2013 in the photos department, group adventure programs, and as a raft guide on multiple rivers. She graduated from Appalachian State University with a degree in recreation management and was coordinator for adventure programs at Illinois State University before leaving to pursue an MBA.

SECTION VI
Early Leaders of the NOC

HORACE HOLDEN: AN APPRECIATION

By John Burton

Author's Note: Horace Holden has had a rich, interesting, and varied life, built around his family and his passions for people, theology, outdoor adventure, sports, youth, and starting things, like businesses. He is also a marvelous storyteller. I interviewed him in early 2013 as he approached his 80th birthday. Here are some highlights of his path through all these interests. (*Name notes:* Jody is his wife and the mother of their four sons, Charlie, Howard, Horace Jr., and William.)

Why I Love and Admire Horace

Horace has had a tremendously positive influence on many people, myself included, both in direct interactions and as a result of his endeavors creating strong, value-driven, visionary, influential organizations, like Chattahoochee Camp and School, the Georgia Canoe Association (GCA), and the NOC. Horace is the actual founder of the NOC, one of the three people whose values and philosophy influenced the how and why of its existence. He has been at the heart of the NOC for 45 years.

Long ago, Horace was a counselor at Camp High Rocks in Western North Carolina, another first-class adventure-learning camp, when he first ran the Nantahala in 1956 at age 22—most likely not in an aluminum boat, but in a wood-and-canvas boat that was state of the art in those days. I think we probably met for the first time in the summer of 1970, my last year as a counselor at Camp Mondamin after my junior year in college, and after I had been racing canoes internationally for three years. Horace put together the first Nantahala River slalom races, which eventually became the Southeastern US Slalom and Wildwater Championships and were always known as the GCA races. Having been on the US team and having gone to the last two World Championships in whitewater, I was thrilled to have a race on my home river. I remember Horace setting up his own mimeograph machine with carbon paper and his typewriter, in room 1 at the Tote 'N' Tarry motel, printing start lists and results, organizing everything.

I have always enjoyed and been drawn to Horace's beautiful spirit. He is almost childlike in his enthusiasm for his ideas and his next plan, and I would say often naive about what it will take to make it happen. But I have benefited in many ways from being in Horace's galaxy. His efforts nourished my racing career in the 1960s, and his founding of the GCA in the late 1960s helped grow the

Horace Holden at the NOC (photographed by Pat McDonnell)

sport and enhance its safety through group efforts to run safer trips and attend to safer gear and paddling trip practices. Of course, the main impact Horace had on me was his founding of the NOC so I could spend most of my working career in North Carolina and get paid to be involved in the sport I loved! He and Jody also raised four wonderfully grounded, charismatic, kind, adventurous boys, all of whom are friends and have influenced me as I seek to operate compassionately in this world.

My appreciation for Horace is grounded in his personal character traits. I experience him first of all as a kind person, and someone who always finds the best in people. He is loyal to a fault, compassionate, gentle, loving, and naturally trusting of people.

While he has always been a strong advocate for the little guy and the less powerful, he also (in the case of NOC staff and guests) framed his outlook in terms of what was best for the company and its core of dedicated people. On many occasions when he was questioned about a policy or issue related to programs or people at the NOC, I could almost see his mind processing the answer through the filter of, "What will be best for the most people here, for the company, and for anyone who does not have a voice in this question?"

He sees possibilities where others see the old way or what has always been there. He sees opportunities to bring together people he likes so they can enjoy each other and perhaps create something they didn't know they wanted to do together!

I think I learned some of whatever grace and kindness I have toward all kinds of people from Horace, who always accepted my redirections of his random storytelling with good humor and trust. Because we trust and like each other in a very fundamental way, it usually fell to me in meetings to rein in his stories, get him back on track, get him to "land the plane" as he digressed into vignettes unrelated to the issue at hand. I believe his motivations are honorable, unselfish, and people-centered, and he's inherently kind, loyal, and trusting.

Horace Holden: TRAVELER, MINISTRY STUDENT, HUSBAND, FATHER, AND ALLIANCE BUILDER

Alliance builder is one of Horace's amazingly consistent roles; he is passionate about bringing people together. People he likes, or he thinks should meet others he likes, or he thinks would be good at something that needs doing, or would be an asset to some venture he is involved in.

JOHN: Why did you go to Scotland in 1956, right after you got married?

HORACE: We went over there to study theology at the New College, which is not very new[1], now called the University of Edinburgh. We went over there to do graduate work, as we had both finished college. Jody was studying also; she didn't want to sit at home while I was studying, so she took some classes. At one time she was sort of leading the class, had the best grades, and made this Scottish guy sort of mad, so he studied harder and became number one.

We did that for the first year, and the second year we were going to have a baby, so she didn't go to school, and we moved out of town to a small town called Pathhead about 10–12 miles south of Edinburgh, where I had gotten a job as an assistant to a minister there. The pastor in a town not far from there had been called down from Inverness to join these three churches in the community of Pathhead. One was several miles out of town, and he needed some help. I met him for lunch. Roger Murchison, and he wanted me to meet the scout leader, a fellow named Willy Ramsey, William H. W. Ramsey.

JOHN: Now Willy Ramsey is a name I remember from somewhere!

HORACE: He's dead now, but I got him to come to the States. Willy and the minister and I made the deal for me to start after the summer, because Jody and I had plans to travel all over Europe that summer, which we did. So we returned the 15th of August, and the caretaker (the Beadle) said the minister and Mr. Ramsey were out of town, and would I take the first service—which I had never done!

I took the service, then there was a funeral, which I also did. Then the minister got sick, and I did some more services. Then Willy's father died, and within 10 days

---

[1] A mild understatement. Founded in 1582, New College is the sixth oldest university in the English-speaking world and one of Scotland's oldest universities.

the minister died, so I ended up taking over the churches. So Willy had two major losses all at once; we became good friends, even though he was 10 years older than I was. He ended up coming over to the states and went to Union Seminary with me, worked for two summers at High Rocks with me, then he worked at my camp in Atlanta. I asked Sumner[2] to hire him, saying he was a super guy, very personable, a hard worker who could fix anything, and he could hike! Sumner said he usually didn't hire folks he did not interview. So Willy flew into New York, and I went up there in my little Volkswagen and picked him up, brought him to Brevard, where Jody's from. So I took him out to meet Sumner, who was working on his truck; Willy jumped in immediately to help, showed him how to fix it, and in a few minutes showed Sumner all of the qualities he hoped for in a counselor—Sumner hired him immediately.

At High Rocks, Willy had the son of the president of Westminster School, William Pressly, as one of his campers. Willy was so highly thought of, had done such a good job with the kids, that Mr. Pressly sought him out to be his director. Willy turned him down, saying he was coming back to the States to help Horace Holden with his camp (he did theology in the winter in Scotland). That was something that just was not done to Mr. Pressly! I had been working at Westminster before I went to seminary, and Pressly asked me if I wanted to make a career out of teaching. I said no, gave up teaching there.

JOHN: Why Scotland? What was the draw there?

HORACE: In Atlanta [as a teenager] I went to the same church as Aurelia, the first Presbyterian Church. Payson would go on Thursday nights when we played volleyball, and the two of them became good friends. I'm only a year older than she is; our fathers were both elders, our families were good friends—the Holdens and the Turpins. The minister, Davison Phillips, had spent time in Scotland and was one of the first of the Presbyterian ministers to go there, to one of the four great theology schools in Scotland. I think he was the inspiration for me to connect to Scotland.

The Founding of the Georgia Canoeing Association (GCA)

At 80 years old, Horace has an amazing memory for people, names, places, and events. His active mind keeps interjecting little vignettes and memories that sometimes seem to take him far afield but make sense in the tightly interwoven labyrinth of his heart and mind. His ambitious entrepreneurship seems always to be tempered

---

[2] Sumner Williams, legendary founder of Camp High Rocks, married to Jane Bell Williams (daughter of Frank Bell, founder of Camp Mondamin in 1922).

by his heart. In his own words, this is how Horace described starting the GCA, almost 50 years ago.

HORACE: The way that all started was in response to a tragedy. There was a camp near us in Roswell that had high-quality programs in gymnastics, diving, and swimming, and an indoor pool. They also had canoes on a lake but did not have a high-quality canoeing program with experienced instructors.

It was probably in 1967 or 1968, before our first Nantahala Races. They had some kids go to North Georgia on a river, without really strong counselors. It started out nicely, it was a warm day, and I think they camped for the night. The leader was young, perhaps 18 to 19, with a much younger assistant, maybe 14. The leader decided he had to walk out and call the director to come get them, leaving the kids there by the riverbank. Two of the boys decided to try to warm themselves by sitting in the water because it was warmer in the water than out in the air. One of them drowned in about 3 feet of water; the other got severe hypothermia but survived.

That accident is what triggered the start of the GCA. That prompted me to say, "Let's start an organization that can teach canoeing and water safety and first aid and how to handle cold conditions." Payson was working for me at the camp, as was Aurelia. Payson got involved from the start, along with Claude Terry and others.

The first GCA race, which evolved into the Southeastern Championships, was 1970. Race HQ was room 1 of the motel, the old Tote 'N' Tarry, next to the office. I brought up my Gestetner mimeograph machine, paper, typewriters, and carbon paper. I was race chairman the first three years. In the fall of 1971, I came up to try to buy the Tote 'N' Tarry—it wasn't a whim, I planned the weekend to feel him (Vincent Gassaway) out and see if he was inclined to sell.

Sharing NOC Ownership

The story of the founding of the NOC has been told many times. The untold story is how committed Horace was and is to the success of both the company and the people who joined it, and how he backed up his and Payson's beliefs with action.

While there are many stories of his generosity and concern for individuals who needed a helping hand or just a willing ear, the main tangible demonstration of his values was the fact that he essentially endorsed turning the NOC into an employee-owned company, for philosophical reasons. The Kennedys and the core staff were the two main partners in the union of fairness and generosity that have defined Horace for so long, and have remained core values of the company.

Originally, in 1972, Horace was sole owner of the NOC. Very soon, Horace found himself giving away more and more of the ownership of the NOC in service to Payson's philosophy of what it took to attract the best people, provide the best service, and keep staff and guests loyal for the long haul. That is, Payson believed so strongly that owners behaved differently than employees, he pushed hard to share the ownership of the NOC with as many people as possible.

Horace, Father to Four Amazing Boys, and the Tragedy of Howard, His Second Oldest

Howard Holden, in his late 20s, was an amazing athlete, paddler, and energizing leader. At some point in his abbreviated NOC career, he was a raft guide, trip leader, lead kayak instructor, and Ocoee Outpost manager. He was one of the most charismatic, energetic, good-natured, and leader-by-example staff in the first two decades of the NOC, until his accident in the fall of 1989.

Try to imagine how you would respond to the phone call that tells you your son has had a horrific accident, is paralyzed, and is in critical condition. Then try to imagine how you would behave over the next 30 years. This is Horace's (and Jody's) story:

JOHN: Can you tell the story of Howard's injury, how you heard about it, what you did, what your involvement was, what it meant to you.

HORACE: I was in the Tree House, by the pool at camp. It was early in the morning, and I got a call from the hospital in Amarillo: "Mr. Holden, I think you should come out here. Your son has been injured in a car accident." I got some details, called Jody, who now had a house in Alpharetta, Georgia—we had separated by then. I told her we need to go out there. I had heard that his life was in serious danger, that he could die. This girl who had been on the trip had a small pickup that her parents had given her, and she asked Howard to help her drive back east.

JOHN: I had been on one of those two NOC trips that year, with Howard, Kathy Bolyn, Jim Holcombe, and Eric Nies, and the four of us drove back in the van. We had planned a loose caravan back across the country but agreed that if we got separated, we would just go on—this was before the days of cell phones, 1989. We got separated in Amarillo, and I believe the accident happened right then. In fact, it may have been literally in our rearview mirror, but none of us noticed and we just kept on driving.

HORACE: The story I heard was that at one gas stop during the long drive, the back seats in the van were occupied by the other sleeping guides, so he decided to stay in the pickup and try to sleep while she drove. There was a tape player that may not have been installed as original equipment but may have been loose—perhaps on the dashboard; this is what I heard, and I don't know if it's true or not—and she leaned over to turn it on or something, and the truck went off the road to the right. She jerked it back to the left and then to the right and it flipped.

JOHN: I think I remember she had a seat belt on and he didn't because he was trying to sleep.

HORACE: And she was fine, pretty much uninjured, but Howard ended up with a broken neck. I'm not sure how long they were by the side of the road, but they got good care from the EMTs, taking good care of his neck injury.

JOHN: I remember we just kept going in the van, heading home after two great Grand Canyon trips, young river people in the prime of our adventurous lives— they were behind us. We drove the remaining 1,200 miles of the trip knowing nothing, unsuspecting, thinking they would pull in an hour or two behind us. Before we came to a stop in the fort, beyond the motel, Bunny was there to meet us. As we opened the door to climb out, she was very somber, near tears, and we were clueless as to why. She told us of the accident and how grievously injured Howard was, and she said that the family was on the way to Amarillo and he might die. It was just a stunning revelation on top of the travel weariness—hard to process and grasp. It was an incredibly sad, scary, shocking moment.

HORACE: We spent something like a week [in Amarillo], and people started showing up—a lot of people came to see him and us. We didn't obey hospital rules about visitors; someone got balloons and put them on the ceiling so he could see them while in the halo that was securing his head and neck. He was making some progress. Horace Jr. knew a guy who was an attorney who had a house there and who opened it up to us, so that's where we stayed. After some time they took out some of the tubes; I think they may have done it too soon. After three to four days we got a call at the house: "Mr. Holden, we think you should come down here."

JOHN: Good gracious.

HORACE: Jody and I went down there. His pulse had stopped, his heart had stopped, but they brought him back. They put all the tubes back in. We came close to losing him then. I think up to that time death wasn't that close or imminent, but that was it.

We stayed out there a little while longer, maybe a total of 10 days, and my dad made arrangements—he knew the people who ran Coca-Cola, and I think they had an airplane, which went out to get him. I met him at the DeKalb Airport and an ambulance took him to Shepard Spine Center. That's where he stayed, I guess for three months. They did a good job. That's my memory.

JOHN: How's he doing now?

HORACE: He does pretty well. For a while, he went to paralegal school, worked with a lawyer. I asked him if he wanted to make this a career, working for a lawyer. He said no, that he wanted to use this to write about political, legal things. So he worked for a paper in Decatur.

JOHN: So you and Jody organized your lives from then on around taking care of him, meeting his physical needs. Did you move, change houses?

HORACE: Yes, eventually we moved to Decatur, to a place closer to the city. We remodeled the house. Jody's house was out in Alpharetta—she was still teaching at High Meadows—about 30 miles farther out of the city. When he was in Alpharetta, he had a job; he worked for the local paper there.

Author's Note: For the last 27 years since the accident, Horace and Jody have been Howard's primary caregivers, along with numerous other major players, mainly oldest brother Charlie. Howard is a full quadriplegic, with a little use of his hands, so that he can steer a motorized wheelchair and was even able to drive a specially outfitted van for a while. He remains a great friend to many of us, and an inspiration for his courage and his coping. If I get lazy or sore or winded or whiny about some physical activity or challenge, it doesn't take but a brief thought of Howard's challenges to turn my attitude around.

Horace's Legacy, in His Own Words

JOHN: You've started a lot of things: the camp, the GCA, the NOC, others. What's the thing you are proudest of in your career?

HORACE: Well, I'm proudest of the family. The success they've had, the life they've had, the joy they've brought. But, other than that, I think it would be NOC. But, one thing just led to another. I probably wouldn't have done NOC if I hadn't had the camp, if I hadn't been teaching school, going to camp. I've never even thought about it [nervous chuckle].

JOHN: Yes, what's your legacy? What do you want on your tombstone?

HORACE: I think to serve humanity. As things come along, you know, we look and say, "Is this good, is it positive, does it make a difference in somebody's life?" I think that, no matter what the outcome is, no matter what position you're in, you know, if the opportunity comes, be prepared, get education for it, get experience. All along, my teaching, giving swimming lessons, kids would say, "Mr. Holden, have you ever saved a life?" I would say, "Yes, I save lives every day teaching them how to swim."

 About the Contributor

See page 3 for more information about John Burton.

PAYSON KENNEDY: AN APPRECIATION

By John Burton

P ayson Kennedy has led the NOC, in one role or another, for all of its 45 years. He put it together, built it, gave it its philosophical and purpose-driven underpinnings, and influenced thousands of people along the way. Ultimately, it is really millions: the NOC now takes roughly 120,000 guests a year down all its rivers and has been taking adventurous folks down rivers for four decades. Go figure. That doesn't include the millions who have taken instruction, eaten a meal, bought something in a store, stayed in a cabin, or traveled around the world with the NOC. He has made a big impact.

I have had a very strong, rewarding personal and professional relationship with Payson since 1973. That was when I first wrote him about working at the NOC, having caught a glimpse of a future in which I could get paid to work in an outdoor environment with the one skill I was really good at: paddling a small boat in whitewater.

In 1971 I had taken my UNC Chapel Hill MBA to Philadelphia and found a job in the trust department of a bank, so I could train for the Olympics with my partner, Tom Southworth, who already lived there. Post-Olympics, I was drawn to the NOC. My first in-depth experience was to lead a whitewater-racing clinic in the spring of 1974 as a guest instructor, along with Tom and Les Bechdel. The three of us had been the US Team coaches in 1973, but we weren't the first racers to show up at the NOC.

My dad was an advertising executive, my older brother was an investment banker, so I took my MBA and became . . . a raft guide! Actually, I started at the NOC in 1975 as assistant director, even though we didn't have a director. Pretty quickly, and in ways that lasted 40 years, Payson took on the role of visionary, CPO (chief philosophical officer), and steadfast leader, and I took on the role of chief operator, and CIP (chief interpreter of Payson). I grew to admire him very quickly, and grew to love him and Aurelia and Horace very shortly thereafter. That admiration, respect, and love has remained strong ever since.

Payson Kennedy at home
(photographed by Pat McDonnell)

I would like to share several stories to shed some light on our relationship and why he has meant so much to me, to the thousands of staff he has inspired, to the millions of guests he has served, and to the outdoor adventure/business world of which he is such an icon.

A Man of Principles and Values, Driving the Company and the Community

Payson and Aurelia and many early core staff created a community of like-minded individuals committed to providing the best experiences possible in outdoor recreation and education. They were determined to create the highest quality of life for staff as possible. They were determined to make a positive contribution to all the communities of which they were members. And they knew they were running a business that had to be self-sustaining, so they had to make enough profit to do all those things and to provide some kind of return for those who had invested in the company.

That paragraph is actually a narrative of the NOC Statement of Purposes (see below), created in 1981 by all the staff and adhered to virtually unchanged for more than 35 years. The fundamentals of the principles, and their order, flowed from Payson's brain, heart, and soul. The wordsmithery, the details, were left to others; once the main points were in place, Payson paid attention but did not demand to have his way. The full Statement of Purposes is as follows:

PURPOSES OF THE NANTAHALA OUTDOOR CENTER

To provide the highest-quality programs in outdoor recreation and education

- To offer a wide variety of activities
- To provide high-quality equipment and auxiliary services for persons participating in these activities
- To maintain leadership in our fields with experienced staff contributing to the state of the art
- To foster in all our staff an attitude emphasizing helpfulness, personal attention, and flexibility toward our guests
- To serve the interests and needs of people of different age, sex, race, physical ability, and income level
- To provide these programs and services at a cost that represents good value to the customer as well as a fair return to the NOC

- ≋ To carry out our programs so as to be fun and educational to all

- ≋ To observe high ethical standards

- ≋ To plan and control growth so as to uphold the quality of the NOC community and programs, and to reflect NOC ideals and values

To provide the highest quality of life for our staff

- ≋ To enrich our community through mutual endeavor, trust and understanding, and open and effective communication

- ≋ To move toward complete employee ownership and control

- ≋ To operate our programs in a manner that encourages staff involvement and pride in NOC

- ≋ To provide salaries and benefits sufficient for a simple lifestyle, to link pay with profitability, and to keep a narrow range between the highest and lowest wage

- ≋ To provide year-round employment, and to use our resources to foster off-season opportunities

- ≋ To provide opportunities for personal growth for our staff

To participate actively and considerately in the larger community

- ≋ To serve the community through contributions of work and money, and to encourage and support individual staff contributions

- ≋ To respect and care for the environment and to foster environmental awareness in our guests

To earn enough profit to accomplish the first three purposes and to increase the value of ownership in the NOC

It turns out that Payson's vision, his purity of adherence to principles as laid out in the Statement of Purposes, was powerfully attractive to many—people want to be inspired by a higher purpose, and we want to believe we are making a difference in peoples' lives. He would move heaven and earth in pursuit of goals and in adherence to principles he held dear. Three examples stand out for me.

One is pretty simple. In the early days, we were still finding our way philosophically, and not always sure about which economic decisions were ones of principle. NOC staff photographers were paid an hourly wage to sit at the bottom of key rapids and shoot pictures that we would sell to our guests. Sometimes those pictures turned out to be great for a marketing brochure, slide show, or poster. Soon an experienced photographer advocated for staff being paid extra for such photo use. It seemed innocent and logical enough to many, but not to Payson. After considering it long and hard, he concluded that, as a matter of principle, people on the NOC payroll should not be paid extra for use of their photos on behalf of the NOC. In fact, it was an emotional issue for him: he actually believed that staff in the NOC family should want to have their photos used to benefit the NOC, whether they were taken on the clock or not.

I remember a meeting when it got heated, and Payson sat virtually alone in his conviction, yet he insisted and that became policy. It left a bitter feeling in some people, but he was willing to endure that for the principle. I think it fit in with his overall framework of sharing ownership with the employees, of a very flat pay scale, of fairness in a one-for-all community. I didn't feel that strongly about it, but I supported him.

The second example is about the "low" pay of the NOC. There has always been pressure to raise the pay scale, to reward returning staff, yet we kept pay low for the very viable reason that we couldn't afford more. Payson and I were regularly fighting the battle to keep our payroll expense (roughly half the total) in balance with revenues. This was pretty doable in the years we were growing, and became much harder as growth slowed.

The truth is, to be financially successful in a long career at the NOC, you had to live a pretty frugal lifestyle. This was a core value of the Kennedys, and it worked well for many. Others simply could not afford to live on NOC pay, and realized it was not the NOC's fault, just the cost of working in a very seasonal industry. (I believed in it in principle, but it was hard for me to live within my means. I liked traveling, eating in restaurants, owning a nice home, staying in motels vs. camping, and playing golf, so eventually I had to change jobs to support my lifestyle.)

The third example involves the principle of taking on all relevant challenges, which is best illustrated by the international raft rally we hosted, called Nantahala '90. In 1989 a number of NOC staff, including Payson, went to Russia to field a team in the Chuya Raft Rally. Compared to well-organized slalom and wildwater kayak races we had attended in the United States and Europe, this event was wild: all sorts of inflatable craft, many homemade, many barely recognizable as boats, but all entered to support the idea of international cooperation, peace, and understanding.

The Soviet Union had just come apart, and the spirit of camaraderie and working together was strong among those who attended the Raft Rally. The organizers were looking for a host for a follow-up event the next year, preferably in the United States. Payson saw this as an amazing opportunity for the NOC, and sank his teeth into the idea of hosting it on the Nantahala.

He came back excited to share this great idea with all NOC staff, and while many were enthusiastic, many were hesitant, some downright resistant. Many said, "We can't do it in the summer; we're too busy." (That argument resonated with Payson the businessman because the NOC made all of its profit in the summer, which allowed it to survive the other nine months). Or, "We can't do it in the fall. The water will be too low on the other rivers. No one will want to come, and we will all be too tired from the summer."

Then there was, "We can't do it in the spring. That's too soon. We don't have enough time. We'll have to work overtime. Staff will be stressed." And so on. That was the argument that Payson would not entertain. The idea of hosting the international event was too big, too important, too much aligned with the NOC's mission and place in the paddling universe for us to miss this opportunity. So, Payson argued, cajoled, and eventually won the day, much to the chagrin of many support staff who would have to make it happen.

Payson just could not reconcile the opportunity with the complaint that it would be too much work. No surprise there—he usually worked longer and harder than anyone else, seven days a week, and when he found the zone, he was unstoppable. It was a glorious feeling for him, and he wanted others to have it, whether they knew it or not. Hosting this rally, with high purpose and incredible good energy and goodwill along for the ride, would both produce and result in that feeling of extraordinary productivity and accomplishment, the holy grail of work for Payson.

And, it turned out he was right. It was an extraordinary amount of work for many people. And, it was one of the absolute highlights of their careers for many NOC staff. Competitors from many countries, including from behind the former Iron Curtain, descended on Atlanta and then the NOC and the Nantahala River, for a week of festivities, music, international camaraderie, and cultural bridge building. Despite the fact that mega-rains flooded all the rivers, including the Nantahala,

Payson participating in a log-sawing contest during Nantahala '90
(photographed by Villa Brewer)

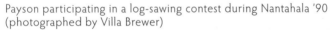

and turned the NOC parking lots into a lake, the event was a great success. It would not have happened without Payson's insisting on banding together and doing whatever it took to get the job done.

Perhaps the highlight for me personally was an emotional moment driving to Atlanta to pick up the athletes from all over the world who were gathering there for the opening ceremonies at the Carter Center. I was simply a bus driver that night, and I'll never forget the pride I felt as I and three other drivers, in big blue rafting buses with Nantahala Outdoor Center painted in white letters on the side, caravanned down the interstate into Atlanta in a driving rain storm. It was dark and windy, with rain thrashing the windows and no other rational people on the roads that March evening, and there we were sending four big buses to bring everyone back to our place. It was a magic, memorable moment for me.

Loyalty, Pride, Humility, and Excellence

Once Payson and Aurelia and their family committed to the NOC after the summer of 1972, his involvement was total. He worked seven days a week but didn't consider it work. He led by example. His vision of community demanded that he, and everyone else, do any job that needed doing. Driving buses, washing dishes, mopping floors, repairing rafts, digging ditches, cleaning motel bathrooms—this was all honorable work. Payson's faith in himself, in Aurelia and his family, and in the people he hired to work with him at the NOC was unwavering.

The most gifted paddlers, the most audacious hikers or runners or climbers, the hardest workers, the most focused leaders—these were the people he wanted to attract to the NOC. So if difficult situations arose, he was willing to trust his people and go for it. We ran tough rivers. We developed new teaching techniques. We explored new adventurous places around the world. We tried difficult climbs and hang gliding. We built challenge courses and an Alpine Tower. We repaired our own buses and rafts. We printed our own newsletters. We built our own lodging. If a job could be farmed out to an expert, Payson would ask us to see if we could do it ourselves first. If it took a little longer, or wasn't quite as neat, clean, and perfect, at least it was ours, and that was good—better than paying someone else to do it.

In fact, it became NOC legend that if a job could be done by hand, even though a machine (like a backhoe) could do it faster, Payson would argue that we should just start digging. With shovels. If rocks needed moving, we should gather enough strong backs and heave-ho until they were moved. Men and women, young and old, it didn't matter—everyone did whatever needed doing. Payson was often the first one out there, so there was no excuse for someone who thought they were above such work. If such folks made the mistake of starting to work at the NOC, or we made the mistake of hiring them, they did not last long.

Payson's Pond, the Work That Does Not Stop

Perhaps the best example of his work ethic and Zen-like pursuit of knowledge and peace is the story of his residence and his pond, on a small, extremely steep acre of rocky land adjacent to the easternmost corner of the NOC property. The land looked at the oxbow, the old riverbed of the Nantahala that was cut off by the railroad more than 70 years ago, forcing the main river flow into a new rapid, Wesser Falls. The old oxbow was a marsh that filled up (through a pipe under the railroad tracks) when Lake Fontana filled up each spring/summer.

To me, the house and pond are symbolic of him and how he went about building a company. Not flashy, not arrogant, just step by step, with total dedication to the process rather than the outcome. It's a place of great serenity, a project that has been going on for 25 years, has no planned completion date or form, and in fact cannot ever be finished. That's the point. It is there to be worked on. To deem it finished would ruin it, or at least display the dunce-ness of the beholder.

Payson and Aurelia's house, with a timber triangle foundation, balances precariously on 8-foot-tall concrete pillars at the end of the driveway. The main horizontal location requirement was so they could walk to work. The main vertical location requirement was that it had to be built above the Tennessee Valley Authority (TVA) floodplain of 1,723 feet above sea level—the problem being that the ground leading to the area, which became the driveway, was at about 1,705 feet.

Payson and John Howey, perhaps his oldest friend, came up with a foundation plan that resulted in a number of tall, poured-concrete pillars holding up a quartet of triangular trusses made of very long 3-by-12-foot rough-hewn timbers. This gets the first floor to exactly 1,723 feet, so the TVA signed off on it! The house is mostly wood and glass, with a beautiful stone fireplace and an outdoor shower, and it sits next to a waterfall.

The land above the house is so steep that it must be protected from careening boulders by a stout chain link fence.

Framing Payson and Aurelia's house (photographed by Villa Brewer)

How do you get the concrete up the nearly vertical hillside to the fence line above the house? No problem—you carry it up in buckets. Or, Payson and other family members do. How do you dig the holes for the concrete footers holding those posts in the rock face? Of course you dig them by hand, with pick and shovel.

If you visited, you'd find the house unique and amazing enough. Then, you'd notice a curious earthen structure in the old riverbed. As you get closer, you see that it is indeed a serpentine wall, perhaps 15 feet wide at the base, 5 feet wide on top, and roughly 7 feet high, with small rocks on both faces. Some have called it the Great Wall of Wesser, or Payson's Great Wall. It is quite beautiful, spectacular even, to someone who appreciates one-of-a-kind creations.

The wall is perhaps 150 feet long, meandering, curving from one bank to the other, and it has been constructed by one man, one shovelful of dirt at a time, wheelbarrowful by wheelbarrowful, every rock moved by him, over the last 30-plus years. He has worked alone on this wall virtually every day for the last 15 years, and every day he could for the 15 years before that, when he was working full-time at the NOC.

The design has changed over the years, but no one remembers previous intended outcomes. They don't matter. Really, the current design doesn't matter, other than to be pleasing to the eye of the builder. It keeps the vegetation from taking over the pond right in front of the house, or maybe it helps the vegetation. I'm not quite sure which. It helps the fish and the turtles, and it once harbored the legendary attack swan.

But really, it is there to be built, to be worked on, to provide occupation and proof and challenge for the man building it. At Christmas and other Kennedy family get-togethers, it usually provides a period of shared activity, as most family members don their oldest clothes and join Payson in the pond. It is an engineering challenge, mainly in how to control the water flowing into and out of the pond through a pipe under the railroad tracks. Vegetation control is always evolving, as is critter and fish control and nurturing.

I love the wall and the pond, and love telling the story of how Payson has built it. Most days when I am showing a visitor around and I take them down the driveway to the house and pond and wall, Payson will be there, in his tall waterproof boots, dirty jeans and T-shirt, and ragged gloves. He is happy to take a break, shake hands, and answer any questions, but before long, he'll get a bit antsy, conversation will falter, and it is obvious that he wants to get back to work while the weather allows. He usually works half days, mornings in the summer, afternoons in the winter.

I believe if the wall fell apart, or the pond filled with mud somehow, he would be sad for a moment, try to figure out what happened and why and how to prevent it, say, "Hmm, perhaps I can do it better now," and start back again, moving rocks and mud one shovelful, one wheelbarrowful, at a time.

Payson's True North: Simplicity, Frugality, Knowledge, Community, Ownership

I think Payson's unshakable integrity and faith in his principles were the key traits in making him a leader so many of us chose to follow. He is absolutely reliable in applying his underlying values and beliefs to his decision-making. He believes owners of businesses or property behave differently from non-owners. They care more. They attend to the details (like picking up litter) automatically, not as a duty. They do better work and are willing to work harder and longer for themselves and their enterprise, rather than because they are getting paid. He backed that up by widely sharing the ownership of the NOC. We can debate the success of that plan from many angles, but fundamentally it demonstrated his belief that owners produced better work and better service to guests.

He believes in democratic enterprises in the arena of pay. He modeled his pay hierarchy after Mondragon, the cooperative enterprise in the Pyrenees that is generally recognized as the most successful and largest worker-owned cooperative in the world. An economist who studied it reported, "I saw no signs of poverty. I saw no signs of extreme wealth. I saw people looking out for each other. . . . It's a caring form of capitalism." That was Payson's model: everyone pitching in together and everyone benefiting, not one owner or CEO getting wealthy off the work of lots of people. To that end, he instituted a pay scale that put the top person's pay at no more than four times the lowest pay. It was eventually discarded when he retired.

His business principles flow from his avid reading habit. He devours books about philosophy and human and economic performance. Perhaps his most famous attachment to a book/philosophy is to *Zen and the Art of Motorcycle Maintenance* by Robert Pirsig (abbreviated here as ZAMM). It is basically a treatise about quality, what produces it and what gets in the way of it, with a cross-country motorcycle trip as the vehicle.

In the early years, Payson and I thought it necessary to talk with new staff at orientation about NOC philosophy, history, and values. Payson usually read his favorite passages from ZAMM. I'm not talking a few sentences. I'm talking pages. Not a few minutes, but 15, 20, or more. Articulate, precise reading by a man who values accuracy more than performance. These readings became legendary. He would also read these passages at veteran staff meetings. ZAMM became the source of much amazed joking, eye-rolling, fun-poking—"Have you gotten your dose of *Zen and the Art* yet"—and head-shaking cynicism. The true, hard-bitten, closed-up cynics could never get on board, but they were few. The rest of us figured out we were in the presence of something special and had been given a rare opportunity to be part of a special place led by a special man, who believed in excellence and quality and the rewards of working hard and playing hard together. He was not afraid to demand that every new staff get this introduction, and he was willing to philosophize and read to make sure they got it.

But he didn't just *read* about philosophy; he explored it through personal growth, most notably through workshops with Farr-Cruickshank & Associates (abbreviated Farr here), a consulting firm in Greensboro whose workshops required a deep dive into self-awareness. Payson, the buttoned-up intellectual who had previously been all about thinking and the brain, got a peek into the world of feeling and the heart. He could not have come up with higher praise for the Farr workshop: "They do as good a job at their work as we do at ours."

His exploration again influenced others; key staff, myself included, started going to Farr workshops as well. At the heart of our years of "being Farr-ed," we did some fun stuff. My favorite stemmed from the advice to pay attention, to value silence, not to have to talk all the time. One year, Payson and I and about 10 new staff members did a unique exercise in orientation: After the ZAMM reading, after talking about quality and paying attention to one's work, after talking about focus and not being distracted and not having to have the music blaring in the kitchen, we went outside and washed and waxed a bus. In silence. No talking. Just pay attention.

Payson's Awards

Payson has won many awards, but these three stand out for me: In 2005 he was in the first class of inductees into the International Whitewater Hall of Fame, along with Charlie Walbridge, Rob Lesser, Jon Lugbill, David Hearn, Bob McNair, and Bill Endicott—all legends in the world of whitewater sport.

In 2010 he was awarded the American Canoe Association's Legends of Paddling Award for his decades of pioneering service to canoeing.

Payson Kennedy racing downriver K-1 in Nationals—1985

In 2014 he, Aurelia, and Horace were honored by the North Carolina Department of Commerce with the Winner's Circle award, for their impact on the state's travel and tourism economy over the span of four decades. Fittingly, when asked to speak in front of 600 people at the awards banquet at the Governor's Conference, Horace spoke of his family, Aurelia spoke of the joy of feeding weary hikers and paddlers in the NOC restaurant, and Payson spoke of others, not himself, who had been influential in shaping the NOC. Their inspiring humility confirmed once again how fortunate we all were to have worked with them for so many years.

Following Payson's Lead, Wanting to Be Like Him

Sometimes a moment or an event looks normal or insignificant, but with a little historical perspective or awareness it can grow.

Thursday, April 26, 2012, was a spectacular day on the Chattooga, but not your typical NOC raft trip with typical guests. Five rafts guided by the best: Ryan Dale, Curt Roth, Dave Perrin, Christy Cochran, and Cathy Kennedy, plus me and Payson bouncing down in our HPDs, high performance ducks! Neither of us had ever been in one with thigh straps, toe braces, comfortable butt, and hamstring padding, and a hull design made for quick turns and relatively high speed (for a duck).

Dave Perrin, the NOC's 30-year-veteran Chattooga Outpost manager, had four important people in his boat. Sutton Bacon, the NOC's young, experienced CEO, a whitewater expert in his own right, was here mainly to experience the river with three of the new owners of the NOC: brothers Brad, Clay, and Malon Courts. They had just completed a complicated stock purchase that resulted in the four of them and two other new investors owning roughly 80% of the NOC. Payson, Aurelia, Cathy, and several other long-term employees owned the remainder. So, we had the founders (absent Aurelia and Horace) and the new owners together for a day on our favorite river, the Wild and Scenic Chattooga.

And, Payson and I were in our cool ducks. Never thought I'd say that, but I'm about to be 65 and all sorts of things look good to me now that I couldn't imagine in my testosterone-laced, ego-driven, macho youth.

Section IV is a magical place. Completely remote, completely undeveloped, with a powerful and well-deserved reputation as a place that does not suffer fools gently. It welcomes rookie and veteran alike with a combination of anticipation, fear, no-fooling-around consequences, and respect—kind of like meeting a likable-but-serious, aged-but-rambunctious headmaster of the school into which your parents just enrolled you. He has a twinkle in his eye, a ready, friendly smile, but an extraordinarily stout handshake, and he carries the aura of someone on whose bad side you do not want to be, ever.

The Chattooga won't let you get away with anything, unless you are Dave Perrin and have earned the right to play. So here he is with Sutton and the Courts brothers in his raft. While they are now in charge of the NOC and effectively control the company, in this venue they are the rookies (except Sutton, who knows his way around the river), and wonderfully willing paddlers and students in Dave's hands. Dave is at least 20 years older than all of them, and they know he is legendary, so they feel they are in good hands. They are, but they don't know that he has permission to be a little more playful than most, because he understands the consequences and chooses his moments wisely.

Which brings us to Seven-Foot Falls, a scenic, fun, yet daunting rapid. As one approaches the lip of what is in fact a 7-foot vertical drop, it is just breathtaking. Getting it right takes months if not years of practice, and even then the rapid will often just decide you don't have it right and either dump truck the raft or flip it entirely, even though your run looks just like the one before and after, which were smooth and upright.

On this day, however, Dave cannot control his mischievous nature, and the opportunity to dump the new owners is just too tempting to pass up. Conditions are perfect—the water level is medium, the weather is warm, the guys are all hardy and game for just about anything (and completely, if naively, trusting), several photographers are ready, and the trip is full of veteran staff watching the new guys. A Section IV trip is the perfect lens through which to view a person's nature. A scary, dangerous whitewater trip can build character, and it can also reveal it. How one handles fear, and a headfirst dive into a whitewater maelstrom from a potentially embarrassing raft flip, can tell quite a story. Everyone is watching to see how the new leaders handle just about everything.

So Dave does his expert thing and turns what looks like a perfectly set up run into a huge photo opportunity by catching the bow of the raft on the guard rock at the last moment, just enough to make the raft not turn down the drop forward but to stay sideways. This is actually a very difficult move to get just right, but with eager rookies paddling their asses off, he has all the tools he needs. The raft plummets sideways to the bottom of the drop. Sutton and Brad Courts, who started sitting on the right tube, have no chance and rocket vertically to the left, bodychecking Malon and Clay Courts into the water and submerging them with great momentum in a jumble of arms, legs, paddles, and so on—no helmets in view, they're under water.

Dave, knowing what was coming, and having rigged his grab line off his right hip, grabs and waits, hopes, for a brief instant thinks he can dump them all and stay in the raft as it rights itself, but not today—he pulls it over on top of himself and everyone else, so now they have to try to remember what he told them to do if they come up under the raft. No problem—the raft is upside down, and its banana shape lifts the tubes and floor way out of the water, so everyone comes up into air, not fabric. The water is deep and slow, the perfect place for a flip, so everyone relaxes when all five heads appear quickly. Then, of course, the laughter and raucous shouting begin, and the baptism by Seven-Foot is complete. The boys are a little amazed, not quite sure if Dave did this on purpose, but happy to be where they are, snorting water out of their noses in the spotlight of the Chattooga.

Symbolism is everywhere on such a trip. New staff, lots of veterans, three generations of the founding family performing beautifully on their favorite river, which they have shared with thousands of people throughout 40 years of the NOC, and the new owners being introduced to Section IV for the first time with great adventure.

The trip ends at Lake Tugalo, which, for the first 25 years that we ran trips there, meant a 45-minute, 2-mile paddle across for the rafts. Some guests in the early days would protest, but not too loudly, because they knew it was coming, and for all but the laziest and whiniest, it turns out to be a pleasant, though sometimes tiring, extension of the adventure. Then, some time in the 1990s, one of the two other Chattooga outfitters decided they could gain a competitive advantage by bringing a small motorboat to the lake and towing the rafts to the takeout. Blasphemy! This is the Chattooga, our beloved retreat to the past, to the elemental experience of human-powered transport—it's not to be defiled by a stinkpot motorboat! We (the NOC) held out for a couple of seasons, but eventually had to join or risk losing the modern rafting guest to competitors who were eager to tow them. This was a hard transition for many of us old-timers.

It is hardest for Payson. Actually, it is not hard—he just doesn't do it. When guiding, he gets his crews psyched up to paddle the lake, with whatever works, a combination of inspiration, cajoling, challenging, betting, appealing, and so on (that is, whatever it takes to avoid hitching his raft to the motorboat). Occasionally he has to submit, but it is against his will, and he mumbles about values and exercise and wilderness the whole way across.

So we approach the lake and the motorboat after the last rapid, Charlie Laws and I having just had the old-timers-are-tougher conversation, and I see that Payson has taken off ahead. He's way out there, almost out of sight around the first corner, chugging away, getting his daily workout, having plotted this private exercise so that he was first to the lake and could get a head start, and the slightly faster flotillas of rafts, now motorized, would not pass him.

Having not had the slightest inclination to paddle the lake before seeing him, I immediately take off after him. He's 79; I'm 64. I used to be in paddling shape, so it is a beautiful challenge. It is also, in retrospect, extraordinarily symbolic, at least for me. Here I am, 37 years after starting to work for Payson, following his lead yet again. Trying to emulate him, be like him, inspired by him. His motives are consistent and without pretense, pure to his unwavering philosophical compass. He knew, before he got on the bus this morning, that he would paddle the lake, on

Passing on his spirit of adventure: Payson tags his grandson Andrew Holcombe.

principle. I hadn't thought about it. He planned it with an intentional strategy. I liked what I saw, thought it would be good for me. Thought people would notice me being the hardy, fit, river man. Thought I would have bragging rights when it was over, and so on. All sorts of contrived reasons to chase Payson. And sure enough, we finished together, right ahead of the flotilla, and I (not he) gave them a "we wondered when you all were going to show up" barb. He just picked up his boat, shouldered it, and carried it uncomplainingly up the steep takeout ramp, despite the very painful arthritic feet and ankles he now puts up with.

I'm not sure who or how many people noticed, but my experience is that all of it was noticed by some of the people, in their own way. As I look back on it, I'm glad I did it for so many reasons.

And one of the Courts brothers said he wants to do it with us next time.

About the Contributor

See page 3 for more information about John Burton.

AURELIA KENNEDY: AN APPRECIATION

By John Burton

Introducing the Heart and Soul of the Center: Aurelia Kennedy

The NOC-origin story goes that Horace was the visionary investor and prospector, Payson the principled visionary business leader and philosopher—what else was needed to form the NOC community? The heart, the generosity, the caretaking, the love. Look no further than Aurelia Kennedy, the most beloved member of the team. She brought extraordinary values and energy to the NOC, and it brought out of her the love of community, the grounded ability to serve others (mainly through food), a compelling humility, and a true love of all kinds of people. Her rich life demonstrates goodness, caretaking, selflessness, and good-spirited fun.

The interview in the next section gives some historical detail about and perspective into her early years and how they shaped the woman she would become. She was a lover, not a fighter, but she fought fiercely for her family, her husband, her values, those who were suffering or less fortunate, and anyone who came into her purview and could be served. Her main assigned role at the NOC was food service, though before she arrived here she had no formal experience in serving food, other than to her family and her Girl Scout troop in Atlanta. She learned the skills, but these were less important than the example she set of quality, goodwill, hard work, and doing whatever it took, for however long it took, to be of service and do it right.

A couple of vignettes will hopefully provide a window into this extraordinary woman, the heart of the NOC over four decades of dedicated service.

Aurelia Kennedy

"Hi, John, I'm Aurelia. You look hungry. Come in and have something to eat."

In those early years, and actually throughout its existence, the true heart of the NOC was the restaurant, with its riverside views, red vinyl booths, jukebox, small kitchen, staff meal plan, cleanup duty (we didn't want to pay for dishwashers, so all staff on meal plan rotated end-of-day cleanup duties), and the River Runners Special. There was even a motellike room between the store and the restaurant that served as living quarters for various store or restaurant workers in the early days.

I first met Aurelia in 1974, when I came to North Carolina from Philadelphia at the invitation of one of my oldest friends, Frank Schell, the founder of Mondamin Wilderness Adventures. He was attempting to make year-round use of the facilities at Camp Mondamin in Tuxedo, North Carolina. Now the trip from Mondamin to the Nantahala Gorge takes about an hour and a half on four-lane highways, but in those days it took 4 hours in the back of a cattle truck towing a wooden trailer full of Grumman canoes. We didn't care; we didn't know any better, and the long drive on twisty two-lane mountain roads over Soco Gap and through the town of Cherokee was just the price we had to pay.

After that trip we were tired, and the headline of this story ("Hi, John, I'm Aurelia. You look hungry. Come in and have something to eat.") is actually the first words I ever heard from Aurelia Kennedy, as I was introduced to her—or I introduced myself, or she stopped me as I was wandering around checking the place out, I don't remember. The important point is the welcome I received: simple, open, bright-eyed, with a generous smile and energetic handshake. I believe Aurelia had already invented the River Runners Special, and most likely the soon-to-be-famous loaf of bread on a breadboard with knife and butter. I don't remember those details, but I do remember the feeling of ease, of inclusion, of family, of food-as-healer, or food-as-connector.

Aurelia had started a day care center in Atlanta in the 1950s, and she became an elementary school teacher there and in the North Carolina mountains after moving to the center. She was always a giver, always incredibly generous, and she always encouraged young people to pursue honorable things. She was very competitive underneath all that sweetness. She was a gifted canoeist, and perhaps her most amazing trait is that she was a risk-taker in the face of fear and the unknown. She paddled all sorts of hard rivers, not to mention being one of the first to run Nantahala Falls, as a Camp Merrie-Woode counselor in 1954 (before me, before Payson, before Bunny!), and she was a raft guide on Section IV of the Chattooga in the early days of the NOC. She won many races, mostly with Payson or Cathy or John, and not just short slalom races. She and the rest of her family were always willing to push themselves in the long downriver races prevalent in the 1960s and 1970s around the Southeast, up to several hours long. She was tough to beat.

Later I would learn about these traits of hers and about her history. Here, in the summer of 1974, when she was 40 and I was 27, I was taken in by her charm, her humble charisma, her down-to-earth-ness, her fundamental open-armed welcome. She was famous for offering hungry, penniless hikers a peanut butter and jelly sandwich, something that would buck them up but not cost too much.

Bill Baxter and Gary Duven, rough-but-charming University of Florida grads hiking the Appalachian Trail around that time, showed up at the restaurant late one cold spring night, claimed hunger, and were welcomed and fed by Aurelia after closing hours. She may have even heated up some meat loaf for them, while the rest of the crew cleaned up the kitchen and dining room around them. Not a bad investment: Bill and Gary kept hiking but came back, to many years of working at the NOC and then putting roots down as key members of the NOC expat community. Gary started one of the early NOC spin-offs/competitors, Rolling Thunder River Company, and has been a stalwart member of the community for 40 years. Bill built Payson and Aurelia's house in the early 1980s, built most of the NOC buildings over the next 25 years, and became one of the most important and successful residential and commercial builders in Western North Carolina, which he remains to this day. Bill openly acknowledges that the meal and welcome he received from Aurelia was a huge influence in bringing him back to Wesser to live and work. Aurelia's welcoming two exhausted hikers into the NOC was one of many instances that built the NOC community into its unique position as a bastion of good people, good works, and good business.

"Will We Make It Through Memorial Day?"

Aurelia and I worked together for 16 years, 1975 to 1990, in many relationships. I was operations manager of the NOC, she was the restaurant manager and then food services director, as we added Relia's Garden in 1986 and Slow Joe's, by the river, in that era. She and I were both on the board of directors throughout that period, seeking to provide long-term direction and vision for the company. She and I were very involved in the creation of the Statement of Purposes (as were many leaders). We served on various executive committees and operations committees in the 1980s as the NOC grew exponentially, requiring much more staff. The scale of the bureaucracy and of the guest services we offered grew and at times became unwieldy and frustrating, as we were experimenting with employee ownership, democratic decision-making, inclusion vs. top-down hierarchy, voluntary simplicity, and all the nuances of a complicated business serving many constituencies and growing so fast. For both of us, it became trying and sometimes exhausting and even debilitating, but we worked together and I would say we loved and respected each other throughout.

While Aurelia hired most of the restaurant staff, we often collaborated on hiring restaurant managers and assistant managers. This was a tough assignment in such a seasonal business, where we were open in the winter mostly to feed staff on the meal plan, and where business ramped up in the spring with dead weekdays but busy Friday nights, Saturday nights, and Sunday mornings. It then morphed into crazy-busy mornings, lunches, and nights for about eight weeks, until mid-August, then it crashed as schools started back.

Many truly ambitious racer-heads figured out that working a regular shift in the restaurant, a.m. or p.m., allowed them to create the best training schedule, but restaurant managers were a different breed, and a different challenge to attract. Most had no interest in the core outdoor activities that attracted so many other NOC staff. They didn't care about gear, hiking trails, boats, paddles, racing, or adventure. They cared about making a living, and they were usually older and had bills to pay.

Restaurant managers work long hours, so no racers were interested in this position—they were at the NOC for its unique geographic and competitive environment. Plus, the NOC did not pay particularly well for any leadership positions, so money-motivated career restaurant professionals did not come our way. Most of the managers we attracted back in those days, it seemed, were getting away from something, and were willing, at first, to deal with our crazy seasonal schedule. We would get through a season with some sort of manager surviving through the fall, then have to hire a new manager to start in late winter and get the restaurant up and ready as spring business grew.

Memorial Day weekend was usually the acid test. After previous weekends got busier and busier, the three-day weekend at the end of May would explode with double or triple the number of guests, and staff members were often overwhelmed with new experiences of busyness, long lines, and no breaks—all the classic symptoms of impending panic and doom—and the kitchen's often slow order fulfillment made the guests cranky. And sure enough, more than once, I would come into the River's End during Memorial Day weekend and Aurelia, with a bus pan full of dishes in her hands and her signature red bandanna practically flying with the pace, would tell me that the manager had quit, walked off, or simply not shown up for the shift. So, Aurelia would have to step in and take over, and others of us would put on an apron and start washing dishes or busing tables or, God forbid, cluelessly wait tables.

Sometimes we would wait too long to try to recruit and hire the next manager, because we were so busy and the work in front of us needed to get done, and doing it ourselves was easier than going through the often-unrewarding hassle of interviewing and hiring. In those instances, Aurelia would work incredibly long hours doing whatever it took to keep the place going and the guests happy, but eventually we would have to pull back and find the next manager.

Sometimes we got lucky, and we could always count on some stalwarts to hold the fort together. The current director, Ron Mitschke, has brought stability and an amazing work ethic to the normal upheaval of the food service world at the NOC, and he has lasted far longer and done a better job than any former manager. Other employees, like Patrice Price, who came in 1974 and is still at the NOC, have been reliable stalwarts of the NOC food service businesses for virtually all of its existence. But through all the years, and all the changes, the linchpin has been Aurelia.

Payson and Aurelia Kennedy guiding together on the Sun Kosi River

Aurelia the Adventurer

Many NOC staff members have gone with Aurelia on adventure travel trips around the world to Guatemala, Nepal, China, the Grand Canyon, and dozens of other remote locales. My favorite memory of Aurelia the Adventurer was less far away, lasted only a couple of hours, and is memorialized to this day on the wall of historical pictures at River's End.

It is a picture of a woman in a climbing harness, life jacket, helmet, bathing suit, river shorts, and river shoes. With ropes all around her, she dangles 20 feet in the air over Nantahala Falls. It is Aurelia (in the mid-1980s, I think), in one of our early River Rescue clinics. I'm not sure if she was a student of the clinic, or if she made a guest appearance, but here was this 50-year-old, fit, strong, fearless, willing woman showing all the young kids what courage and belief could make happen. She was attempting a Tyrolean traverse, crossing from one side of the river to the other, on a rope she and the rest of the clinic had just thrown across the river and pulled as tight as possible. The idea was to experiment with how to get people out of stranded situations on remote rivers or treks, where ropes but not boats were available. Perhaps the water was too rough, the gorge too deep, or other obstacles awaited to block the crossing.

The NOC was famous for conducting these rescue classes, in which everyone was in on the challenge to think up new strategies or techniques to handle whatever situation might arise. The main principle of the clinics was that everyone had to participate, mentally and physically. Anyone, teacher or student, could come up with an idea that might eventually prove useful. Aurelia, dangling over the biggest rapid on the river, working hard to follow the instructions from shore as to how to move or how to

Aurelia Kennedy demonstrating a Tyrolean traverse

drop a rope to a (simulated) pinned rafter who could not be reached any other way, would offer invaluable perspective on the difficulty, the stresses and strains, the ways that looked easy but just were not feasible from her position. Had she volunteered for this assignment? Had the clinic leaders picked her? Not sure. We all learned by watching, doing, by contributing, by discussing and debating—hopefully not

Aurelia Kennedy and Ramon Eaton prepare a rattlesnake skin for drying.

too long while she bounced around in the (not blissfully comfortable) harness, the circulation to her legs beginning to falter painfully.

The point is, she could hang in there with the best of us, most not knowing that she was a Section IV guide, a downriver racer, a school teacher, a civil rights pioneer in segregated Atlanta 30 years earlier, and had probably just come off a double shift in the kitchen to stand in for someone who didn't show up for work or who had talked her into a weekend off so s/he could go racing.

She would give herself to anything and anyone who needed her, especially if it was in service to a guest or, by extension, to the NOC. We were her next family, just outside her Kennedy family, but all within her big heart. I am honored to have called her a friend for four decades.

 About the Contributor

See page 3 for more information about John Burton.

JOHN BURTON: AN APPRECIATION

By Gordon Grant

Full disclosure: Abandon all hope of journalistic objectivity here. This is a chance for me to appreciate a man who has been a major part of my life, first as hero whom I flat-out idolized as a 14-year-old summer camper, then as a mentor who guided me into the world of canoe slalom, then as a partner in C-2 racing, then as a supervisor when I was a young manager of the Chattooga Outpost, then best man at my wedding . . . and now, after all these years, as a training partner again with whom I share weekly check-in calls to hold each other to the goals and intentions we are setting to become who we yet might be. So, yeah, I know the guy pretty well, but he keeps on changing, so I plan to follow his lead and see where it goes for a few years more.

John came to the NOC in 1975, lured by Payson in the hopes that both his business training and his boating skills as a member of the 1972 Olympic Team would provide a perfect package of resources to move the NOC forward. It was a good catch. When John arrived in 1975, he was, well, a little intimidating: tall, blond, wide-shouldered, and impressive in his Olympic sweats, with Ivy League credentials (Dartmouth) and an MBA from the University of North Carolina Chapel Hill.

John Burton and Gordon Grant paddling C-2

He quickly proved that he was one with us common folk by flipping a raft on one of his first trips through Nantahala Falls and being endearingly good-natured about the howls of delight this feat generated in the rest of the guides. That's pretty much the standard that he set throughout the following 41 years in which he has helped lead, inspire, and influence the influencers of one of the most influential places for whitewater sports in America.

This combination of practical skills popped up early in his tenure in NOC leadership, when he became aware that the NOC had no health insurance for its employees. At the time, we operated on Payson's belief, somewhere south of Leonidas's Spartans, that if you worked hard and stayed fit, you didn't need to worry about minor medical issues: just get a good night's sleep and get back after it the next day. John said no, we've got to fix that, and we did.

John Burton, Bill Baxter, and Ramon Eaton offering congratulations at the conclusion of Nantahala Outdoorsman Triathlon

Payson knows this, and has said so, but it is often overlooked that it was John's combination of qualities—success and accreditation in the world of business and leadership; world-class credentials in whitewater competition; and a willingness to play, question, and challenge these successes with the humility of a servant leader—that were the connective tissue holding everyone who worked at the center to Payson and Aurelia's radical vision of an intentional community.

He stayed athletic, outright winning several of the Nantahala Outdoorsman Triathlons, paddling on several US teams in 1977 and 1979, and skiing.

Though seduced by golf at an early age, and continuing as a lifelong addict, he was—and is—capable of getting off the couch, into a kayak or canoe, and running difficult whitewater on the Upper Nantahala or on trips to the New and Gauley Rivers.

His outward journeys were accompanied by inward ones of introspection. He was a leader and participant in the personal growth work offered by the Greensboro company of Farr-Cruickshank & Associates—which involved having all NOC leaders take courses in learning more about their own behavior patterns and processes to understand better those processes in the NOC community. This work, which he has continued through meditative and introspective practice, has allowed him to further his application of Kipling's injunction to "trust yourself when others doubt you, but make allowance for their doubting too."

The NOC was, and continues to be, a place of strong-willed, highly skilled, highly opinionated, and self-directed people. John's ability to navigate the rapids of commerce with this rowdy crew and get them to paddle well together was a mark of the application of his own work in learning his own behaviors. He was innovative and willing to try anything, even some activities that bring to mind the purposeful lunacy of a Zen monastery, like getting all new guides to wash the NOC buses during staff training, in silence: soap on, wash off. Joy in the doing of the thing itself.

Here are some vignettes of what he did—and how—that seem to be indicative of the quality of the man.

US Nationals Road Trip: NC to Kernville, California, 1976

We drove across the country to race in Colorado and California at the Kern River Nationals, driving a battered NOC Ford van whose battery had fallen out, which we then ran over, on the way to a local mechanic, Troy Wall. Troy helped us out a lot; I recall John watching him intently and asking him lots of questions. More on this in a moment. . . .

Throughout the trip, John took pains to send postcards back to Troy Wall's Garage to note our unlikely progress. I was struck by that gesture: the follow-through to a person we barely knew, to say, "Thanks, you helped us out; we're thinking of you." It has stayed with me in my lifelong habit of sending postcards, like prayer flags fluttering from across the country, to family, friends, and fellow travelers to say the same: "Thanks for being in my life; thinking of you." This habit started with John, and it has pleased many people since and is an indication of the way he has always thought outside the narrow bubble of self.

Returning to his attentiveness in the mechanic's shop: Somewhere in the deserts east of Barstow on the road home, the van's engine quit and we rolled to a stop in a vast wasteland extending in all directions to the margin of the sky. John leapt out of the van with a meager toolkit, announced that somehow the engine wasn't getting fuel, and produced a fuel filter, which he then installed. The van coughed into life, and we were all dumbfounded with respect for his abilities as a mechanic. To this day, he can't say why he even had a fuel filter with him. This willingness to just jump in and try to solve a problem with the tools available, and the breezy optimism that it would work, stayed with me as long as the habit of sending postcards: just be willing to try something—just begin!

Deep Play: "Rules? We don't need no stinkin' rules!"

At one of the Open Canoe Nationals held on the Nantahala in the 1980s, there was an experiment with open canoe freestyle, a crowd-pleasing event where open boaters had a chance to play and do tricks in Nantahala Falls, including surfing Top Hole, rolling, catching the micro-eddy, and back-ferrying across the drop while eating apples. Because the sport was young and ill defined, it was hard to have rules about it.

John and John Kennedy entered as a C-2 pair, with the sole aim of being outrageous. As the pair came into sight, the announcer Dave Moccia intoned: "These guys have not submitted a list of tricks because they have no idea of what they are going to do!"

At which point, John came into view, paddling alone in the bow of a Blue Hole canoe. Kennedy appeared sliding out over the river from a slalom wire and dropped, Batman-like, into the stern of the canoe, to a roar of approval from the crowd. Approaching the falls, John went into a headstand on the bow seat, an astonishing maneuver that wowed the crowd, and wowed them even more when the boat stopped cold in the bottom hole, causing John to do a backflip out of the boat into the water, narrowly missing an impact on the bow plate that would have resulted in a spinal injury.

John Burton doing his legendary headstand

Clearly a crowd favorite, their routine was disallowed even for consideration in the rankings, to which John cheerfully raised his eyebrows in mock outrage to claim, "We were robbed!"

Muotathal, Switzerland, Summer of 1978

John and I took another battered van, a Comer van (the English Dodge) around Europe for a month with Steve Holmes and a crew of young paddlers to race in various slaloms, from Tryweryn in Wales, through Augsburg, Germany, to Tacen in what is now Slovenia. John and I were racing C-2 together. At the Swiss race, we were hopelessly out of line to make a sharp set of offset forward gates. John reached out with his paddle and batted one of the poles out in a wide arc so that we could make it inside the gate. It was a desperate move, and a flagrant intentional foul that should have gotten us a 50-second penalty. But somehow, the judges missed that and just gave us a 10-second penalty for hitting a single pole, so that when we carried back up the course, there we were, number one on the leader board, winners of the race. John looked at the board, and said, "You know we fiftied that gate, don't you? Got to tell the judges that."

So he went over to the head judge's table and told them, just before the arrival of the German coach of one of the C-2 teams we had we had beaten with our illegitimate score. The German coach was red-faced and indignant at the injustice of our victory, but when it was explained that John had self-reported the error, the German's indignation turned to admiration, and one of the C-2 paddlers, Dieter Welsink, pumped my hand and said, "This is how a true sportsman behaves!"

It has always been this way for John. As a 23-year-old, I watched and made mental note of the behavior, the ethical bedrock of it. I wanted to make it my own, and have tried to in the years since.

One of us—he is one of us forever. Across all his years at the NOC, John lived the belief that drove us then—that the leadership of the NOC should be servant leadership. Despite all impressive credentials that one brought from the outside world, what mattered at the NOC *was the doing of the thing itself, the tissue-thin difference between a thing done well and a thing done ill.* Guiding rafts, renting them, repairing them, teaching clinics in canoe and kayak, waiting on people in the store or at the restaurant, fixing the plumbing, cleaning the buildings or sometimes building new ones, sweeping floors, pounding nails, balancing the books. All equal work. John Burton lived the ideal of the leader of a community where he served as first among equals, and he remains, for me and for many, a hero.

 ## *About the Contributor*

See page 12 for more information about Gordon Grant.

THE OTHER SIDE OF THE RIVER:

AN INTERVIEW WITH WHITEWATER PIONEER BUNNY JOHNS

By Gerald Thurmond

Elizabeth "Bunny" Johns is one of the most skilled women whitewater canoe-ists and kayakers to have ever put a paddle in an Appalachian river. When she worked at the NOC, she was an innovator in whitewater instruction and a tandem canoeist of international standing.

Once when she was CEO of NOC, I spoke to her as she was leaning on the bridge railing looking down at the flowing water. Bunny seemed preoccupied and a little sad. She talked about the peace she still found paddling the Nantahala, even though she had kayaked it hundreds of times before. I thought that she was just being philosophical or perhaps that she was exhausted from the demanding job of running a multimillion-dollar business. I didn't realize until later that the NOC was in trouble and that she was about to leave an organization and a career to which she had devoted 26 years of her life.

Bunny grew up in Atlanta, Georgia, and went to Stetson University, and her career in outdoor recreation started by accident. As she recalled, "The summer before I left for college I'd gotten a job as a waitress. When I got back from school they told me that I didn't have a job. I had friends who had worked at a girls sum-mer camp called Camp Merrie-Woode in the North Carolina mountains, and two of them didn't want to return. They were swimming teachers, and I was a compet-itive swimmer, so I said, 'I'll do it.'" She laughs.

This was in the early 1960s. Bunny's introduction to paddling came about as the result of a camp requirement: "Camp Merrie-Woode has a very extensive canoeing program. At the last step, when the girls get to become a captain, which is a very big deal, they have to teach somebody else how to paddle. They don't let them teach other kids, so they teach one of the counselors, who doesn't know how to paddle. So the kids taught me."

The wilderness program at Merrie-Woode was one of those rites of passage that put the steel in the budding steel magnolias of the South. This is the way Bunny describes the camp's whitewater paddling program when she was a coun-selor there. "We had a number of wood canoes that we used on the river. One thing the kids had to know how to do was repair a wood-canvas canoe with air-plane glue and linen sheets and then paint over it. Midway through my career, we were primarily using Grumman aluminum canoes. They had no flotation other than the end tanks—no padding, no life jackets, no helmets. That was the standard at the time. We did use towels to kneel on for the wussies [she laughs]. Actually most people ended up bringing towels and then kids started coming back to camp with basketball kneepads. That was the big increase in comfort.

"That's how we paddled. You know, people look at what we used to do and they say, 'You were crazy.' But the kids were very well trained. The progression was very slow compared to what it is now or even [what it was] in the 1980s. They had complete control over their boats on the lake before they even got on whitewater, and there was a very slow progression from moving water to whitewater, and they really didn't have all that much trouble. Not that we never upended canoes, but I can't remember a single instance when I thought someone was in danger."

Bunny was a counselor at Merrie-Woode for six years, all through her undergraduate years, and while she was getting a master's degree at the University of Richmond. She only stopped returning to the camp when she went to NC State University to study for her PhD in plant pathology. Even these studies didn't stop her paddling. Bunny remembers, "When I got married, which was my second year at State, my husband and I would come up to the mountains for one week a year. There was a race on the Nantahala when we went up there that Payson and Aurelia Kennedy almost always won."

Bunny first met the Kennedys on the river, and after learning about the plans for the fledgling NOC from her friend Ramon Eaton, Bunny went to work for the company. I asked her what made her decide to work for the NOC after she finished her PhD, rather than playing it safe and becoming a college professor. "What I told myself at the time," she said, "was that I really didn't want to depend on the taxpayers of the state of North Carolina. I wasn't sure that what I was doing was worthy of tax support, so I wanted to do something different.

"In the beginning, people were so excited to go rafting because there weren't that many places that would take you rafting. It was a sense for me of being part of something new. To be on the cutting edge of all of that was very exciting for me.

"It was . . . I use the word *commune* lightly. *Community* would be a better word. As a community we were expected to do whatever we were asked to. So while my expertise was in whitewater paddling, I made up beds, I worked in the restaurant, I cleaned up, I was a waitress. I even cooked one night. I didn't ever have to do that again for reasons that were obvious at the time. Basically there was a schedule and whatever you were scheduled to do you did.

"It didn't take very long before there was more specialization. It was hard to clean a restaurant from midnight to 1 a.m. and then get up the next morning, drive to the Chattooga, and be a raft guide. So gradually it became departmentalized, but you were always expected to pitch in and do whatever needed to be done in the evenings."

The nature of whitewater boating at the time was one of the things that made the NOC attractive to staff like Bunny: "When people came to do raft trips on the Chattooga Section IV, they were there for adventure. I remember being up above Soc-em-Dog. Payson was leading the trip. He went over the drop, and everybody exploded out of the raft. He came out too. It ended up he had a broken rib. The next guide goes over and his raft does the same thing and he's hurt too. Fortunately, none of the guests were hurt. I was the third raft up there, and my guests were just chomping at the bit to run that rapid. We were going to do it. About that time, Payson walked up and said, 'No more rafts.' They were very disappointed. Those first groups, they were very fit and they were there to experience it. They didn't even care that we had to paddle across the lake to get out."

Bunny remembered fondly the development of whitewater instruction at NOC: "Early on I became the manager of the canoe/kayak instruction program. There were great people in it: Kathy Bolyn, Ken Kastorff, Eric Nies, and so many others. In those days there wasn't much material on how to teach people to paddle, other than the Red Cross books, and they were basically about flatwater. To be there during that time when we had so many excellent paddlers who became so involved in trying to be excellent in teaching, it was a real thrill. You'd be sitting out there at night and somebody would come up and say, 'I taught the roll this way and you know what happened?' It was an exciting time for somebody like me, an academic who actually liked teaching, to learn to teach a physical sport well."

Bunny credited the instructional crew with the development of a new roll and the kayaking technique of holding the body upright while surfing rather than hanging out of the boat and bracing against the water with the paddle as had been traditionally done. Bunny said, "There were other places doing it, but I don't think at that time there was another place that had that number of people thinking about teaching."

Bunny later completed a nursing degree and had a job at District Memorial Hospital in Andrews, North Carolina, while also working for the NOC. Although she got along very well with the people she worked with in the hospital, at times some of them would let her know just how they felt about the new whitewater industry: "One night this orderly comes up to me and says, 'When you are on the river, what color life jacket do you wear?' I didn't tell him that all of them were orange. I just said, 'It's orange. Why do you want to know?' He says, 'Well, I want to know who not to shoot.' And he was only half joking [Bunny laughs]. There were incidents during that time of people shooting BB guns at paddlers.

"Basically we were characterized—how did they put it? We didn't go to church, we didn't get married, and we used drugs. But there were a lot of us who didn't use any drugs whatsoever. And, over time, we did get married and we had children and those children grew up and went to school in Swain County. And over time things have changed. I'd say the problem was that they looked at us as outsiders coming in and bringing with us a different way of life."

From the onset, founder Payson Kennedy wanted the NOC to be an egalitarian community. His move to formally create employee ownership was part of that vision, an innovation that Bunny did not think was needed.

"He wanted it to be a community," she said. "He wanted people invested in what they were doing so much that they would act like they were owners of the business. He was overwhelmingly successful at creating that. And I think he never quite realized he had really done it. That's why he went into this whole employee ownership thing; he wanted people to have an ownership mentality. In fact, they already did and he didn't know it, in my opinion. I was not a great proponent of employee ownership. I went along with it just like a lot of other people did, but I never thought it was necessary. We were spending a lot of money to do the legal structure and all of that stuff. It was something he really wanted because Payson is Payson."

Bunny became the chief operating officer and president of the company in 1991. Payson Kennedy held the position of CEO, and they were both on the board of directors. Bunny says, "It was a very good time for me because Payson is a true visionary, and I liked doing the operations."

While she was at the NOC, she gained recognition as a competitive wildwater canoeist in the mixed couples class. Bunny and her paddling partner, Mike Hipsher, ran a race in 1981 in the Wildwater World Championships at Bala, Wales. That race has become known as the perfect run. They won the gold medal. John Pinyard, Georgia Canoeing Association member, called their victory "perhaps our greatest single achievement" in American canoeing. Bunny simply characterized that period as a "wonderful time in my life." She said, "It's hard to make this sound right, but we actually enjoyed the training and getting better as much or more than we did the races. The races often became, as we put it, the reason that allowed us to put in so much time in on our training. Not only did we train in the morning and night, but in between time we were lifting weights and running. We went about it seriously, seriously enough that we did get quite good."

Good enough so that their skills proved to be embarrassment to some of the male canoeists. She describes one race on the Ocoee River in which she and Mike Hipsher beat all of the men's boats. "And of course," Bunny says, "word came down that the stopwatch must be wrong." In the US Team Trials, they not only came in first for the mixed class, but they beat the fastest men's boat by 30 seconds. "One young gentleman said if a woman beat him he would give her his paddle. He didn't say it to me. So after the race, all his friends came and told me I ought go and collect it."

At the Wildwater World Championship in Wales, Bunny and Mike won the gold medal for the mixed class by 75 seconds, a huge margin. They were the fastest US boat even in the men's class. If they had been competing against the men's teams, they would have come in twelfth overall. Bunny and Mike also anchored the three-boat men's tandem relay race for the United States, leading them to a fourth place finish.

Age, an injury, and a rule change ended Bunny's international competition. Bunny was 40 years old at the time. Her injured back required surgery, which put her out for a year. The next year the Wildwater World Championships cut out the mixed class and then prohibited women from competing even in the men's class. Bunny says, "We thought that was kind of silly that they made those rules—strange, actually, after we had competed so well." I tell her that maybe the men didn't want to have to give her their paddles.

Once voting rights and employee ownership of the NOC was established, the elected members on the board expressed dissatisfaction with the direction the organization was going in. According to Bunny, they were unhappy with some of the expensive projects that Payson had pushed, like building Relia's Garden restaurant and a climbing wall made out of all natural materials. Bunny said, "You know those were all very laudable things, but they cost us a lot of money. Payson truly did ask people's opinions, but I think the perception was that he drove everything and that they didn't have any say. So this new structure gave them what they wanted, an opportunity to change things. I'm not sure what they really wanted to change, other than a few key decisions. I think people did want to make more money. Think about having a family with the pay scale the way it was.

"The downside of employee ownership was that we had raft guides, many of whom were only there for 125 days out of a year, making decisions that they had no basis for. Some people would really take the time to know the issues, but a lot of them just went on rumor and innuendo."

In 1998 Payson resigned and Bunny took his place. In one of her efforts to be community minded, Bunny decided that the NOC would pay thousands of dollars in U.S. Forest Service (USFS) fees that the company could have avoided paying. The USFS charged the outfitters for access to their property for rafting. The NOC was exempt from some of those fees because they launched their rafts and took them out on private land on the Nantahala. Bunny chose, on a year-to-year basis, to pay the fees anyway. She thought it would look bad if the largest outfitter on the river did not pay its fair share. She also wanted the NOC to financially support the maintenance of the USFS's parking lots, bathrooms, and launching and takeout areas that helped to protect the river from the hundreds of thousands of people who visited it each year. As Bunny says, "I did things that weren't bottom line oriented. I wanted to take a wider view and bring the NOC into a more collaborative pattern."

As president, Bunny lasted three years. Bunny describes it as "a time of real turmoil." At first people on the board were civil, but later their arguments became more heated. "This is when we got to where people wanted to make more money and cut all of these programs."

I asked Bunny if this conflict was what finally pushed her to resign. She paused. Her voice dropped, and she said she didn't resign. "The board asked me to leave. That's how bad it had gotten. You know, it's not like we didn't have issues, but anyway, obviously my opinion about that would be very different from people that were on the board at the time."

One thing Bunny remains certain of is her love of rivers and her continued pleasure in paddling them: "You know, I've never really known why I like [paddling] so much, but the very first time I experienced it when those kids taught me to paddle at the camp, something about the movement, the physical endeavor to make it all happen, the complexity of the water, the thrill of seeing if I could do something, even if wasn't difficult water, to see if I could make a move. The whole beauty of it. Even though the water might be released through a turbine, it's a naturally flowing river. Using the energy of that river to do fun things. I think the real reason is that it's totally absorbing. I can't think of another time when I am so engrossed in what I'm doing."

It's been a pretty incredible run for the NOC, and for Bunny as well, with more to come. And to think that it all started with a waitressing job that fell through, two friends who didn't want to return to their summer camp jobs and suggested that Bunny apply, and a camp's requirement that the girls teach an adult how to canoe.

About the Contributor

Gerald Thurmond is a professor in the sociology department at Wofford College in Spartanburg, South Carolina. He's an avid birder, snake enthusiast, canoeist (he had his first real whitewater experience on the Nantahala paddling an old Blue Hole canoe in the early 1980s), and hiker. He's editor, with his friend John Lane, of *The Woods Stretched for Miles: New Nature Writing from the South,* published by the University of Georgia Press. His essay, "Pipe Dream: The Wild Nantahala," published by *Isle* in 2005; his interview with Payson Kennedy, first published by *Appalachian Journal* in 2006; and his interview with Bunny Johns are part of a larger manuscript, reworked and retitled *Kephart's Mountains.* His essay "Snake Bit on the Ogeechee" appears in an anthology edited by Douglas Higbee and David Bruzina and published in 2018 by the University of South Carolina Press.

SECTION VII
Zen and the Art of Running a Rafting Company

A CHAUTAUQUA ON NOC PHILOSOPHY AND PRACTICES

By Payson Kennedy

Finding Flow

The idea of finding a job that one enjoys so much that it seems like play rather than work is one that I have always advocated and have tried to follow in my own life. The paradox is that when work feels like play, the person is able to work effortlessly but with full concentration that produces high-quality results and great internal satisfaction.

As an undergraduate, I majored in philosophy and came to agree with Plato that the pinnacle of the career pyramid should be occupied by philosophers. While I never aspired to be a philosopher-king, I did aspire to be a philosophical leader. Not so much philosophy in its academic sense but the more popular idea of philosophy as a search for wisdom regarding questions like what is the good life and what is the nature of good work. Back in the early 1990s, I actually got permission from the NOC board of directors to change my title from CEO (chief executive officer) to CPO (chief philosophical officer); John Burton called himself CCO (chief cultural officer) and CIP (chief interpreter of Payson). I never thought of myself as an executive, and I truly believed these titles described how John and I worked together to guide the NOC.

In my 15 years as an academic before coming to the NOC, I noticed an occasional phenomenon in which I got into a state of complete focused concentration on some problem. On one occasion, I needed to teach a paper-tape to punch card mechanical converter how to count to 10 so that the sequence of the sets of punched cards being produced could be electronically checked and corrected in case the cards had somehow gotten out of sequence. To do so, I'd have to internally rewire some terminals on the programming board, but doing so would void the machine's warranty (I'd talked my boss into buying the machine for $30,000, which was quite a sum in the 1960s). Put simply, the stakes were high. After much intense consideration, I made the internal changes and it worked. Later I realized that this experience, while of trivial importance in the overall scope of my job, had been one of the most personally satisfying of my career, and while I was working on it, nothing else intruded on my thoughts. This experience also recurred fairly often when I was working on a challenging computer program. In this state I lost track of time, could work for hours productively and without fatigue, and afterward I had a euphoric feeling of accomplishment and satisfaction.

During the 1960s, I was a faculty advisor for the Georgia Tech outing club; a scoutmaster; an advisor for an Explorer Scout post, whose members built their own kayaks and became accomplished kayakers; and a very active member of the Georgia Canoeing Association (GCA). I was canoeing, backpacking, climbing, or caving almost every weekend. I began to notice that experiences similar to those described above occurred more frequently in these activities than in my work. My most vivid memory of such an experience was on my first trip paddling on the Upper Nantahala between the Cascades and the power plant. The river was in flood and definitely at the upper limits of my paddling ability. I started out feeling intensely nervous, but as I moved downstream I soon reached a state in which all fear and nervousness disappeared and I felt I always knew exactly where my next stroke should go. I forgot everything except the next 20 feet of the river in front of me, but I saw everything in that visual cone that extended 20 or 30 feet ahead. I don't ever remember another paddling experience in which I felt more confident and at ease. After the trip we went for dinner at the Tote 'N' Tarry, and I was in a state of complete euphoria.

Similar experiences, less intense but still satisfying, occurred most frequently in challenging situations, such as when paddling a new river near the limits of my ability, when there was a situation in which a rescue was needed, or in competition. The result was always the same: nervousness disappeared and I was able to perform at a level beyond my normal ability. When I got into this state during races, I discovered I could beat many paddlers whom I thought normally surpassed me in paddling ability. I was never aware of fatigue and was always left feeling exhilarated.

Gradually it occurred to me that the people who were most successful must be those who most regularly attained this state of focused concentration in their work. Because these experiences were most common for me in outdoor recreational activities, I thought I should change careers. About this time, several of us GCA members were invited to canoe through the Okefenokee Swamp with the directors of the various US Outward Bound schools. As I learned about their philosophy and programs, I started discussions with the director of the North Carolina Outward Bound School about developing a whitewater paddling program there.

On the Chattahoochee River north of Atlanta, my friend Horace Holden, who knew I was thinking of changing careers, operated a day camp where Aurelia had sometimes worked. In the fall of 1971, Horace purchased the Tote 'N' Tarry property and asked Aurelia and me to consider managing the new operation on the Nantahala. After some thought and family discussion, Aurelia and I decided to try it for the summer of 1972, but without resigning our jobs at Georgia Tech and the Atlanta Public Schools. We intended to go back to work in Atlanta in the fall.

In the mountains, I worked with a group of family and friends and taught some of the skills I most enjoyed to people who were really interested in them, rather than in working for academic credit. I frequently reached that psychological state of focused concentration that I sought. Once I had experienced this life, there was never a real possibility of returning permanently to city life, even though we went through the motions of thinking about the risks and trade-offs involved. Aurelia was a bit more cautious because we had four teenage children who we wanted to help attend college soon, but the three older children were enthusiastic and in time Aurelia became so. We moved permanently to Wesser, North Carolina, and the NOC at the beginning of the summer in 1973.

In 1974 *Zen and the Art of Motorcycle Maintenance: An Inquiry into Values* by Robert Pirsig was published. I immediately felt that I had discovered a philosophical companion. The book is loosely autobiographical, and on the surface it's about a motorcycle trip from Chicago to Montana that Pirsig takes with his adolescent son as a bonding experience. Along the way, Pirsig includes Chautauquas, or essays about the nature of quality and how to achieve it in our work. These Chautauquas are the real heart of the book.

Early in the book, Pirsig describes a motorcycle shop where the mechanics were listening to the radio and not seeming to be focused on their work, so they butchered Pirsig's cycle. Later, working alone, Pirsig not only fixed the damage, but he also found and repaired the initial problem. Although not a trained mechanic, Pirsig thinks he succeeded because he cared about having a reliable motorcycle for his trip, and therefore he was focused. For him, focused concentration always produces high-quality work, and high-quality work is always a product of caring and focused concentration. He also maintains that this state is always accompanied by peace of mind.

Pirsig's descriptions mirrored the same experiences that had led me to change careers, and during my early years at the NOC, I pretty frequently attained the state of focused concentration that I was seeking. In the summer, I usually worked 80–100 hours a week without feeling fatigued or put upon. Because about half my working hours were usually on the rivers, that time in particular felt more like play than work.

Inspired by my experiences and Pirsig's philosophy, I talked incessantly about the book in staff meetings and orientations. I know many were bored by my obsession and joked about it, but I am confident that some also took it to heart, and I felt great satisfaction and pride in the culture of quality that began to develop at the NOC. Each year it seemed that many of the less talented and less hard-working staff members didn't return; many of the best returned and attracted folks of similar quality.

Though this focused state can occur in most if not all activities, the element of perceived risk in many outdoor recreational activities tends to help bring about focused attention and works to make these powerful experiences common. I told new staff that if they did not experience this state frequently in the work that they were doing at the NOC, they should seek work in which it did occur, either in a different role at the NOC or elsewhere. I realize that today many people will perceive this as unrealistic and impractical advice, and for some it probably is. In some circumstances, survival might be all that is possible. Nevertheless, I continue to believe that for someone to be truly successful in their career and happy in their life, it is necessary to find such work or learn to attain that state in the work that they have chosen. Both the staff and guests at the NOC had frequent experiences of that state of focused concentration Pirsig had described. I felt it was at the heart of life at the NOC.

Abraham Maslow, a respected academic psychologist who served as president of the American Psychological Association, gave academic credibility and recognition to the importance of this psychological state, which he called peak experiences. In his book *Religions, Values, and Peak-Experiences,* he acknowledges that these experiences are probably universal and occur in all religions and "for priests and atheists, for communists and anti-communists, for conservatives and liberals, for artists and scientists, for men and for women, and for different constitutional types, that is to say, for athletes and poets, for thinkers and doers." I was also impressed by the emphasis he put on the importance of peak experiences in the process of self-development, becoming fully human and fully functioning individuals.

Another academic psychologist, Mihaly Csikszentmihalyi, probably did the most to bring knowledge of this psychological state into mainstream thought and coined the term by which it is commonly known today: flow experiences. Though I referred to Csikszentmihalyi's work in a reading list that I passed out in new staff orientations (see page 279), a more useful book was *The C Zone: Peak Performance Under Pressure,* a very simple and clear book describing the flow experience and how to attain it. For several years I relied on it as heavily as I had previously relied on *Zen and the Art of Motorcycle Maintenance* in my talks to staff. The authors, Robert J. and Marilyn Harris Kriegel, describe a Type C experience in the following way:

> *Have you ever had one of those days when everything you did worked? Things just seemed to fall into place. You were more productive with less effort and completely in tune with what you were doing. You felt great, on top of everything.*
>
> *That's a Type C experience. It's a high performance episode in which you transcend your normal level of ability. Type C behavior enables you to perform at your peak whatever the situation. And although you are more effective at these times, it feels as if you aren't working nearly so hard as usual, for you are vital and full of energy. (p. 1)*

The Kriegels helped me understand the importance of balancing challenge and mastery. They begin with a diagram (see below) that uses the perceived difficulty of a situation as the vertical axis and the perceived ability to handle the situation as the horizontal axis.

The upper left area, where there is too much challenge and not enough mastery, they call the panic zone. The lower right area, where there is too much mastery and not enough challenge, they call the drone zone. The area along the central

PANIC ZONE

Too much challenge
Not enough mastery

Overcommitted
Overconfident
Out of Control

Nervous
Scattered
Hyper

"I GOTTA"   **"CAN DO"**

THE C ZONE

Challenge
Risk and
Innovation

Mastery
Competence
and Quality

Committed
Confident
in Control

Calm
Focused
Energized

**DRONE
ZONE**

Not enough challenge
Too much mastery

Lethargic   **Uncommitted**
"DON'T   Sluggish   **Underconfident**
CHANCE IT"   Bored   **Overcontrolled**

Perceived
Difficulty
of a
Situation

Perceived Ability to Handle Situation

Diagram of C Zone

diagonal, where challenge and mastery are balanced, is the zone in which the actor feels calm, focused, energized, and in control and is most likely to have a C Zone or championship-level experience.

Below are some crucial factors to reaching the C Zone:

Balancing Challenge and perceived Competence (or skills, or mastery)

Caring (as in Pirsig's book)

Commitment

Concentration

Control

I realize that much of this may sound overly academic, but after we decided to move to the NOC but while I still worked at Georgia Tech, I heard people express their own feelings about the drone zone. When I shared our plans with friends and colleagues, most of whom were successful professionals near the peak of their careers, I was surprised that several of them confided that they no longer found their jobs challenging or satisfying. They had dreams of a different career but felt trapped by family circumstances and financial responsibilities. One had dreams of becoming a musician, another of becoming a writer, and a third of becoming a shrimp fisherman. They had all formerly found the demands of their work challenging, frequently inspiring them to work in the flow state, but as they mastered the demands of their jobs, they had not found new challenges and were now in the drone zone much of

the time at work. Their jobs paid well and they felt that it would not be fair to their families to give up their comfortable positions to follow their current dreams into an uncertain financial future. I wonder how often in our society individuals do not realize their potential because they feel trapped in jobs that once were challenging and inspired them to work in the flow, but as their mastery exceeded the challenges of the job, they have not succeeded in finding new challenges and they no longer work in the flow state.

There was one other aspect of flow experiences that the Kriegels didn't mention but that I have found to frequently be critical. I noticed that on early Chattooga trips when swims and flips were common in the small rafts we were using and the perceived challenge was high, participants often seemed to have flow experiences, and they came off the trips exhilarated. Whenever this occurred, it typically happened for everyone, guides and guests, on

Negotiating the high ropes course. This is the NOC's second high ropes course; the first was in a bowl above the old motel offices on river right. It had to be moved because the trees on which they were built were decaying.

the trip. In later years, I noticed that this seemed even more regularly true of the longer duration adventure travel trips. On some trips, everyone seemed to get into the flow, to form friendships that still endure, and to have experiences that created lasting memories. It seemed to me that if a few people began to have flow experiences, it became contagious and everyone was brought along. If, on the other hand, there were one or two whiners in the group, they might bring everyone down and no one got into the flow state. I have observed this regularly on our ropes courses and Alpine Tower. I decided that there was definitely a social aspect to flow, and to make it fit the C Zone mnemonics, I usually referred to it as a Communal aspect.

Many of those coming from team sports illustrate the communal aspect of the flow experience, and I found evidence of this in *In the Zone: Transcendent Experiences in Sports* by Michael Murphy and Rhea A. White. This book is a compilation of accounts of flow experiences, what the authors call being in the zone, from a great variety of sports and challenging physical activities. The one that I most often liked to read to staff was an account they quote from Bill Russell, former center for the Boston Celtics and five-time NBA MVP:

> *In his autobiography Bill Russell observed that something magical happened in certain games. It would usually start with three or four of the top players serving as catalysts. Then "the feeling would spread to the other guys, and we'd all levitate. . . . At that special level all sorts of odd things happened. . . . It was almost as if we were all playing in slow motion. . . . I could almost sense how the next play would develop and where the next shot would be taken. . . . My premonitions would be consistently correct, and I always felt then that I not only knew all the Celtics by heart but also all the opposing players, and that they all knew me. . . . These were the moments when I had chills pulsing up and down my spine."*

The Boys in the Boat: Nine Americans and Their Epic Quest for Gold at the 1936 Berlin Olympics is Daniel James Brown's thrilling story of how nine individuals came together and learned to get in the swing or to find group flow as they trained over a four-year period. Their training and competition culminated in a come-from-behind victory against all kinds of obstacles in the eight-oar crew finals at the Berlin Olympic Games.

My favorite book on flow during the final years that I was doing new staff orientation talks was *Bone Games: Extreme Sports, Shamanism, Zen, and the Search for Transcendence* by Rob Schultheis. In 1964 Schultheis, an anthropology student at the University of Colorado Boulder and a relatively new rock climber, took a serious fall while attempting to climb Mount Neva alone. After the fall, he had a transcendent experience in which he suddenly acquired supernatural climbing ability as he downclimbed to safety. Chapter one of the book describes the fall and miraculous subsequent events, and I highly recommend it as the most vivid account of a flow experience I have encountered. For several years, I enjoyed reading it to new staff just as I had read to them from *Zen and the Art of Motorcycle Maintenance* in earlier years. The remainder of the book is an account of Schultheis's various attempts to learn how to re-create that experience through extreme sports, shamanism, Zen, and other avenues. Because of the many parallels in our lives as anthropology students, runners, trekkers in Nepal, climbers of Popocatépetl, and seekers of flow, I felt an especially strong tie to this book.

With its focus on extreme sports, Steven Kotler's *The Rise of Superman: Decoding the Science of Ultimate Human Performance* pushed the science of flow a bit further and is currently the best summary statement of what has been learned about the flow experience and the triggers that bring it about. Kotler's thesis is that over the past two decades, extreme sports athletes have learned how to reliably attain the flow state, which had previously been attainable only occasionally and accidentally. As a result, feats that had previously been regarded as impossible became routine for these athletes. Kotler uses numerous examples from extreme sports, including an account of various kayaking runs of the Class V Stikine River by Doug Ammons, Rob Lesser, Lars Holbeck, and Bob McDougall, and a short account of the kayaking of waterfalls from Tao Berman's 1997 run of an 87-foot drop in Mexico to Tyler Bradt's 198-foot plunge over Washington State's Palouse Falls.

By the time of my final retirement from full-time work, I was thinking of the primary mission of the NOC as using outdoor recreation activities to bring about flow experiences for the staff and guests. I believed that if staff members were working in flow, they would very often be able to create an atmosphere in which guests were also likely to have flow experiences, and as Maslow emphasized, this would produce self-development as a human being. If this occurred, then guests would usually want to repeat those experiences with us, and they would often want to tell others about these powerful and potentially life-changing experiences, thus ensuring the continued success of the NOC.

Some Influential Books in Developing the NOC Philosophy

Editor's Note: This is the latest iteration of a book list compiled by Payson Kennedy to distribute at new-staff orientation sessions some years ago.

BOOKS RELATING TO THE FLOW EXPERIENCE

1. *Zen and the Art of Motorcycle Maintenance: An Inquiry Into Values* by Robert M. Pirsig. New York: Bantam, 1974. The book that stimulated my thinking about the flow experience during the NOC's formative years. It has continued to fascinate me through numerous rereadings since the early days of the NOC.

2. *The C Zone: Peak Performance Under Pressure* by Robert J. and Marilyn H. Kriegel. New York: Fawcett Columbine, 1984. A short and clear account of the flow or C Zone experience and techniques that can lead to more such experiences.

3. *Bone Games: Extreme Sports, Shamanism, Zen, and the Search for Transcendence* by Rob Schultheis. Halcottsville, NY: Breakaway Books, 1996. Schultheis's account of his life-changing flow experience and his continuing efforts to understand the conditions that bring about similar experiences so that he might re-create them. My current favorite book about flow because of the many similarities in his attempts to find flow and some of my own experiences.

4. *The Rise of Superman: Decoding the Science of Ultimate Human Performance* by Steven Kotler. Boston: Houghton Mifflin Harcourt, 2014. This recent book summarizes most of what has been learned about the flow experience, and it uses examples from extreme sports such as kayaking, climbing, and skateboarding to show the levels of performance possible while in the flow state.

5. *Religions, Values, and Peak-Experiences* by Abraham Maslow. New York: Arkana, 1994. An early discussion of flow under the name peak experiences by a well-known psychologist. Maslow also discusses peak experiences in his best-known book, *Toward a Psychology of Being*.

6. *In the Zone: Transcendent Experience in Sports* by Michael Murphy and Rhea A. White. New York: Penguin, 1995. The first edition was published in 1978 as *The Psychic Side of Sports*. A compilation of accounts from athletes describing flow experiences or experiences in the zone, arranged according to the special qualities experienced and emphasized in the accounts. Includes an extensive bibliography.

7. *Flow: The Psychology of Optimal Experience* by Mihaly Csikszentmihalyi. New York: Harper & Row, 1990. The best known and most systematic, if not the most interesting, book about the flow experience.

8. *The Boys in the Boat: Nine Americans and Their Epic Quest for the Gold at the 1936 Berlin Olympics* by Daniel James Brown. New York: Penguin, 2014. Although Brown never uses the term *flow*, this book seems to me a fascinating account of the attainment of group flow.

OTHER INFLUENTIAL BOOKS IN THE HISTORY OF THE NOC

1. *Small Is Beautiful: Economics as if People Mattered* by E. F. Schumacher. New York: Harper & Row, 1973. A book of essays by one of

the wisest writers I have encountered. He puts economics, business, and development in a broader philosophical perspective.

2. *Islandia* by Austin Tappan Wright. New York: Farrar & Rinehart, 1942. A Utopian novel describing a communal society that provided a model to me for an ideal NOC community.

3. *In Search of Excellence: Lessons from America's Best-Run Companies* by Thomas J. Peters and Robert Waterman Jr. New York: Warner Books, 1982. When this came out, the management team at the NOC read it together and discussed how it applied to the NOC. We were reassured to find that we were on the right track, or at least the same track that Peters and Waterman thought America's best-run companies were on. It proved to be a useful practical guide.

4. *Good to Great: Why Some Companies Make the Leap . . . and Others Don't* by Jim Collins. New York: HarperCollins, 2001. Another book the NOC management team read together and found useful. Collins had to strain a bit to fit all 11 selected great companies into a conceptual framework of characteristics that distinguished them from the 11 comparison companies.

On Leadership

As of this writing, this will have been my 45th year of talking to new staff as they begin their stay at the NOC. I always regarded this as one of my best opportunities to set expectations so that they got a strong start as a worker and community member, and I have always believed it was one of the most important parts of my job. In these talks I have always included a description of the flow experience and its benefits and triggers. When I have spoken about the NOC as a community of friends who enjoyed working and playing together, I might just as well have said a group of friends enjoying flow experiences together.

During my tenure, with varying titles such as president, CEO, chairman, and philosopher, I have never thought of myself as a manager. The very word is itself disagreeable to me, with its idea of managing other persons. When asked about the NOC, I usually responded that it was a community of friends who enjoyed working and playing together in an environment that they loved, and who liked teaching others about this environment and about the activities that they enjoyed. I took this seriously and believed that it was inappropriate to try to manage friends or to tell them what to do. As long as we all shared the same broad purposes and a desire to do our jobs in the highest-quality fashion, I felt that there was room for lots of variation and experimentation in finding the best ways to do various tasks. I believe that if one truly cares about doing quality work, they are more likely to find flow, to be innovative and ultimately successful when they are allowed the freedom to find the ways of accomplishing it that work best for them, rather than being given step-by-step instructions on just how they must do their job.

This sometimes brought me into disagreement with those at the NOC, as elsewhere, who believe the key to success and efficiency lies in better systems and procedures that are written out in manuals to be followed by everyone. In teaching new staff, I like phrases such as "This is how I like to do it" or "This is the way we have found that usually seems to work best," rather than "This is the way to do this task" or "This is the way to guide a raft."

Most of those who have written about flow have included a feeling of being in control of the situation as one of its characteristics. I found this to be true. I thought that a person who has detailed rules on just how to do his job will possibly make fewer mistakes, but there is little chance that he will feel that he is in control of the situation and will work in flow. I believe that to be an excellent coach or an excellent supervisor one should attempt to guide and motivate more than to manage and control in an authoritarian manner.

Contrary to standard business practices, I wanted the NOC to err on the side of freedom and innovation rather than on the side of efficiency. I think Bunny Johns and Kent Ford's account of the success of the NOC instruction program illustrates the manner in which this approach worked out to develop new paddling techniques.

Another corollary of our emphasis on the NOC as a community was that we often found it difficult to fire people who were not being as successful in their job as we wished. Of course if they displayed dishonesty or a lack of caring about their job, there was no difficulty, but if they wanted to be at the NOC and seemed to be motivated to do a good job but were unsuccessful in achieving their goals, we had a problem. I believed that as long as a person wanted to be at the NOC and cared about doing a good job, it was our role to give them the assistance they needed to succeed, coach them adequately to enable them to do their job, or, failing in these measures, to find another job that they could do successfully.

We often compared the NOC community to a family in which when a family member had problems, one didn't try to get rid of them but rather tried to help them deal with their problems. No one seemed to disagree with these practices as long as things were going well, but in years when cash was short and raises small, talk about the need to get rid of deadwood always increased.

After Bunny and I were succeeded by leaders with a background in more conventional businesses, I think it came as a severe shock to the community when members were treated as parts of a machine that could be discarded readily when they were not working with maximum efficiency. To carry the machine analogy a bit further, it seemed to me that John Burton, Bunny Johns, and I were like third-world mechanics who rebuild and repair parts to keep an old automobile running when replacement parts are not readily available, rather than like mechanics in a large US dealership who discard and replace any malfunctioning parts with replacement units.

A Question of Community: Seasonality

Several perennial problems have come about throughout the history of the NOC. Perhaps the most basic of these has been the seasonality of most of our activities. While a few hard-core paddlers paddle year-round and a somewhat larger number enjoy spring and fall trips, the majority of the public seems to only want to go on rivers during the hot months of summer. Other activities that we have offered, such as biking, backpacking, fly-fishing, climbing, horseback trail riding, log cabin–building workshops, and ropes courses are popular in the shoulder seasons, but we have not been able to attract nearly as many participants for those activities.

The two most successful activities we have offered to produce some income through the winter months have been our adventure travel trips and certification courses for wilderness first responder, emergency medical technician, and others. Retail sales and food service stay open through the winter, but the activity is only a small fraction of what it is in the summer months. This situation meant that while we were always able to operate very profitably through the summer and at a breakeven or small profit level through the shoulder season, there were always about five months of the year when we saw much of that profit trickle away. The majority of whitewater businesses deal with this problem by closing down and retaining only a skeleton staff through the off-season. Our goal of building a permanent community prevented us from adopting this approach.

Over the years, we continuously struggled to find the best balance between the desire to provide year-round employment to build a community and the need to limit winter employment in the interest of conserving cash. In good years, we could often afford to provide work through building projects. Scheduling vehicle and building maintenance, doing mailing list work, and producing publications for winter months also helped. I always tried to err on the side of providing as much work as possible, even if it was not always the most efficient course.

Another approach was to build relationships with counter-seasonal businesses, such as ski resorts, Christmas tree lots, or outfitting companies in more southern locales, which might provide guiding and teaching jobs. These arrangements enabled a sizable group of people to remain at the NOC during the warmer months for quite a few years, but they really didn't solve the problem because eventually almost everyone felt a need to settle down in a year-round home.

During these years, I read extensively about employee ownership and cooperatives. One of the books that most interested me was Hal Hartzell Jr.'s *Birth of a Cooperative: Hoedads, Inc., A Worker Owned Forest Labor Co-op* (Hulogos'i Press, 1987). The history of the Hoedads began with three friends from the University of Oregon deciding to bid on their own for a small tree-planting contract with the Bureau of Land Management, rather than continuing to work for larger contractors. Over the following years, many others joined them and some stuck with the work through the difficult learning period. By the end of 1974, there were 150 members in nine crews, and they became a cooperative corporation. By the end of

1978, over 1,000 members had participated in the work and they had completed more than $6 million worth of contracts.

I was struck by the similarity in backgrounds of the Hoedads to the people in the NOC community, by the similarity in their aspirations, and by the parallels in the history of the Hoedads and the NOC. Because we were surrounded by national forests, which contracted for tree planting and brush clearing work in the colder months, and because we had many physically strong young staff members who needed off-season work, I thought we might successfully follow the example of the Hoedads and begin doing contract work for the U.S. Forest Service. For a couple years we contracted in our off-season to plant seedlings and to cut back the brush that had grown up around previously planted seedlings. Hartzell quotes the State of Oregon Employment Department's description of this work:

> It is the hardest physical work known to this office. The most comparative physical requirement is that of a 5-mile cross-mountain run, daily. If all body joints are in very good condition, a person has excellent persistence and at four-and-a-half miles of your self-trial run, you know you can do it, and can persuade the foreman, you may make it the three weeks it takes to really learn how to be a team member on a planting crew. . . . Of those who adequately persist to get on the 2-hour crummy ride for a trial, 1 person in 50 succeeds for the three-week training period. It is actually a good job for some. (pp. 27–28)

During the Thanksgiving-to-Christmas season, our same crew would work at a local Christmas tree farm, harvesting, sorting, and loading trees for the market. The jobs were very demanding physically, and after a couple years, most staff members decided that the earnings were not worth the long hours of hard labor. I was disappointed because I believed that eventually I would become better at bidding for the contract work, we would become more efficient at the labor, and our earnings would improve as had been the case with the Hoedads. Perhaps if a few more members of the crew had read about the Hoedads, they would have been inspired to stick with the hard work, but during the period of contract work, we were all working from dawn to dark, and we were too tired afterward to do anything except eat and sleep. During the warmer months, we were all too busy working and playing on the rivers.

We were never able to solve the problems resulting from the seasonality of our activities. This created some tensions between those who had year-round work and tended to value efforts to support the community and those who found it necessary to move between jobs. The latter tended to think it would be fairer to cut the winter staff back to the most cost-efficient level, which they argued would make us more profitable annually and thus able to pay higher salaries to everyone.

We continued to debate numerous related issues, such as the value of keeping the restaurant open through the months that it was not profitable primarily because it enabled us to keep skilled staff. I often thought that those who believed they were making hardheaded business decisions about seasonally shutting down nonprofitable operations were usually failing to consider all the indirect costs of doing so: having to always recruit and train new staff without having much of an experienced cadre to do the training, losing returning customers, and so on. For this reason, I favored regularly keeping River's End Restaurant, the store, and all our lodging open year-round.

A Question of Community: Short-Term Dividends vs. Long-Term Investment?

Another perennial issue was the balance between devoting a larger proportion of our earnings to higher pay versus investing more funds to support longer-term revenue-producing activities. Soon after we initially became profitable, we decided that none of our earnings would be used for shareholder dividends. I argued that over the long term, since all year-round employees were acquiring stock in the NOC, all of us as shareholders would benefit more by the long-term increase in the value of our shares if we devoted all of our available earnings toward growth rather than paying dividends. When the board approved this policy, it narrowed the choice of the best use of earnings to that of immediate increased compensation or investment in capital projects.

Of course, capital improvements were paid for by earnings, and pay increases came out of our operating budget, but I felt this distinction only blurred the choice because increases in payroll one year decreased the earnings available for capital spending in future years. The basic issue was between those in favor of better immediate compensation and those in favor of greater deferred benefits. I realize that it was much easier for those of us who expected to remain as permanent members of the community to support deferred compensation than for those who thought they would likely stay around for only a few years. So once again the argument was closely tied to the importance of building a permanent community.

I think it was easier for me because when we moved to the mountains I decided to forgo the attractions of a consumer-oriented lifestyle in favor of a life of voluntary simplicity.[1] We made much less money at the NOC than we had in Atlanta, but we needed only one car rather than two, and we put very few miles on that car. In Atlanta, Aurelia and I had each spent about an hour and a half daily driving to and from work, and much of our weekends driving to and from the mountains to play. At the NOC, we spent almost nothing on clothes or entertainment. Initially food was included as part of our compensation, and when that was discontinued, we continued to eat all our meals on a low-cost staff meal plan for many years. And we could acquire our outdoor toys at a very low cost,

---

[1] I was largely inspired by *Voluntary Simplicity: An Ecological Lifestyle that Promotes Personal and Social Renewal* by Duane Elgin (New York: Bantam Books, 1982).

either through our discount at the NOC store or at the fall used-equipment sale. Hence a good life at the NOC really didn't require much cash. It was difficult to save much for retirement years, but I believed that because everyone was able to acquire stock, we would all be able to use our stock to provide retirement funds, and this did work out well for Aurelia and me, as well as a few others.

The idea that complicated the issue for me the most was the argument that our low pay caused many good staff members to leave the NOC and that this weakened us both as a business and a community. Compensation did increase erratically but at a rate faster than the rate of inflation over the years, but naturally it was never at a fast enough rate to quiet the continuing discontent. Initially we kept the range between the highest and lowest pay rates at a ratio of three to one, but over the years it increased to five to one, although I kept my own pay at the four-to-one ratio. We continued to struggle to find the right balance on this issue throughout our first three decades.

A Question of Community: An Outdoor Center or a Whitewater Center?

Another of the perennial arguments was whether we should follow our original wish to be an outdoor center offering a wide variety of outdoor activities or restrict our offerings to whitewater paddling. Our canoe and kayak courses seemed to be the most popular for-profit whitewater instructional programs in the United States and were the pride of our staff. We conducted several thousand user days of instruction each year, and we were able to price these courses so that they remained consistently profitable, even though the margin was never high. Rafting was always our highest volume, highest margin activity by far. At our peak in the late 1990s, we had a total of more than 80,000 participants a year on Nantahala rentals and guided trips alone. On peak days we offered a guided trip every 15 minutes and two to three bus rental shuttles every half hour. This volume and our ideal location at the takeout on the Nantahala enabled us to operate extremely efficiently and with a good profit margin. While our other rafting operations were less popular and less profitable, they did all operate in the black, offered opportunities for variety and progression to staff, served as backup options when the Nantahala power plant went down, and provided a variety of rivers of differing difficulty and scenic qualities for guests.

Over the years, a number of senior staff argued that we should stop offering such a variety of activities, should concentrate on what we did best and what offered the highest profit, and should shut down through the winter. Their idea was to greatly reduce our overhead and concentrate on further improving the quality of our core programs, which would enable us to become profitable enough to afford better pay, which would help staff make it through the winter without working at the NOC.

Once again, the position that individuals took frequently depended on how much value they placed on creating and supporting a permanent community at the NOC. Those who placed the highest value on community often wished to provide as many jobs as possible throughout the year. In many cases, we also enjoyed the variety of activities and teaching different skills. I, as well as others on this side of the argument, maintained that because each of the activities we continued offering had a positive, even if small, margin when considering only direct costs, they each made some contribution to supporting our overhead costs and there would be little if any improvement in profitability from discontinuing them. We were never able to objectively answer the question of whether by simplifying operations we could reduce overhead costs enough to more than offset the contributions made by those less profitable operations, but I was always dubious.

I also felt that the complexities resulting from the variety of activities made life more interesting and challenging. I especially enjoyed participating in some of the great variety of adventure travel trips we offered in the off-season and felt that continuing to offer them even though they contributed little, if anything, to profitability enabled us to keep many of our best trip leaders challenged and excited and therefore more likely to stay around.

On Growth

The perennial issue that possibly generated the most continuous interest and heat over the years was that of how much growth was most beneficial. This was not an issue for the first few years when our survival was at stake. We accepted that all aspects of our business needed to grow as rapidly as possible to allow us enough income to pay our bills and to make the mortgage payment each spring. For the first four years, trip numbers sometimes doubled from month to month, and revenues more than doubled from year to year. Our psychology began to change after our fourth year, in which we first showed a profit and began making decisions about how to allocate our surplus funds.

The issue of using the surplus for higher pay versus investing for future returns has been described above. A related issue that was barely mentioned at first but gradually became prominent was how rapidly we wanted business, revenues, and profit to increase. As we became busier, the pace of work became faster and unanticipated problems more frequent. Some people found this stressful. Some of them argued that we should control our growth so that it came at a slower and more regular pace, which we could better plan for. This was usually stated in terms of allowing us to be able to ensure higher quality experiences for our guests.

We also began to worry about overcrowding the rivers, especially the Nantahala. On August 13, 1977, the U.S. Forest Service counted 1,008 paddlers on the

Nantahala. This called our attention to the overcrowding issue, and we decided to limit our business on busy days in 1978 to a total of 800 rafters. We soon realized that this did little or nothing to decrease overall numbers but simply resulted in the folks we turned away going with one of the other two new outfitters on the Nantahala. The following year, we stopped turning people away and began trying to work out a voluntary agreement among the growing number of outfitters to limit numbers on busy days. This was an unsuccessful effort, but in 1984 the U.S. Forest Service finally restricted the number of commercial outfitters to the 13 then in operation and the number of rafters that each outfitter could take on the busiest days. Each outfitter received a different allocation of allowed rafters based on historical use records. After the unsatisfactory effort to limit growth in 1978, we didn't make further efforts to limit our growth, but the discussions continued unabated.

This was probably the most difficult issue for me. Philosophically, I agreed with those who argued for limiting growth. Some of my favorite books of the time were *Small Is Beautiful, Voluntary Simplicity* (Duane Elgin, Morrow, 1981) and *Muddling Towards Frugality* (Warren Johnson, Sierra Club Books, 1978) and I was committed to the idea of voluntary simplicity and limits to growth. Yet temperamentally I seemed to enjoy the challenges of rapid growth, rather than finding them stressful. When folks talked about becoming overly tired and burned out, I usually thought, even if I didn't say it, that it was because they were not really focused on what they were doing, so they were able to get into the flow. The challenges of growth helped me achieve a flow state and were therefore energizing rather than stressful.

Some of the days I remember with the greatest pleasure and pride are those when high water or problems at the power plant forced us to shift trips from one river to another. For example, on one busy Saturday when a power plant fire caused the water on the Nantahala to be shut off unexpectedly, we offered all our Nantahala guests the option of going on the Pigeon River. About 20 of us and several buses traveled together to the Pigeon for the day. There was a feeling of camaraderie and excitement on the bus rides to and from the Pigeon, and I thought there weren't many companies that could have pulled this off and created a good experience for guests and guides. I think most of us were in the flow.

According to the Kriegels' description of the panic zone, the drone zone, and the C Zone, the newer staff members, who hadn't yet mastered their jobs, should have experienced the stress and anxiety of the panic zone. But it appeared to me that it was the older, more experienced staff members with a high level of mastery who were complaining about burnout. I thought that it was actually the boredom of the drone zone that was more often the problem than the stresses of rapid growth. I argued that we needed to grow to earn the profits that were enabling us to improve the quality of life for staff and the quality of our equipment and facilities. John Burton was more sympathetic to the point of view that our rapid growth was overly stressful for many staff members.

The argument against continued growth that was most compelling to me was that with the increase in staff size, the strength of community weakened because one simply could not know so many staff members well. Yuval Harari in *Sapiens: A Brief History of Humankind* (Harvill Secker, 2014) says that sociological research has shown that the maximum number of persons in an organization based on intimate acquaintance rather than on ranks, titles, and rules is about 150. In the late 1990s, our number of year-round staff was approaching this threshold and the number of summer staff was over 600. We all agreed that it was becoming more difficult to know all of the year-round staff and that loyalties to the NOC were being displaced by loyalties to individual outposts or departments. The discussion finally ended only when the popularity of whitewater paddling and rafting decreased at the end of the 1990s. With the difficulty of maintaining profitability when our regular growth ended, no one seemed to think this was a good thing and we all became focused on how to bring about growth again.

I think that if most folks who have spent time at the NOC are asked what has been most different and most valuable about their time here, they are likely to answer in terms of the strong community and the incredible group of people who make up that community. Just as in the most cohesive military units, individuals are likely to say that what usually motivates them to perform at an exceptional level is the wish not to let their comrades down. That often seems to be the strongest motivation for folks at the NOC to strive for exceptional levels of performance.

Over the years, I have heard with increasing frequency folks using expressions such as "having one another's backs" and "looking out for their wingman on the river." And when I receive communications from former employees about their time here, they most often speak about what an incredible community it was and how they still feel a part of that community, even though they no longer live at Wesser or one of our outposts.

As I have gone through the exercise of thinking and writing about some of the issues that we disagreed about, I have come to realize how very often the arguments revolved around the effects that different policies would have on this community. There were always financial arguments as well, but they were usually couched in terms of what greater financial success would enable us to do for our community and for the quality of our programs rather than as an end in itself.

After John, Bunny, and I were no longer in full-time leadership roles at the NOC but I remained on the board of directors, there was actually a motion made for the board to modify the Statement of Purposes, which had guided us for our first three decades, to change the priorities of the purposes. Our first three broad purposes were:

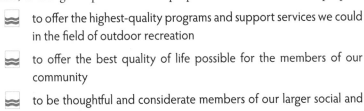

≋   to offer the highest-quality programs and support services we could in the field of outdoor recreation

≋   to offer the best quality of life possible for the members of our community

≋   to be thoughtful and considerate members of our larger social and ecological communities

The fourth purpose was explicitly instrumental, rather than being an end in itself. It was to earn enough profit to accomplish the first three purposes. The motion was to change the fourth purpose to become the first in priority and recognize it as an end in itself. My recollection is that this motion was defeated in a five-to-four vote and that in the next few years those board members who had supported it all left the board. By the time I returned to full-time work as CEO and CPO (chief philosophical officer) in 2004, we once again had a board that was unified in priorities.

Warren Buffet has long been my greatest hero among business leaders, and he has argued persuasively that he views his top priority as achieving the best possible return on investment for Berkshire Hathaway shareholders. I accept this as a valid argument in the case of a large impersonal conglomerate with thousands of shareholders having relatively little interest in the company other than the return on their investment.

On the other hand, the NOC was founded with the goal of being a community and a company consisting of friends working together in an environment they love and teaching the activities they love to share. All shareholders invested with the knowledge that this was the intention and that no dividends were anticipated in the foreseeable future. Almost all shareholders were employees, and the few who were not were personal friends who wished to support the recognized goals of the center. I continue to believe that in this context our emphasis on community and achieving the best quality of life possible for our employees and community members at the possible expense of maximizing profitability was justified.

I could continue with this discussion of various issues that we debated over the years, but I am sure I have already exhausted the patience of many readers, so I would like to end this Chautauqua on our philosophy and practices with one remarkable observation. As I have been thinking and writing, I have realized that I never doubted the positive motivation of any of those I disagreed with. When the board was frequently divided on a five-to-four basis, I had no doubts that all of those I disagreed with had the best interest of the NOC and its employees at heart. We simply had honest disagreements about what was in the best interest of the employees or how best to achieve those interests. I also found that those with whom I disagreed were a remarkably capable and intelligent group of adversaries, and in the case of outside directors, persons who were willing to devote a tremendous amount of unpaid time to a business and community they loved. I think this is a remarkable and unusual business environment, and it reflects the strength of the community we built.

About the Contributor

See page 81 for more information about Payson Kennedy.

GOOD THINGS NEVER END:
A POEM FOR PAYSON'S 70TH BIRTHDAY

By Gordon Grant

From Journal, 8/29/02

I went to sleep and dreamt that I was standing on the table in the Deep Creek Campground, looking down at Payson and Aurelia and all those whose lives they had brought together, and I said the following, borrowing from Robert Frost's "The Silken Tent":

You two are, as in a field, a silken tent
At midday, when a sunny summer breeze
Has dried the dew, so all its ropes relent,
and in guys it gently sways at ease,
And whose supporting central cedar pole
That is its pinnacle to heavenward, and signifies the sureness of the soul
Is tightly held by naught, but loosely bound
By countless silken ties of love and thought the compass round
And only by one's going slightly taut
In the capriciousness of summer air
Is of the slightest bondage made aware.
Then, I stood up and kept speaking, and these words were my own:
When you are gone, may your bones
Transform with time to stones
Rebuilding mountains, so that those
Who are descendants of descendants of descendants
Of followers of you two
May come to a strange familiar space:
A clear quick stream, where
At the water's edge there is another chance
To build a place anew,
Where all who come to work in play
Find again that all the joy that's in the world
Is in the joy of loving what you do.
And then I woke up. I swung my feet over the bed, grabbed my journal, wrote the words exactly as they are here, and went back to sleep.

 ## *About the Contributor*

See page 12 for more information about Gordon Grant.

Epilogue

By Payson Kennedy

B unny did her best to satisfy the board of the Nantahala Outdoor Center (NOC) for three years beginning in 1998, but unfortunately the decline in rafting numbers that had begun in 1996 continued. For the first two years, we all assumed that the decline was one of the minor fluctuations that we had repeatedly experienced over the years, but by 1998 it was becoming increasingly apparent that this was a more general and lasting decline in interest than we had seen previously. Numbers were declining on all the rivers we ran, except the Pigeon, on which rafting was relatively new. From what we heard and read, this trend seemed to be occurring nationwide.

Responding to these declines in rafting numbers and revenues, Bunny began trying to make adjustments in a company that had grown used to relatively steady growth for 24 years. She managed to keep the NOC profitable in those three years of declining numbers. After 2000, Bunny left employment with the NOC, and David Ennis, who was chairman of the board, took over as CEO.

Just as the NOC was attempting to negotiate a tumultuous period of declining interest in whitewater activities, the company had now lost the accumulated experience and knowledge of John Burton, Payson Kennedy, and Bunny Johns, the three primary leaders during its first 29 years. In 2001 staff morale suffered as we experienced our first year with a financial loss since 1974, and David Ennis eliminated many of the less profitable operations and several supervisory positions to reduce overhead expenses. In 2002 we had a small profit again. David recruited Larry Pitt, who had been director of the North Carolina Outward Bound School, to take over at the NOC in 2003. The NOC experienced another losing year, morale was declining precipitously, and many senior company leaders were ready to leave. The board asked for Pitt's resignation. After 26 profitable years, we had at that point experienced losses in two of the last three years.

I am convinced that forcing Bunny's resignation was the greatest mistake that the NOC board ever made. I am confident that if Bunny had remained as CEO she would have figured out how to adjust to the declining interest in whitewater without the damage to staff morale, leadership turmoil, and declining profitability that occurred the following three years.

In 2004 the board asked me to come back to work as CEO, and I began full-time work again. We experienced three years of slowly increasing profitability and slowly improving staff morale. During these three years, our leadership group studied together Jim Collins's books, *Good to Great* and *Built to Last*. In talks to staff, I frequently used the metaphor from *Good to Great* that the flywheel had begun to turn in the right direction and was very slowly beginning to gather momentum. But I was now 73 years old and had learned to enjoy the time in carefree travel, bicycling, and working in my pond that retirement allowed. The chastened board and I struggled to find a successor who would maintain the values that had made the NOC successful.

We eventually found Sutton Bacon, who took over as CEO in 2007. In 2012 he brought in several investors who were interested in outdoor recreation to strengthen the company's balance sheet after several more years of losses. A new partnership was formed, which included all of the prior owners who wanted to stay involved but was controlled by the new investors. Under the leadership of Sutton and these new partners, the NOC has again become profitable and it is my great hope that they will continue to support the values that made the NOC so incredibly successful during the years leading up to Bunny's departure.

APPENDIX
Chronology of Events: 1971–1997

By Payson Kennedy

T his chronology is based on fading memories and some historical documents, including the book of minutes from the NOC board meetings, various notes that I kept, minutes of some executive committee meetings, a file of race results, and a list of past NOC employees. It is at least generally true but almost certainly contains some inaccuracies.

It has surprised me to see how vividly I remember many events and staff from the first 10 years and how blurred my memories of the later years and staff have become. As the staff grew larger, it became increasingly difficult to know them all, and my memory also seems to have become poorer. As a result I have recorded more detail about the early years and mostly the events that I find recorded for the later years.

I chose 1997 as a cutoff date because that was the last year I worked before I first retired from full-time work at the NOC. Overall, this record shows how growth occurred throughout the first 26 years of the NOC's history and something about the people who brought about that growth.

Editor's Note: If you notice inaccuracies or can suggest additions, we would love to learn of them so we can make corrections. We would also be interested to hear from former staff about what you have been doing since leaving the NOC.

1971

H orace Holden reached an agreement with Vincent and Dorothy Gassaway to purchase the Tote 'N' Tarry, a complex located on US 19, where the Appalachian Trail crosses the Nantahala River. It included a 14-unit motel, small restaurant, gas station, and souvenir shop.

1972

W inter. Horace recruited Payson and Aurelia Kennedy to manage his operation at the Nantahala, and the three of them began making preparations to operate a recreational facility at what had been the Tote 'N' Tarry motel complex. The three agreed on the name, Nantahala Outdoor Center (NOC), and that the new facility would serve the general public as well as groups from Horace's camp and family club.

We created its first NOC brochure, which emphasized rafting on the Nantahala but also stated that by special arrangement NOC could lead one- to three-day group trips on the Chattooga, Chattahoochee, Hiwassee, Little Tennessee, and other rivers in the area.

Spring. Horace closed on the property, and four Rubber Fabricator 12-foot, single-thwart rafts were purchased. About 20 staff members were recruited, largely from Explorer Scout Post 49, which specialized in whitewater kayaking and for which Doug Woodward, Claude Terry, and Payson were adult advisors. Crucially, Jim Holcombe, a veterinary medicine student at the University of Georgia, also agreed to come work at the new NOC.

Summer. Payson was granted a leave of absence for the summer from his job at Georgia Tech, and Aurelia, as a public school teacher, had her summers free. The initial staff numbered about 20, including Aurelia and Payson and their four children: Cathy (16), Frances (14), John (12), and Stewart (10). Besides Cathy and Frances, several other Explorer Scouts worked at various times through the first few years: Charley Holden, Marc Reimer, John Stephenson, Laurie Greiner, Ron Greiner, Bruce Lowell, and Hugh Hilliard.

Several Georgia Tech graduates who had been active in the outing club at Georgia Tech also worked during the first several years. These included Jim Shelander, Gary Lewis, Tom Doyle, Tom Gonzalez, Ken Simonton, Jim Karwisch, and Steve McDaniel. (Payson notes: I'm unsure who worked the first summer, who worked only weekends, and who worked in subsequent years.) A Kennedy cousin, Linda Percival began working that first summer and came back for about six additional years. Finally, a kayaker named Jim Beyers somehow found his way to this new river operation, and a local man, Larce Mashburn, who had worked in the store for the previous owner, continued working for the new NOC.

Larce always worked in the store but the other staff did whatever jobs needed to be done, whether it was guiding a raft, cooking, waiting tables, washing dishes, cleaning motel rooms, or driving a shuttle. The high-school-age guides from the Explorer Post were paid $20 per week, plus room and board. I think the Georgia Tech students got $50 per week.

Rafting trips were conducted on the Nantahala and Chattooga Rivers. Lunch was included on both trips, and the cost was $10 for a Nantahala trip and $20 for a Chattooga trip. Raft capacity was three guests and a guide in each of the 12-foot rafts, so our initial trips were limited to 12 guests.

The NOC vehicle fleet consisted of the Kennedy's 12-passenger 1970 Ford van and two used Camp Chattahoochee GMC vans.

The NOC began taking North Carolina Outward Bound School (NCOBS) crews on multiday raft trips on the Chattooga. NCOBS turned over their four Avon Redshank rafts to the NOC, increasing its raft fleet to eight boats with a capacity of 24 guests. Three NCOBS staff members worked on all their trips. Two of them, Paul Yeuell and Don Haldiman, joined the NOC staff the following year.

The movie *Deliverance* was released in August. Payson made a trip to Atlanta to see the movie and hand out NOC brochures featuring trips on the Chattooga River, where the movie was filmed. The NOC got a flurry of interest in Chattooga trips.

Doug Woodward was race chairman this year for the Georgia Canoeing Association–sponsored races that had been held annually on the Nantahala since 1969. Against the advice of many more conservative paddlers, Doug shifted the site for the slalom competition from Patton's Run to Nantahala Falls. He also managed to get sanction from the American Canoe Association to designate the races as the Southeastern Championship Canoe and Kayak Races. Eventually Doug also obtained sanction from the 1972 Olympic Slalom Committee to make this race the last qualifying race for the US Olympic Team Trials.

There were 312 entries in the race, including many of the top Olympic contenders. Lots of the NOC staff participated, especially the Explorer Scouts. In the championship slalom classes, Jim Holcombe placed third in C-1; Payson was sixth in K-1; Cathy Kennedy was fourth in K-1W; John Stephenson, Hugh Hilliard, and Bruce Loehle were first, fifth, and seventh in the K-1 Jr. class. In the slalom team races Payson, Hugh Hilliard, and John Stephenson were last of the four K-1 teams. In the wildwater championship races, Payson and Cathy were second in the C-2M

John Stephenson

class, Cathy was first and Frances Kennedy second in the K-1W Jr. class, and Hugh Hilliard and John Stephenson were fourth and fifth in the K-1 Jr. class.

Whitewater slalom competition was included in the Olympics for the first time in 1972, and it was held on an artificial course constructed at Augsburg, Germany. Over the next several years, seven of the paddlers on that US team came to work at the NOC.

Rates in the motel were $8 for a room with one double bed and up to $18 for a room with two double beds and a kitchenette.

The most problematic area of operations was the restaurant, because no one on the staff had previous restaurant experience. As the most experienced cook, Aurelia took over the management of the restaurant. The menu was quite abbreviated. All staff members except Larce ate family-style meals in the restaurant. The dinners cooked for staff were available to the public as the River Runners Special.

Rafting numbers totaled about 800 persons on the Nantahala and 400 on the Chattooga, but revenues from rafting were under $5,000. Restaurant revenues were about $14,000, store revenues (including gasoline sales) just over $15,000, motel revenues almost $7,000, and revenues from shuttles, instruction, and miscellaneous sources made up the remainder. Total revenues for the summer were about $45,000. Our checkbook, showing bank deposits and expenses paid by check, was essentially the only financial record maintained. With amortization and depreciation included, the operations showed a loss, but with Payson and Aurelia taking no pay for the summer, revenues exceeded direct cash expenses by almost $8,000.

Cathy Kennedy recalls that Aurelia had to return to her teaching job in Atlanta in late August, but the rest of the family stayed in Wesser to keep the NOC open through Labor Day. Cathy and Frances were in charge of the restaurant during this period, and each got a raise from $20 per week to $50 per week. After Labor Day, most of the staff left and the NOC at Wesser shut down for the winter. Don Haldiman, who had been a North Carolina Outward Bound staff member that summer but worked with the NOC on all Outward Bound trips, stayed around to keep an eye on the facilities.

After the stimulation of interest by *Deliverance* and the Olympics, demand for raft trips continued in the fall, especially for Chattooga trips, so the Kennedys, with the help of other Explorer Scouts and Georgia Tech students, continued to run weekend raft trips. Payson remembers on several occasions using funds from the previous weekend's trips to purchase additional paddles, life jackets, or helmets for the coming weekend's trips.

1973

Winter and Spring. The Kennedys made the big decision to resign from their jobs and leave Atlanta, selling their house, collecting their retirement funds, and investing all their available cash plus credit for their previous summer's work and their furniture, tools, van, and fleet of personal boats in the NOC to become equal partners with Horace in that operation. Four additional rafts were ordered, increasing the fleet to 12 boats. An order was placed for about a dozen Grumman 17-foot shoe-keel aluminum canoes to be delivered in the summer. A few would be kept for sale in the new outfitter's store, and most would be used for canoeing instruction and rentals.

In March, the NOC's first whitewater instructional clinic was conducted at Camp Chattahoochee near Roswell, Georgia, and on the Nantahala at the new NOC. Members of the Ledyard Canoe Club of Dartmouth, including Eric Evans, who was on the US Olympic Team the previous summer and was a US national champion in slalom kayaking for many years, were the instructors. The clinic

attracted more than 70 participants, mostly from the Georgia Canoeing Association, which Horace had founded a few years earlier and for which Payson was the immediate past president.

Summer. During the last week of May, the Kennedys made the big move to Wesser. The Kennedys began renting the Stone House on river left from the Queen brothers, and a couple other female staff members usually stayed there with them. The Queens were unwilling to rent to the NOC but willing to rent to the Kennedys for their family to use. Hence any additional female staff staying there became "cousins," along with actual cousins Linda and George Percival. Most of the other younger male staff again stayed in the bunkhouse created from the garage at the house Horace owned on Gassaway Road. The Car-

Carter Martin, John Kennedy, and Payson Kennedy on a 1973 Chattooga trip

ter Martin family lived in the motel manager's quarters. The quality of the staff attracted for this season was crucial in attracting even more quality staff in the following years and is largely responsible for the growth and success of the NOC.

Louise Holcombe, Jim's younger sister, and Carrie Ashton, both of whom were kayakers on the US Olympic Team the previous summer, came to work at the NOC in the summer of 1973 and played an important role in getting the instruction program off to a strong start and in attracting other Olympic paddlers to work at the NOC. Both of Louise's children worked at the NOC's Chattooga

Outpost in more recent years. John Holland, who paddled K-1 on the US team at the Olympics, also worked for a time during the summer.

Carter and Jane Martin, canoeists from Huntsville, Alabama, with their teenage sons, Carter Jr. and Doug, came for the summer, and we hoped to convince them to invest in the NOC and stay on as partners. Jane acted as motel and office manager and began fixing up the somewhat rundown motel rooms.

Carter helped get the Outfitter's Store operating and worked on the river. They received NOC stock when it was issued the following February, rather than a salary for their work that summer. Unfortunately, at the end of the summer, the Martins decided the financial prospects of the NOC were a little too iffy for them to give up their regular jobs as a high school librarian and a university professor and gamble their future on the success of the center.

Allie and Florrie Funk, sisters from Atlanta, also joined us this summer. Allie developed a new horseback trail riding program and worked hard building trails and fences. Both sisters joined our first adventure travel trip to the Usumacinta River in February 1976.

Larry and Alex Roberts, graduates of the Baylor School in Chattanooga, also joined us. Larry later went to work at Baylor and recommended the Chattooga River and the NOC to Herb Barks, the Baylor headmaster, when Herb decided to take some of his senior students on an outdoor camping adventure in the mountains. This experience contributed to Herb's plan to begin the Walkabout program at Baylor, in which senior students can spend a week in outdoor activities at the Chattooga, rather than taking final exams. This program has been going now for more than 40 years. Herb has played an important role in NOC history by recommending the NOC to many other private schools and by serving on our board of directors.

Harry and Joyce Allison, our new restaurant managers, were not quite the same kind of folks as the other staff, but they did have years of restaurant experience. They were able to get the restaurant running a bit more professionally and began teaching Aurelia about restaurant management. After a few months, the Allisons moved on.

The NOC sold all the remaining souvenir and craft items from the old Tote 'N' Tarry store at a liquidation price and used the funds to minimally stock the new Outfitter's Store. Payson also sold the jukebox from the restaurant for $50. Horace has never forgiven him for this because Horace said many of the records alone were now collector's items and worth far more. The store cash register was old and hardly functional. The store staff was sure we needed to purchase a new cash register, but Payson told them they could use a cigar box and calculator if necessary until the NOC began making a profit.

Joe Terrell and Jim Shannonhouse, novice kayakers at the time, began paddling along with NOC Chattooga trips and became good friends of the NOC.

In July the US National Wildwater Kayak Championship races were held on Section IV of the Chattooga. In the K-1 class John Holland was third, Jim Shelander was fifth, and Payson was sixth. In the K-1W class Carrie Ashton was second, and in the K-1 Jr. class Hugh Hilliard was second. David Benner was third in the C-1 class.

As Labor Day weekend approached, many staff members were exhausted from working long days, and some had already left to return to school, so the remaining staff came to Payson with an ultimatum. They said that there was insufficient staff to stay open over the Labor Day weekend and that they wouldn't be able to offer quality service. Payson responded that the NOC was just starting to develop a group of loyal guests who expected to be served if they came for the weekend, and he said that the company could lose their confidence if they came and found the NOC closed. As the impasse continued, Payson said that he was going to remain open with whatever help he could get. If necessary, he would cook breakfast for whoever was there and would then take as many people as he could on the river but he hoped the remaining staff would all decide to help. There was a long silence, but finally Jim Beyers spoke up and said that he was staying to help. The others then all fell in line and we had a successful weekend. Payson has always been deeply appreciative of Jim's support at this critical moment.

Fall. Aurelia began a regular job teaching first grade at nearby Andrews, North Carolina, and became the primary breadwinner for the Kennedy family over the next several years. She continued in her role as restaurant manager, working in the restaurant on weekends and often in the evenings after school.

Scott, Russ, and Patrice Price were among the new staff. Scott and Russ took over the management of the store, and Patrice became a mainstay of the restaurant. Patrice has continued to work at the NOC most of the time since then and has managed the River's End Restaurant as well as Relia's Garden restaurant. She raised her two children, Rayne and Heather, as part of the NOC community. Scott became one of the initial stockholders and directors. Robert Harkness became a key river leader and helped to familiarize Les Bechdel with the Chattooga and NOC practices there when Les took over as manager of our Chattooga Outpost. When the NOC was finally incorporated, he and his parents became the largest stockholders after Horace and the Kennedys. Robert continued to work at the NOC for many years, and he also managed the Cullowhee store, along with James Jackson, for several years. He still retains an ownership stake in the NOC.

Joe Cole came to work as a mechanic and photographer. A buddy of Joe's named Donnie Dunton came to the Gorge with Joe, but Payson would not hire Donnie initially.

The NOC continued to run trips on both the Chattooga and Nantahala through the fall, but as the weather turned colder, work and revenues became scarce.

NOC staff created a boatbuilding shop at Horace's brick house and tried to develop a business of providing facilities, molds, supplies, and assistance for people coming to the NOC to build their own boats, but the business did not prosper. They also tried making spray skirts to sell, but neither did this business prosper. Payson bid on a U.S. Forest Service contract for rerouting the local Appalachian Trail, but he didn't get the contract. It was a difficult winter and spring until business picked up in late spring.

Trip numbers grew to 2,719 on the Nantahala and 1,114 on the Chattooga, more than triple the numbers of the prior season. Revenues for August were approximately the same as those of the entire previous summer, and revenues for the June through October period totaled about $135,000. But the NOC again showed a small loss for the year when indirect costs were included.

1974

On March 1, Jim Shannonhouse, one of the two kayakers who had begun accompanying NOC trips on the Chattooga the prior summer, incorporated the Nantahala Outdoor Center in North Carolina. The initial shares were valued at $10. The first board of directors was made up of Horace (chairman), Aurelia, Payson, Jim Shannonhouse, and Scott Price.

Key staff who began work in 1974 included Bunny Johns, who eventually became president of the NOC; John Barbour, who managed the main NOC store for years; Anne Hodgson, who was the first marketing manager; Tom Bolen, who became maintenance manager after Bob Bouknight's departure; Dave Heflin, who was a physical education instructor at Delta State University and who continued to bring groups to the Chattooga for years (his son, Land, eventually followed him to work at the NOC); and Bill and Cece Ussler.

Russ Nichols, a C-2 paddler from the 1972 US Olympic Team, followed his teammates Louise Holcombe and Carrie Ashton to work at the NOC. Miki Piras (Sager), who was a top K-1W competitor, also started work in 1974. Other prominent paddlers who worked that season were Al Harris, a top C-2 competitor, and Charlie Walbridge, who was the national expert on whitewater safety for many years and the safety editor of *American Whitewater Journal.* Al and Betsy Quant and Sue Firmstone from the paddling club at Bucknell University in Pennsylvania also came with Charlie.

Donnie Dunton, whom Payson had eventually hired, traded one of the old Chattahoochee vans for a load of stone at a quarry up Silvermine Road. He used the stone to face the lower part of the pink stucco walls of the restaurant and motel units and then put hemlock siding over the upper portions, which gave the buildings a more pleasant rustic appearance.

The NOC began leasing Hellard's Motor Court for staff housing in Wesser as well as a derelict house on US 76 near the Chattooga for the guides to stay in rather than camping.

The NOC purchased four additional vehicles: 18 open canoes (13 used), 18 kayaks (10 used), 21 rafts (15 used), 90 personal flotation devices (PFDs), and 120 paddles.

The whitewater open canoe nationals were held on the Nantahala at Delabar's Rock rapids. This was the first time the nationals were held in the South. Claude Grizzard, a Georgia Canoeing Association (GCA) member from Atlanta, had won the C-1 class at the nationals in Maine the previous year and suggested that the GCA would be willing to sponsor the nationals on the Nantahala in 1974. NOC staff won many of the slalom events. The team of Miki Piras and Carrie Ashton won the women's tandem class in both slalom and wildwater, while Bunny Johns and Jeannie Bracket were second in both events. Charlie Walbridge won the men's slalom class and Les Bechdel was second. John Kennedy, at age 14 paddling with Payson, won the junior-senior class and had the best time, corrected for penalties, of the boats in all slalom classes. There were 76 entries in the slalom classes and 70 entries in the downriver classes. Mad River Canoe introduced a Kevlar open canoe at this race.

Congress designated the Chattooga River as a wild and scenic river.

Hollowform introduced the first roto-molded plastic kayak at a price of $129 ordered directly from the factory.

Carrie Ashton and Philip Williams—racing through Nantahala Falls

The NOC conducted 10 whitewater paddling instructional clinics and 50 three-day courses for the North Carolina Outward Bound School.

The NOC took 3,443 rafters on the Nantahala River and about 2,100 on the Chattooga River.

1975

This was another critical year in building the exceptional NOC staff. John Burton, who was another member of the 1972 US Olympic Team, came as assistant director and eventually became president. He played a major role in building the NOC. John was especially good at realizing the implications that all decisions would have on staff morale and culture.

Ray and Jackie McLeod joined Al and Betsy Quant in filling many of the roles that Carter and Jane Martin had filled, in supervising the younger staff and supervising the office and store operations. Horace's second son, Howard, began working. Cindy Goodwin, the third K-1W paddler on the 1972 Olympic Team, joined her teammates Louise Holcombe, Carrie Ashton, and Russ Nichols at the center. Cathy Potts was the first of many employees from the outing club at Sewanee: The University of the South to join us. The faculty advisor for the outing club was Hugh Caldwell, an occasional racing partner of Payson's. Hugh also became the director of Camp Merrie-Woode, and over the years guided many good staff from both Sewanee and Merrie-Woode to the NOC.

Dick Eustis, who became a longtime manager at the Ocoee Outpost and later managed the Rocky Mountain Outdoor Center before starting his own company, Rios Honduras, came to the NOC this year. Kathy Bolyn (KB), who remained for many years as a guide and instructor, also started this year. KB has the fastest time that Payson knows of for a woman on the Nantahala River. In the 1989 Southeastern US Slalom and Wildwater Championships, her time was 45:20. Other staff members who began that year were Linda Aponte (who became C2-M national champion with John Kennedy in slalom), Rick Ardolino, and Mike Beesch.

The NOC purchased Hellard's Motor Court, which had been leased the previous season. This was the first property addition since Horace's initial purchase, and the debate about purchasing it was long and intense, even though the purchase price was only $80,000 and the decision seems like a no-brainer in hindsight. Hellard's has remained the site of the NOC's main staff housing complex throughout the subsequent years, and in 2006 the company turned down an informal purchase offer of $1 million for it, figuring it would cost more than that to replace staff housing elsewhere.

The U.S. Forest Service began regulating trips on the Chattooga River. Each of the three outfitters was limited to six rafts and 30 guests per trip, and the number of trips was restricted. The NOC joined the other outfitters in switching from four-person rafts to larger rafts that could take five or six guests. The shift to larger rafts decreased the excitement but increased safety and also proved financially advantageous as it provided a better guest-to-guide ratio.

Anne Hodgson resumed production of the *NOC Newsletter,* which had not been produced since the issues Horace, Aurelia, and Payson produced during the winter of 1972–73, and this time it was improved and enlarged.

The first meeting of what was to become the Eastern Professional River Outfitters was held in the living room of the Stone House in November, and Payson was elected to serve as the first president of the organization.

On a weekend when races were being held on the Nantahala, a major flood occurred and the river rose to 9.5 feet on the old river gauge. A portable toilet that had been rented for the race weekend washed away and must still be at the bottom of Fontana Reservoir. Some staff who lived in the Stone House formed a chain and were able to steady one another while walking through the thigh-deep water to get to breakfast and work on river right. When Sara Ledford, a waitress, tried to follow them an hour later, she was washed downstream by the high water and spent a terrifying time hanging on to a tree above Big Wesser Falls, the Class V rapid downstream of the NOC, until a guest alerted Payson. He was able to rescue her with a throw rope. Stewart Kennedy walked a mile up the railroad tracks to the swinging bridge to cross safely.

Revenues increased to nearly $500,000, and the NOC made a profit for the first time. Payson told the store staff that they could purchase a new cash register. Henry Wallace, a paddler and friend from Prospect, Kentucky, purchased 1,000 shares of NOC stock, and John Burton and his father purchased 290 shares. It was a great pleasure to experience what an improvement in spirit came about as leadership gained confidence that the NOC would survive and were able to begin improvements to our facilities and equipment.

1976

The first NOC employee stock plan was created. Over the years, some employees earned several hundred shares, which they were able to sell for a few hundred dollars a share when they left employment, thus providing a type of retirement plan.

In February 1976 the NOC ran its first Adventure Travel trip on the Usumacinta River in Guatemala and Mexico.

The NOC purchased the present Chattooga Outpost property. Les Bechdel became our Chattooga Outpost manager.

David Dauphine, a CPA, came to work as company treasurer and greatly improved the quality of the NOC's rudimentary accounting.

The NOC sponsored the first triathlon to be held in the United States. It included a mile swim in Fontana Reservoir, a 4-mile run over the Needmore Road hill, and an 8-mile paddle in a solo open canoe down the Little Tennessee River and Fontana Reservoir back to the starting point at the NC 28 bridge. There were 43 entries in the individual classes, and 26 of those finished in under 3 hours.

Flatwater national champion paddler Sperry Rademaker won the women's competition. Bunny Johns was second, Kathy Bolyn fourth, Sherry Spurlin sixth, and Cathy Holcombe was eighth. John Kennedy won the junior class and Payson won the master's class. John beat his dad by a minute and a half. Olympic paddler John Burton won the men's competition. Russ Callen, a Georgia Tech colleague of Payson's, was sixth. Russ has now competed in the individual event in the Nantahala Outdoorsman Triathlon for 41 consecutive years and also in the team event with Jim Hall and Payson most years. Other NOC staff members who competed were Jim Shelander (2nd place), Tom Doyle (7th), Bill Shelander (10th), Les Bechdel (14th), Jim Holcombe (15th), James Jackson (17th), and Jim Shannonhouse (23rd).

On several high-water days, Section IV of the Chattooga was too dangerous, and instead guests were offered a chance to raft the Upper Nantahala at flood stage. On the first of these trips, when the rafts filled with water, guides found that most of the eddies were too small to stop for bailing or dumping the rafts, and they paddled pretty much out of control and without stopping until reaching the power house where they could eddy out. On subsequent trips, guides first ran a fast trip on the lower river to train crews before lunch and then ran the upper in the afternoon. They'd also learned the locations of a few eddies where it was possible to stop and empty the rafts.

On Labor Day, the old flume on the Ocoee River was shut down and water began running regularly in the old riverbed. Paddlers began running the Ocoee on a regular basis.

Bill Master's company Fiberglass Technology introduced the HD1, a solo open canoe for whitewater paddling.

Bunny Johns came to work full-time in 1976. Some of the other exceptional staff who began work in 1976 were Bill Baxter, Les Bechdel (first as Chattooga Outpost manager and later vice president in charge of facilities), Gordon Grant (Gordon succeeded Les as Chattooga Outpost manager and later became head of the NOC instruction program), Becky Grey, Drew Hammond (who came to the NOC from the NCOBS and became the manager of the vehicle shop), Ken Kastorff (who later became a founder and partner at Endless River Adventures), Dante Langston, Helen Langston (who was department head of the NOC reservations office for many years), Eve Mortimer, Russell Patterson, Gail Shoemaker, David Smith, Mike Smith, Ramelle Smith, and Sherry Spurlin (who managed the marketing department for several years).

John Burton joined the board of directors.

1977

"Fort Hammond," the equipment storage area upstream of the motel, was built. It was named for Drew Hammond, the first full-time manager of the maintenance of vehicles and equipment.

The NOC began several new programs: renting rafts without guides for use on the Nantahala, offering rock climbing instruction under Les Bechdel's leadership, leading cross-country skiing trips on the Blue Ridge Parkway and Clingmans Dome Road, and offering its first Grand Canyon trip for rafters and kayakers.

Our first competitor on the Nantahala River, Nantahala Rafts, began running raft trips.

Commercial rafting started on the Ocoee River with several new rafting companies, including Sunburst Adventures.

John Burton effectively became COO with the title director of the NOC, and Bunny Johns became the first department head for the instruction program. Ramon Eaton, who is widely known as the father of whitewater canoeing in the Southeastern United States, was elected to the board of directors. Ramon resided at Wesser for the several months of the paddling season.

The pay for first-year employees increased to $94 per week, plus meals and lodging.

Staff began blowing up rafts at the Chattooga with electric blowers run off of the truck battery, rather than with foot pumps.

On Saturday, August 13, 1,008 paddlers were counted on the Nantahala, and complaints from private paddlers about overcrowding the river increased.

Revenues were approaching $1 million, and we made a profit of more than $80,000 (about 8%, one of the highest margins NOC ever earned).

1978

John Burton and Payson wrote an editorial for the *NOC Newsletter* about overcrowding on the Nantahala, stating that on busy summer Saturdays the NOC would limit its business to 800 rafters. At the end of the season, John and Payson decided that their decision to limit business in order to limit traffic on the Nantahala had been a dismal failure.

The NOC began publishing a mail-order catalog as a part of the *NOC Newsletter.*

The NOC began operating on the Ocoee River with Dick Eustis as the outpost manager. This made a total of seven rafting businesses on the Ocoee. David Brown began coordinating lobbying efforts to ensure regular recreational water releases on the Ocoee after renovation of the flume was completed.

In the fall, the NOC began operation of an outfitter's store in Cullowhee, North Carolina, under the management of Robert Harkness and James Jackson.

1979

Don Weeden and Payson and Aurelia led the first NOC adventure travel trip in Nepal. The trip, which lasted for a month, began with a trek in the Langtang area after a few days of acclimatization and sightseeing in Kathmandu and continued with a rafting excursion for 150 miles down the Sun Kosi River from the mountains in the Everest region to the flat Tarai area near the border with India.

The NOC paddling fleet had now increased to 56 canoes, 30 kayaks, and 103 rafts.

Gordon Grant replaced Les Bechdel as manager of the Chattooga River Outpost. Les became vice president of facilities at Wesser and took charge of construction projects. John Barbour was designated vice president for retail.

The NOC was now offering up to four trips per day on the Nantahala, three trips per day on the Chattooga, and two trips per day on the Ocoee.

The NOC began trying to develop a voluntary agreement among outfitters to limit trip numbers on the Nantahala but met great resistance to the idea.

The NOC suffered a tragedy when Rick Bernard, an NOC guide, drowned on a Chattooga trip.

The 1979 International Canoe Federation Canoe Slalom World Championships were held at Jonquière, Québec. US paddlers John Lugbill, David Hearn, and Bob Robison swept the C-1 class, and Cathy Hearn won the K-1 Women's class in slalom and wildwater.

1980

The NOC made major acquisitions of property in 1980, including the Flint Ridge property of 50 acres on river left extending from Nantahala Falls downstream to Wesser Falls; riverfront property on river right extending from Nantahala Falls downstream to the original NOC property acquisition, which gave NOC ownership of both banks of the river from Nantahala Falls downstream to the mouth of Silvermine Creek; and the previously leased property for an outpost near the Ocoee River.

On Flint Flats, the NOC constructed a large parking lot (essentially as it exists today), public changing rooms, and a large rafting facility.

On busy days, the NOC began running four Nantahala trips. The Chattooga Outpost was now regularly running three trips a day in the busy season.

The NOC began offering log cabin–building workshops during the off-season first in cooperation with the Shelter Institute and later with Peter Gott.

Dave Perrin, who had come from Wildwater Ltd. the previous summer, became Chattooga Outpost manager, a position he still holds today.

Sherry Spurlin, who was now in charge of marketing and producing the newsletter and other publications, convinced leaders to buy a printing press to print brochures, newsletters, and so on. The NOC has historically favored doing most things for ourselves, rather than contracting work out. The primary purpose of this practice was to provide off-season work for permanent staff. It has historically included doing our own vehicle maintenance, much of our own building construction, and cooking from scratch most restaurant dishes. A high proportion of construction company owners and workers in Swain County have had experience as NOC employees. Our vehicle shop now has four full-time employees who maintain our current fleet of about 100 vehicles, including about 50 school buses. In 1980 our vehicle fleet increased to 22 buses, vans, and trucks.

The year-round staff now numbered about 50, and the summer staff about 150.

We replaced the employee stock plan established in 1976 and modified several times with a new employee stock ownership plan (ESOP), with the goal of moving to complete employee ownership of the company.

The 1980–81 schedule of adventure travel trips now numbered 13, including whitewater rafting on the Salmon River, skiing at Telluride in Colorado, kayaking the Grand Canyon, backpacking in the Grand Canyon, bicycling on the Blue Ridge Parkway, cross-country skiing in Vermont, kayaking or rafting on the Usumacinta River in Central America, scuba diving at Cayman Brac, sailing in the Virgin Islands, backpacking and other activities in the Highlands of Scotland, alpine mountaineering in the Alps at Chamonix, and trekking and river running in Nepal.

This was NOC's best year yet financially.

1981

Helen Langston became manager of the reservations office. Les Bechdel and Bunny Johns initiated a program of river rescue workshops.

This was the first year of a severe drought that persisted intermittently through most of the 1980s.

NOC's growth in river numbers dropped to 9%, having been above 35% in the 1970s and about 30% in 1980.

Bunny Johns and Mike Hipsher won the C-2 mixed class in the Wildwater World Championships. Their time was faster than any of the US men's C-2 teams.

1982

Because of the drought in 1981 and the resulting decrease in growth and profitability, we experienced a cash flow crisis in the winter of 1982. After several staff meetings to discuss possible steps to reduce expenditures, we decided that all winter staff (including company officers) would be paid for only a four-day workweek. This was painful for everyone, but at least the pain was shared equally. Many staff members continued to work five or more days a week, even though they were paid for only four.

We closed the Cullowhee Outfitter's Store after several years of marginal operations.

We published our first Adventure Travel Catalog, which included a total of 18 trips, including a new paddling trip to Costa Rica and our first foreign bicycle trip, in southern England. We purchased Smoky Mountains River Expeditions from Rich Wist and began offering French Broad and Nolichucky River trips. John Kennedy became our first French Broad Outpost manager and Brad Howarth, who came from Smoky Mountains River Expeditions, was the assistant manager.

We built a new store building and staff housing at the Ocoee, additional staff housing at Hellard's, an additional rental cabin at Flint Ridge, and our first addition to the Stone House.

We began our spring triathlon. It started from Andrews with biking over Junaluska Gap to Nantahala High School, running from there down to the put-in on the Nantahala and canoeing down the Nantahala to the NOC. Kathy Bolyn won the women's class, Rand Perkins won the men's class, and Payson was third in the master's class. The team of Burt Fields, Rand Perkins, and Mike Hipsher won the men's team event, and Frances Glass's team won the women's team event.

The NOC began sending all department heads to a five-day leadership development and self-awareness program conducted by Farr-Cruickshank & Associates in Greensboro, North Carolina. Ron Cruickshank, who later became a partner at Farr Associates and a director of the NOC, did a staff attitude survey for the NOC. It showed that overall attitudes were the highest ever seen at Farr but that three areas of concern were salaries, staff housing, and opportunities for year-round employment. While none of the three concerns came as a surprise, we believed that because we had aroused expectations by initiating the survey, we had to respond to the concerns.

In response to the concern over salaries, raises averaging 22% were granted for the next year. In response to the concern over staff housing, about $60,000 was spent on staff housing improvements and additions, including a new staff housing complex called Mashburn's during the following winter. We increased efforts to provide winter employment in our adventure travel program and in construction projects at the NOC. We also worked on relationships with ski resort companies whereby they would hire NOC staff for the winter months and we would employ their staff for jobs in the warmer season.

After numerous meetings and much staff input, we published our Statement of Purposes, which effectively guided much of our decision-making for the next 15 years.

Roy Wood, who had recently retired from the U.S. Bureau of Outdoor Recreation, joined the NOC board of directors. After the Georgia Canoeing Association held its first races on the Nantahala in 1969, at which Roy had served as master of ceremonies and announcer, he thought how beneficial it would be if more land along the river were protected from commercial development. Roy visited Percy Ferebee, who was the major landholder along the river, and talked him into willing almost 5,000 acres of land along the Nantahala to "the people of the United States" and the U.S. Forest Service now manages this land along the river. Hence, Roy Wood and Percy Ferebee deserve credit for the natural state that still exists along most of the Lower Nantahala today.

1983

The NOC took about 24,000 guests on guided trips and rented equipment to about 34,000 more rafters. Total commercial use on the Nantahala for the year was 102,618, and estimated total use, including private paddlers, was 130,000. We employed about 200 staff in the summer and 70 year-round. Weekend rafting prices on the following rivers were: Nantahala, $16; Ocoee, $23; Chattooga III, $36; Chattooga IV, $45; French Broad, $30; and Nolichucky, $40. Five-day instruction programs, including lodging and meals, were $350.

We began renting inflatable kayaks, or duckies, for use on the Nantahala.

Ron Cruickshank of Farr-Cruickshank & Associates replaced Roy Wood on our board.

Jan Letendre, who had been working with David Dauphine in accounting, became company treasurer. Angus Morrison became our first full-time Nantahala rafting manager. He continued in this capacity for many years.

The Mashburn's staff housing complex opened.

An older iteration of Slow Joe's Café, mid-1990s (photographed by Villa Brewer)

The NOC invested in the start-up of the Rocky Mountain Outdoor Center (RMOC) on the Arkansas River in Colorado. Dick Eustis moved there as our representative. Dick became president of RMOC a year later.

We operated our first Carolina Cycle Tours trip to England under the leadership of Brett Poirier and Sherry Spurlin.

We opened Slow Joe's Café (named for Joe Huggins, who built the original facility and operated it for several years) and a new day care center on the Wesser campus.

We built Kleinrath Hall, a new meeting space. Because of his commitment to quality, it was named for Arnie Kleinrath, who had come to the NOC from Minnesota and who supervised the construction of several of our buildings on the Flint Ridge property. When we were digging holes for the footings of our buildings, Arnie always said we should dig Minnesota holes. He demonstrated that a Minnesota hole was perfectly round and vertically straight in appearance. When asked why this mattered for a hole that was going to be filled with concrete and then hidden by dirt, he responded that it was a matter of getting in the habit of doing everything in the highest quality manner possible, even if it didn't show.

The extremely rapid and easy growth of the 1970s seemed to have ended with the low water of the early 1980s.

A computerized reservations system, designed and implemented by Russ Meyer, began to be used to take reservations for the 1984 season.

1984

The U.S. Forest Service began a permitting system on the Nantahala. Permits were issued to commercial outfitters and some summer camps and schools that had conducted trips in 1983. Numbers for each company were restricted on peak-use days to the average number that the company had taken on its highest-use days in 1983 plus 10%. These numbers were to be adjusted annually. Permits were issued to 13 outfitters with a total allotment of 2,295 rafters on peak-use days.

David Brown's work to save the Ocoee for paddling was rewarded. Congress made an appropriation to TVA to assure regularly scheduled water releases on the Ocoee River.

John Kennedy, who had become the manager of our Ocoee River Outpost after Dick Eustis left for RMOC, built our Ocoee house.

NOC began offering Blue Ridge Parkway bicycling trips.

Bunny Johns joined the board of directors.

1985

Another drought year. The Chattooga and French Broad staff continued to develop techniques to run the rapids with minimal water, as well as to keep the trips fun at extremely low water levels by doing lots of swimming and playing in the rapids.

Russ Nichols, a C-2 paddler from the 1972 US Olympic Team and a former NOC staffer who had now become a documentary filmmaker, produced the first NOC promotional video, titled *Center Magic.* I continue to believe that it and the promotional video recently produced by Gavin Young capture the spirit of NOC better than any other promotional products we have produced.

Slow Joe's, which had opened under the leadership of Joe Huggins in a corner of the rafting building, moved to the location where it now operates under the name Big Wesser BBQ & Brew.

The first units of our hostel-type lodging known as Basecamp, which had been constructed under the supervision of Rand Perkins during the winter, opened.

In the fall we purchased High Country's Nantahala River operations, which we renamed Great Smokies Rafting Company the next season.

Payson proposed that the board pass a resolution ensuring that the highest salaries paid by the NOC would not exceed a four-to-one ratio to the base pay of new employees. This idea was based on the practices of the highly successful Mondragon cooperatives in the Basque area of Spain. The board agreed on a policy that the ratio would not exceed a five-to-one ratio. Payson stuck to the four-to-one ratio for himself throughout his years at the NOC, even as others' pay went to five-to-one.

Payson was granted a six-month sabbatical for the fall of 1985 and the winter of 1986. He spent the fall and winter traveling in Great Britain, India, Nepal, and Tibet. On his return in the spring, he became chairman of the board and CEO, and John Burton became president.

1986

The drought intensified, with the water level on the Chattooga dropping as low as 0.45 foot on the gauge attached to the old US 76 bridge. With the slower growth resulting from low water, financial results were weak and austerity measures continued.

Great Smokies Rafting Company began operating from the old Tomahawk Trail Texaco Station across from Hellard's, under the leadership of Ray McLeod.

The NOC purchased Sunburst Adventures on the Ocoee River from Marc Hunt and Bill Chipley. Bunny Johns became president of Sunburst.

Planning for Relia's Garden restaurant building was completed, and work began in the fall under the supervision of Bill Baxter. The design was done by Chris Larsen, a former staff member who had subsequently received a master's degree at MIT, for which a version of the design for the Relia's Garden building was his thesis project.

We had to cancel our Usumacinta River trips, which had been our most popular adventure travel trips for 10 years, because of guerrilla activity in the region.

1987

After 15 years, we finished paying off the mortgage on the river-right property that Horace had originally purchased from the Gassaways.

We built our first ropes course up in the trees on the hill behind the old motel and above the spring box that served as the source for our original water system.

The Nantahala Paddling Club, forerunner of the Nantahala Racing Club, was organized under the sponsorship of the NOC.

The NOC created and marketed an American Rivers credit card to generate funds for American rivers.

Over our first 15 years, rafting prices had increased from $10 to $20 on the Nantahala and from $20 to $55 for a Section IV Chattooga trip. Five-day instruction clinics, including food and lodging, were now $440.

We took 3,680 rafters on the French Broad River, 14,311 on the Ocoee River, and 1,216 on the Nolichucky River.

Payson proposed that to further strengthen the sense of ownership and community among staff, the NOC should convert from a corporation to a staff-owned cooperative.

1988

This was the last year of the severe drought that had started in 1985. On days when the Nantahala Power Plant did not operate because of the low reservoir level we began running raft trips on the Little Tennessee River and occasionally on the Tuckasegee River.

The construction of Relia's Garden restaurant building was completed and the new restaurant opened for the summer season.

A water reservoir was built above all our buildings on the Flint Ridge property, except for Cabin E. It was built to provide water for a new sprinkler system required in major new buildings, such as Relia's Garden, but it was intended to also eventually become a swimming pool in which we could conveniently teach rolling, even in the colder months.

Relia's Garden completed

It was 40 by 75 feet with a uniform depth of 4 feet. We thought this would work well for teaching rolling, swimming laps, and for kids to play in, even though it couldn't be used for diving.

The railroad agreed to remove the unused railway spur located on our property, which was taking up valuable flat parking space.

The bike trips we had been offering for several years, along with several new ones, formed the basis for a new department under the leadership of Julie Thorner, called Carolina Cycle Tours.

John Barbour and Bob Gernandt began leading fly-fishing programs and acting as fishing guides.

Bob Gernandt fly-fishing on the Nantahala River

1989

This was a good water year. Both Nantahala and Fontana Reservoirs were full going into the summer.

The land exchange with the U.S. Forest Service (USFS) finally closed. The USFS acquired 35 acres on river right below Nantahala Falls for use as a takeout area for other rafting companies. The NOC received a small sliver of land along Silvermine Creek, where the original store and front office buildings encroached on USFS land; a few acres farther up US 19, adjacent to our staff housing at Hellard's; as well as a few acres surrounded by the oxbow of the old riverbed adjacent to Wesser Falls.

At the same time, the TVA also gave us a permit to use their land lying below 1,710 feet within the oxbow. This land within the oxbow was usually dry but became covered with water any time Fontana Reservoir filled to the spillway level of 1,710 feet. The land within the oxbow became the location of our rope course, Alpine Tower, and eventually the Zip Line Adventure Park.

Our 1989 catalog of programs lists the following adventure travel trips: Bicycling Historic England, Baja Sea Kayaking, Rio Grande Canoeing, Usumacinta: River of Ruins (rafting and kayaking), Costa Rica Whitewater (rafting and kayaking), Mountains and Rivers of Nepal (trekking and rafting or kayaking), Grand Canyon Paddling (kayak or canoe), Bío-Bío's Big Water (rafting and kayaking), Scotland Week of Rivers (kayaking), Southern France Whitewater (kayaking).

In the spring a team from the NOC went to the Chuya River in Siberia for a week of competition sponsored by Project RAFT (Russians and Americans for

Teamwork) with teams from about 15 countries. After the competition was over, the NOC invited participants to come to the NOC the following year for a similar competition in the United States.

The Great Smoky Mountains Railroad began operating excursions from Bryson City to the vicinity of our staff housing about a mile downstream from the put-in on the Nantahala River.

Six children were born to NOC staff during the year. Our community continued to grow.

At the request of the Department of Tourism for the Indian State of Jammu and Kashmir, the NOC agreed to send guides to Kashmir to train a dozen Kashmiris to be whitewater guides. Unfortunately, the breakout of hostilities between Pakistan and India in Kashmir prevented the program from succeeding, as tourists were afraid to go to Kashmir for water sports and rafting.

Alpine Tower at the NOC's second ropes course in the Horseshoe

Herb Barks, headmaster of Baylor School in Chattanooga, and George Snelling, leader of the group planning for conversion to cooperative ownership, replaced Marc Hunt and Bunny Johns on the board of directors. Officers of the company were Payson Kennedy, CEO and board chairman; John Burton, president; Bunny Johns, John Barbour, John Kennedy, and Tom Blue, vice presidents; Marc Hunt, treasurer and secretary; and Joanna Foster, vice treasurer and vice secretary.

The board decided that rather than converting to a cooperative structure, the same goals could be achieved with less expense and risk by restructuring the current ESOP, "so as to include a 401(k) provision," creating what has become known as a KSOP.

Much time and energy during the fall and winter went into planning and raising funds for Nantahala '90, the international peace rally and competition to be held at the NOC under the joint sponsorship of the NOC and Project RAFT in March 1990. Ellen Babers was selected to be in charge of the event.

Payson's annual letter to shareholders summarized the performance for the year in the following words:

1989 was a good year for the NOC. After nearly a decade of drought, the rains seem to have returned in 1989, and so far in 1990. With the return of good water and with lots of staff effort, revenues increased 14% to nearly $7 million, generating a record profit of $297,000. Book value of our stock increased 16.7% from $114.25 to $133.33. The appraised market value of our stock increased 11.1% from $124.29 to $138.14. Particularly pleasing was the improvement in performance of our two restaurants after a difficult first year for the new restaurant.

1990

The Great Smoky Mountains Railroad placed a train car within which bathrooms had been installed between the railroad tracks and our sewage treatment plant. The NOC agreed to install plumbing to the bathrooms and to maintain them for the use of train passengers when trains stopped at the NOC, as well as for other NOC guests.

In March, Nantahala '90 was held. Competitions were held on the Nantahala, Chattooga, and Nolichucky Rivers.

The US Olympic Committee designated the Nantahala Racing Club as a center of excellence for training in slalom competition.

The NOC opened a store in Bryson City.

After a series of meetings of various leadership committees and KSOP members, a policy was approved by the board to use 5% of each year's profit for charitable purposes. An endowment fund was set up at the North Carolina Community Foundation.

Payson's annual letter to stockholders summarized the year's financial performance in the following words:

I hope that two years are enough to point to the beginning of several trends. In 1990 we had another good year. Good water levels continued for the most part and we have had lots of water this winter and spring. With good water and lots of staff effort, revenues increased 16% to about $8 million, generating a record profit of $355,000 (up 19%). Book value of our stock increased 8.4% from $133.33 to $144.51. The appraised value of our stock increased 10.9% from $138.14 to $153.18. Both restaurants continued the dramatic improvement remarked upon last year, and the French Broad, Ocoee, and Nolichucky Outposts, and rentals and Slow Joe's Café also showed dramatic improvements in financial results. The staff bonus increased to 4.75% of pay for eligible employees and a total of $108,000.

1991

John Burton organized a partnership largely composed of NOC friends to purchase Nantahala Village. John, along with his wife, Jan Letendre, left employment at the NOC to manage the village.

Our board expanded to nine members, with three being elected each year for three-year terms. The three members to be elected each year were to be two current employees and one nonemployee outside director. With the KSOP members now having majority ownership, they had enough votes to determine the election outcome. Election to the board became more competitive. Some staff members viewed Aurelia Kennedy and Jim Shannonhouse as being too influenced by Payson, and they were replaced on the expanded board by inside directors Billy Richards, Bunny Johns, and Jim Holcombe and outside director Allen Grumbine.

Bunny Johns became president of the NOC. Other company officers were: Payson Kennedy, CEO; John Barbour, vice president of retail; Aurelia Kennedy, vice president of food services; Tom Blue, vice president of rafting operations; Mark Singleton, vice president of marketing; Al Mandrell, vice president of facilities; Marc Hunt, treasurer and secretary; Joanna Foster, assistant treasurer and assistant secretary.

The Depot Store was built near the site of the old Wesser post office, train station, and general store.

A new off-campus vehicle shop was constructed.

Under the leadership of Julie Thorner, revenues from our bicycling program tripled.

The NOC typically dominated any regional races between the guides. In 1991 in the Ocoee River Raft Races, the NOC men were first, the Sunburst (now owned by the NOC) men were second, the NOC women were third, and the Sunburst women were fourth, followed by the other men's teams.

The NOC sent a team to Costa Rica '91, the Project RAFT international rafting competition.

1992

As the NOC celebrated its 20th anniversary, a new long-range plan restated our ideals in the following way:

The NOC is an intentional community united by commitment to common ideals which include:

 creating experiences of joy and growth for ourselves and one another

 sharing these experiences with our guests

≋ using outdoor recreation as the primary activity for creating these experiences

≋ enjoying a simple lifestyle in a beautiful mountain environment that we seek to preserve and protect

≋ seeking quality or excellence in everything we do

≋ developing compassion and honesty in the way we treat one another.

We bought the property in Walnut, which was close to the put-in for the French Broad River. This became the meeting place for French Broad trips.

After an incident at the NOC in which a supervisor harassed an employee because of the employee's sexual orientation, the supervisor was terminated and the following policy published: "We expect an atmosphere at the NOC where people can express their sexual preferences without fear of judgment or ridicule and where gays, lesbians, and bisexuals can feel as comfortable as everyone else. Harassment of an employee by a supervisor for reasons of sexual preference, gender, race, or religion is not acceptable, nor will we tolerate harassment of a member of the community by any employee. The only appropriate criteria for judging an employee is the quality of that person's work and the respect that person shows other members of the community."

It rained most of May and June. Not many people chose to go rafting.

Three paddlers from the NOC, Adam Clawson, Joe Jacobi, and Scott Strausbaugh, went to the Barcelona Olympic Games as members of the US whitewater slalom team. In the C-2 event, Joe and Scott won the only gold medal that the United States has ever won in Olympic slalom competition.

The value of NOC stock moved above $200 per share.

We had a higher number of staff from 1991 who did not return in '92 than in prior years. In studying the reasons for this and analyzing the past figures, we found that for many years about 25% of the prior year's employees did not return. This seemed to be a reasonable figure because an increasingly large proportion of our staff were college students who worked three or four seasons at most before graduating and beginning professional careers.

1993

The KSOP trust now owned 60% of the NOC stock, and staff members owned most of the remaining shares individually.

We purchased the property at the Nolichucky River, where our outpost is currently located, and built a shower house and sauna there.

Sunburst Adventures was sold to Larry Guy and Keith Judson.

In March we had a blizzard that left 2 feet of snow at Wesser and up to 5 feet on the higher mountains. It was a week before our power was restored. It took us two weeks to clear downed trees from the Nantahala River and about a month to clear the bike trails at Tsali.

Our French Broad store building was constructed.

In the fall, we demolished the original Outfitter's Store building and began constructing a new store designed by Chris Larsen, a former guide who had also designed the Relia's Garden restaurant building. Bill Baxter was again employed as the general contractor for the store, with the agreement that he would employ as many out-of-work NOC staff members as possible for the winter construction season. We also began construction of new facilities for Great Smokies Rafting Company at Nantahala Village.

1994

Windy Gordon replaced Ed Daugherty on our board. He also became manager of our French Broad Outpost. Peter Englander replaced Tom Blue as treasurer. Tom left the NOC to study law at UNC Chapel Hill. The roles of CEO and chairman of the board were separated. The role of the chairman was primarily to plan the agenda for board meetings and to facilitate those meetings. Bill Travitz was elected as board chairman. Payson remained CEO and CPO.

Our new Outfitter's Store opened in April. The new store included a bicycle shop and a much greater inventory in other areas.

Additional land was purchased adjacent to our Ocoee Outpost property, and a new store opened there.

It was a very rainy summer, which resulted in high water for paddling but a decrease in rafting trip numbers. The rain also resulted in a mudslide of land that had been disturbed in building our reservoir for the sprinkler system. The mudslide destroyed our commons building at Basecamp, which had to be rebuilt. River's End cook, Walter Wright, was in the commons building when it was moved several feet and essentially destroyed by the mudslide. Walter was terrified but unhurt.

The River Wild, a movie about rafting starring Meryl Streep and Kevin Bacon, was released. Former NOC employee, Arlene Burns, helped teach Meryl to row a raft. The movie seemed to boost rafting numbers the following season.

1995

We inaugurated a photo system at the Chattooga whereby photographers developed the pictures as soon as they returned from the trip and guests

NOC's second ropes course

stayed for a slide show, after which they could have prints made of the photos they wished to purchase.

We lost a few days of rafting on the Nantahala because of an explosion in the power plant, but it was a hot, dry summer, and rafting numbers boomed. This was the peak year for total use on all rivers at 150,000 river days. This over-all peak was driven by a total of more than 32,000 on Nantahala guided trips, 55,000 rental users on the Nantahala, almost 17,000 on Chattooga trips, and more than 25,000 on Ocoee trips.

Our Outfitter's Store at Wesser and our Ocoee store set sales records.

Our original ropes course in the trees up a steep trail from the old motel build-ing was taken down because the trees were no longer healthy. In September, a new course designed by John Mordhorst and Paul Wolfe and an Alpine Tower were constructed in the oxbow created by the old river course on land acquired

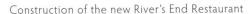

Construction of the new River's End Restaurant

through the exchange with the U.S. Forest Service and on land permitted by TVA for our use.

In the fall we began construction of a new River's End Restaurant building. Again, Chris Larsen did the design and Bill Baxter was the general contractor.

This was a good year financially. This was the last time in many years that our margin reached our threshold goal of 5%.

River's End, new building construction (or it might have been Relia's Garden). Bill Baxter, builder; Aurelia Kennedy, restaurant manager; and Chris Larsen, architect.

1996

B oard meetings were now being held much more frequently than in the past, usually every month. The board was taking a more active role in running the company.

The board spent considerable time during the year in strategic planning for the mail-order business and in considering the acquisition of two pieces of property totaling about 350 acres adjacent to the NOC on river left. In December we closed on the purchase of the Townhouse Creek parcel of 200 acres on river left, downstream of our other river left property, and continued to negotiate with the U.S. Forest Service to acquire the land between our holdings on river left through another land exchange. We also purchased the Simonetti property on Silvermine Creek to provide staff housing within walking distance of the NOC campus. A proposal to purchase wetlands elsewhere to ameliorate for the building of a new parking lot in the wetlands adjacent to our sewage treatment plant proved to be very controversial within our staff and among the public. The proposal was eventually dropped.

River's End Restaurant opened in its new building in early April. A footbridge was also built across the river between the Outfitter's Store and the new restaurant building. The concrete pier supporting the bridge incorporated an older pier that in the past had supported a log flume bringing logs down Silvermine Creek and across the river to the railroad on river right.

We purchased Carolina Wilderness Tours from Paul Breuer. It was a French Broad and Nolichucky Rivers rafting company on desirable property adjacent to our property on the French Broad River at Hot Springs.

For the 1996 Atlanta Olympics, the whitewater slalom event was held on an artificial course constructed in the normally dry section of the Ocoee River above the section where rafting had been taking place since 1977. Four Nantahala Racing

Club members made the US team: Adam Clawson, Scott Shipley, Wayne Dickert, and Horace Holden Jr.

River numbers had boomed the previous two years with the release of *The River Wild* and the excitement of the coming Olympics, with competition to be held on the Ocoee River, but in 1996 numbers declined from 150,000 to 137,000.

1997

We closed on another land exchange with the U.S. Forest Service, which Payson had been working on for several years. We acquired 120 acres between our Flint Ridge property and our newly acquired Townhouse Creek property, giving us a total of 400 acres on river left. We also acquired another 0.5-acre parcel in the oxbow created by the old riverbed. The U.S. Forest Service acquired additional property along the Appalachian Trail, as well as two parcels away from Wesser that we purchased to equalize values in the exchange.

We closed on the purchase of a 74-acre parcel of land adjoining our Chattooga Outpost to be used primarily for a new septic field and staff housing.

Bunny and Payson had spent a lot of time over the previous two years lobbying for a new bridge to be built over the Nantahala River. The old one-lane bridge had been shut down for repairs a couple times and the Department of Transportation had said that it was becoming unsafe for bus traffic or heavy trucks. A new bridge was approved and planning completed this year.

After our purchase of Carolina Wilderness Tours the previous year, our trip numbers on the Nolichucky River peaked at 4,500 rafters and our use of the French Broad River peaked at 18,700 rafters.

With the more slow-moving decision-making processes as committees were appointed to study most issues, the more bureaucratic and rule-driven behavior, the increasing emphasis on maximizing profitability at the expense of other values, and the more contentious divisions on many issues, Payson decided that working off the river was no longer putting him in the flow state very often. He announced that he and Aurelia had decided to retire from full-time work at the end of the year but would continue to guide and to serve on the board of directors. He thought that Bunny Johns was more capable of working harmoniously with the board. It was decided that she would now become the CEO, as well as president.

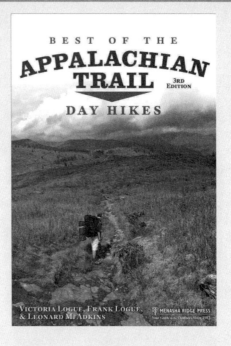

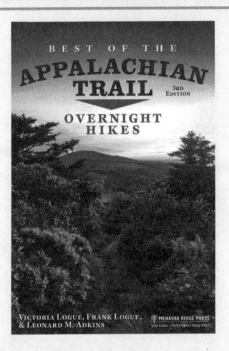

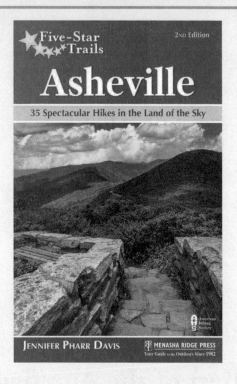

Whitewater River Maps:
Nantahala River

By William Nealy
ISBN: 978-0-89732-354-3

35 inches high by 19 inches wide
$7.95

A hand-drawn river map poster by world-famous cartoonist William Nealy.
Nealy is best-known for his groundbreaking book *Kayak*, which combined
expert paddling instruction with artful caricatures and parodies of the whitewater enthusiasts themselves.

  MENASHA RIDGE PRESS
www.menasharidge.com

DEAR CUSTOMERS AND FRIENDS,

SUPPORTING YOUR INTEREST IN OUTDOOR ADVENTURE, travel, and an active lifestyle is central to our operations, from the authors we choose to the locations we detail to the way we design our books. Menasha Ridge Press was incorporated in 1982 by a group of veteran outdoorsmen and professional outfitters. For many years now, we've specialized in creating books that benefit the outdoors enthusiast.

Almost immediately, Menasha Ridge Press earned a reputation for revolutionizing outdoors- and travel-guidebook publishing. For such activities as canoeing, kayaking, hiking, backpacking, and mountain biking, we established new standards of quality that transformed the whole genre, resulting in outdoor-recreation guides of great sophistication and solid content. Menasha Ridge Press continues to be outdoor publishing's greatest innovator.

The folks at Menasha Ridge Press are as at home on a whitewater river or mountain trail as they are editing a manuscript. The books we build for you are the best they can be, because we're responding to your needs. Plus, we use and depend on them ourselves.

We look forward to seeing you on the river or the trail. If you'd like to contact us directly, visit us at menasharidge.com. We thank you for your interest in our books and the natural world around us all.

SAFE TRAVELS,

Bob Sehlinger

BOB SEHLINGER
PUBLISHER